POSTCARD HISTORY SERIES

Napa County

ON THE FRONT COVER: Visible in this postcard is the Fox Theater, located at the northeast corner of First and Randolph Streets. It began its life in 1920 as the Hippodrome Theater, a 1,500-seat theater complete with a full orchestra pit and a pipe organ. It was renamed the Fox in 1941. The theater closed in the early 1950s and was later demolished. The tall building to the right of the Fox is the *Napa Valley Register* newspaper building, which housed the *Register* from 1863 until the late 1960s. The building now houses a sushi restaurant. (Author's collection.)

ON THE BACK COVER: The Old Bale Mill, located just outside of Calistoga, is an enduring reminder of early life in Napa County. The mill was built in 1846 by Dr. Edward Bale and served the area until 1905. Today the mill has been restored and is part of a state park. (Author's collection.)

POSTCARD HISTORY SERIES

Napa County

Todd L. Shulman

ARCADIA PUBLISHING

ISBN 978-0-7385-7039-6

Published by Arcadia Publishing
Charleston SC, Chicago IL, Portsmouth NH, San Francisco CA

Printed in the United States of America

Library of Congress Control Number: 2009921917

For all general information contact Arcadia Publishing at:
Telephone 843-853-2070
Fax 843-853-0044
E-mail sales@arcadiapublishing.com
For customer service and orders:
Toll-Free 1-888-313-2665

Visit us on the Internet at www.arcadiapublishing.com

To my wife, Stacey, whose trust and creativity inspire me every day

CONTENTS

ACKNOWLEDGMENTS

I began collecting postcards as a young child during the frequent trips that my family took in the western states. Even now, I periodically leaf through my postcard scrapbook and am transported back to the sights and sounds of the places we visited.

When I began working in Napa in 2000, I was fascinated by the rich history of the Napa Valley. While doing research for my prior book, *Napa County Police*, I came in contact with many longtime Napa County residents, some of whom can trace their roots back to the pioneer days of the 1840s; their reminiscences of bygone eras piqued my interest in chronicling this history using the medium of postcards.

This book would not have been possible without the gracious cooperation of other local collectors and of several historical societies. In particular, I want to single out collectors Stan France and Mike Vanwormer, lifelong Napans whose passion for the valley's history and postcard collecting is contagious. I would also like to thank Dennis Gonslin of the Napa Firefighter's Museum, Elke Strunka of the Sharpsteen Museum of Calistoga History, Pat Alexander of the Napa Valley Museum, and Amanda Dareing of the Napa County Historical Society. Thanks also to the St. Helena High School AP English classes of 1996 and 1998, who compiled narratives about unique aspects of St. Helena history.

Many of the postcards in the book are the work of noted local photographers, either made as photographic prints or used as the basis for hand-colored cards. The excellent talents of I. C. Adams from Calistoga and Mark Strong from Napa are both featured. Many postcards show the mark "Zan," denoting that they were the work of Alexander J. Stark, a photographer who traveled the Pacific Coast during the first half of the century.

In addition, I owe a debt of gratitude to other historians and authors who came before me, whose works have chronicled Napa County's history with detail and clarity. I hope the postcards I have chosen for this book will open a window to the history of the destination and the way of life that is Napa Valley.

INTRODUCTION

Napa County is a unique and historic part of California in ways beyond the area's claim to fame as the epicenter of the wine industry in America. Nearly half of the participants of California's 1846 Bear Flag Revolt against Mexico came from Napa. A great many of the rescue party that came to the aid of the ill-fated Donner Party in 1847 were from a wagon train bound for Napa.

Perhaps Napa's first explorer, Fr. Jose Altimira, best described the beauty of Napa when he said, "We saw on the plain and hills large groves of oak trees, and went over large spots of land proper for the cultivation of wine. We climbed the slopes of a mountain [Mount St. Helena] which, with its adjoining hills, could furnish good stone, abundant enough for the building of a new Rome."

The term "destination resort" may not have originated in Napa, but it was surely perfected there. Early pioneer entrepreneurs such as Sam Brannan recognized the health benefits of Napa's climate and the curative potential in its natural hot springs.

Many of the postcards in this book come from the golden age of postcards, from 1907 to 1915. It was during this time that many factors came together to enhance postcards, including technological advances in printing, the advent of postal rural free delivery (RFD) to unincorporated areas of the United States, and the expertise of German artisans who hand-colored many of the cards. As you will see while reading this book, many of these cards are truly works of art.

The golden age of postcards coincides with the end of the first golden age of tourism in Napa County. The institution of prohibition in 1919 and later the Great Depression would have profound and lasting impacts on the resorts and wineries of Napa. It is only since the 1960s that tourism and the wine industry have rebounded to the multimillion-dollar industries they are today. Today nearly five million visitors a year travel to Napa to take in the sights, sounds, and tastes that have made Napa County famous worldwide.

One

In the Country

When the first white settlers came to the Napa Valley in 1823, they found a vast, untamed expanse inhabited by Wappo and Patwin Native Americans. Herds of elk and antelope roamed free, hunted by scores of mountain lions and bears.

Even after settlers began to leave their mark on the valley by planting crops and populating towns, the area was still a wilderness in many ways. Hardy souls shunned the populous areas such as Napa and St. Helena, instead preferring to live on the fringes, closer to the natural beauty of the valley that enthralled early settlers and present-day tourists alike.

Development and population growth have encroached on some of these areas, and others, such as the town of Monticello, have vanished completely. Yet Napa County still remains relatively rural and attracts those seeking to escape from the rigors of city life. In 1968, vintners and civic leaders in the county seized an opportunity to preserve farmland. They took advantage of a new state law to create an agricultural preserve, the first of its kind, on the floor of the valley in unincorporated areas between Napa and Calistoga. Initially the preserve encompassed 23,000 acres. It has now grown to more than 30,000 acres.

In a nod to Napa County's raw beauty, the default wallpaper entitled "Bliss" provided with the Microsoft Windows XP computer operating system shows a rolling hillside in Napa.

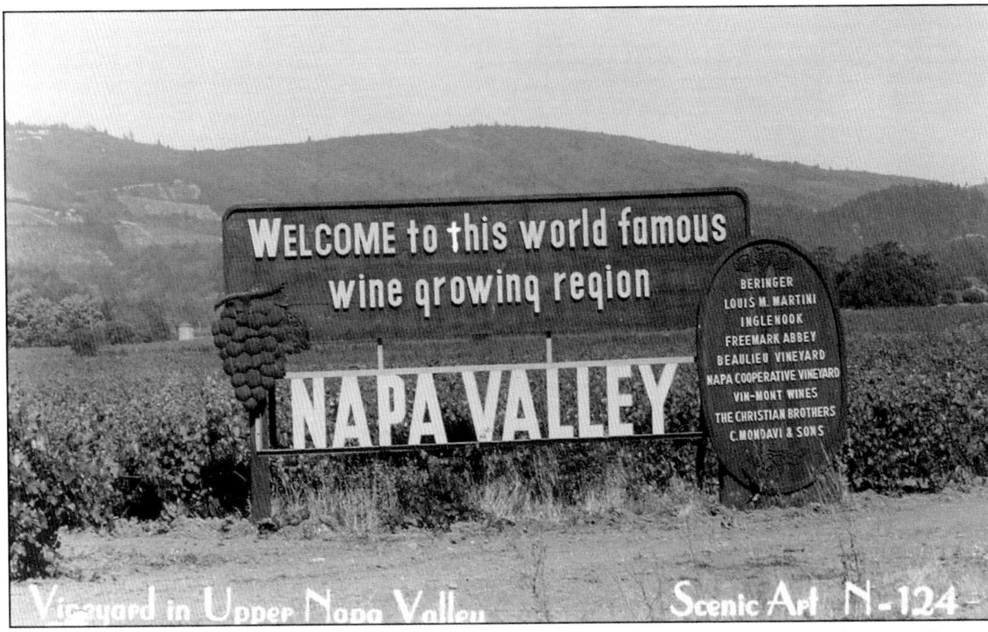

There are two signs that welcome travelers to the Napa Valley, one just north of Yountville and the other just north of St. Helena. The picturesque backdrop makes them popular photographic opportunities for tourists. (Courtesy of the Sharpsteen Museum of Calistoga History.)

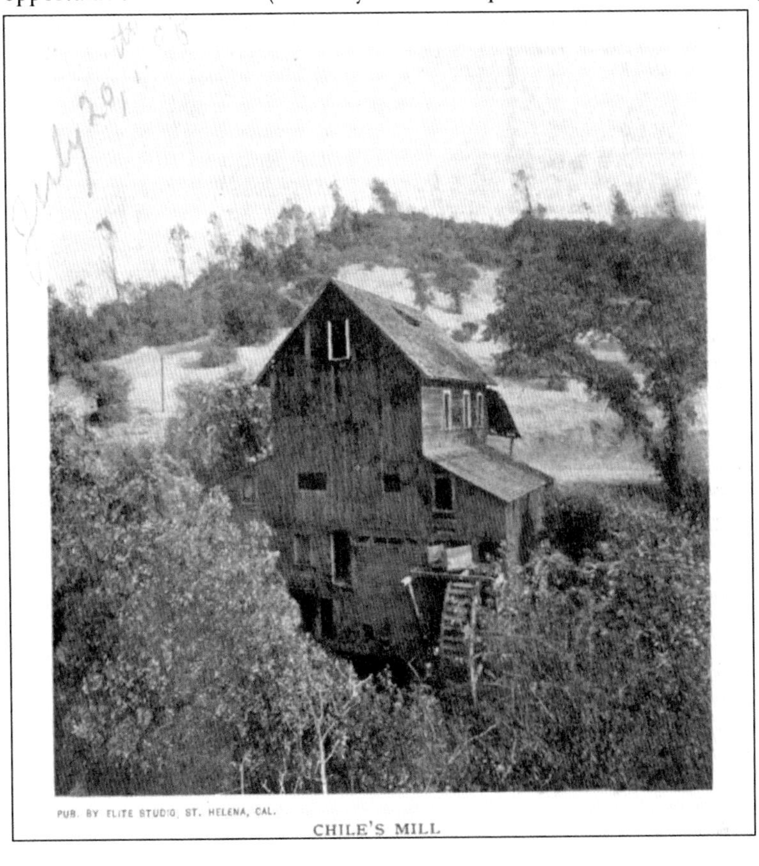

The Chiles Grist Mill, the first American gristmill in Northern California, was built by Joseph Chiles in 1845 on land he received from Mariano Vallejo. The millstone was brought over the Sierra Nevadas; it is currently on display outside the state capitol building. The mill was located in lower Chiles Valley near present-day Highway 128. It burned to the ground in 1955; the site is now marked as a state historic landmark. (Courtesy of the Napa County Historical Society.)

Napa County has seen its fertile valley used for other agriculture besides the well-known grape industry, as this 1908 postcard attests to. At the start of the 20th century, Napa and neighboring Sonoma County were major producers of hops, an important ingredient in beer. Mechanization in the 1960s consolidated hops production in the United States to the Pacific Northwest states of Washington and Oregon. (Courtesy of the Napa County Historical Society.)

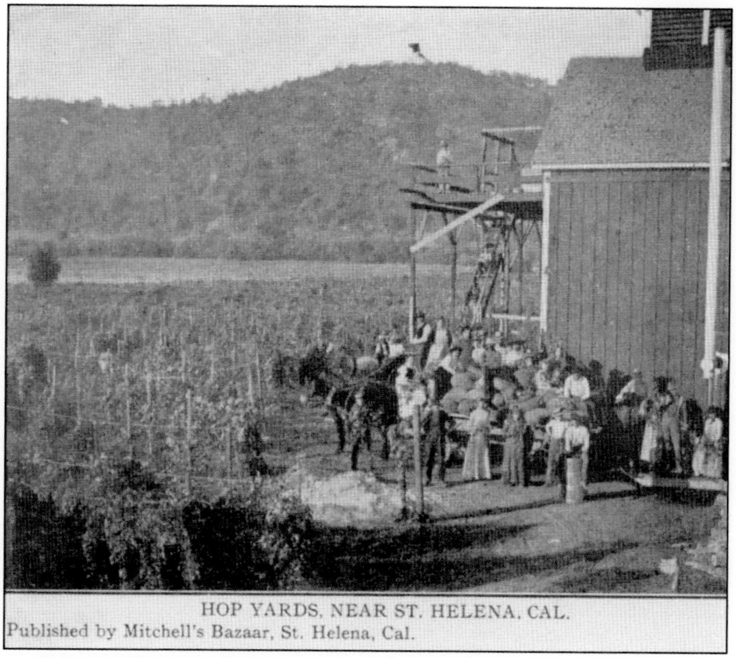

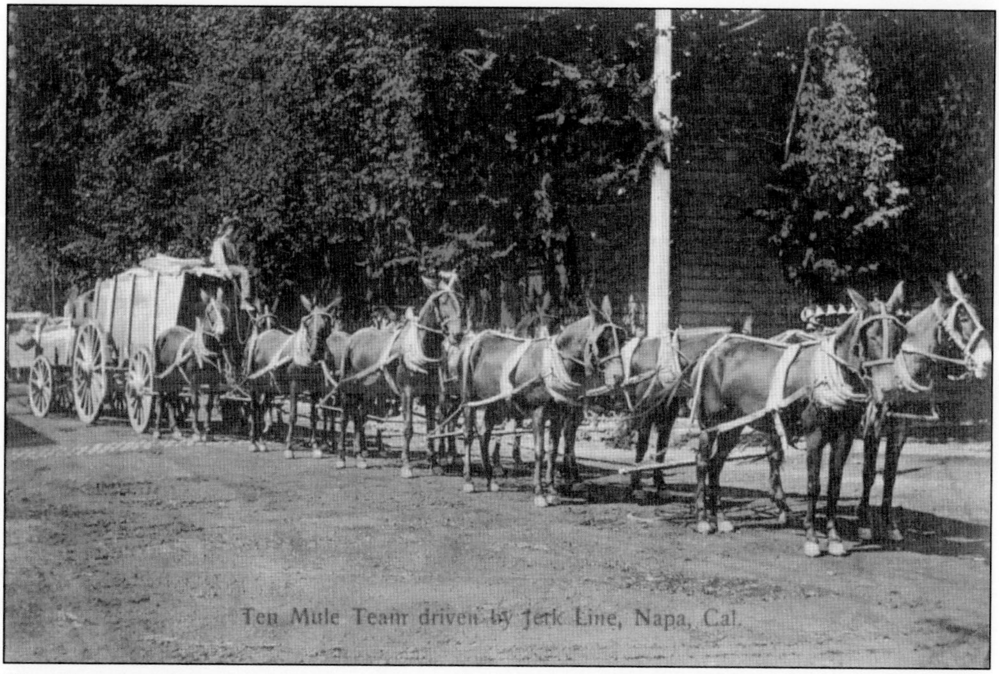

The 10-mule jerk line transport wagon was the 18-wheeler of its time, transporting the harvested grapes or prunes to their respective wineries or processing facilities. The term *jerk line* refers to the method used by the driver to steer the mules, that is, jerking on the reigns. (Author's collection.)

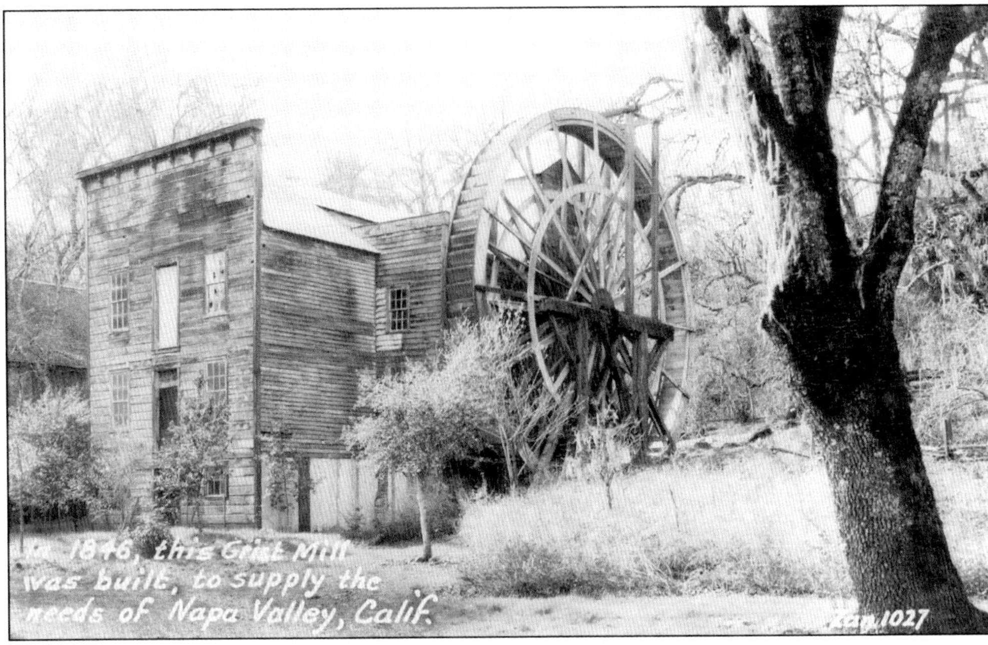

Edward Turner Bale, a surgeon by trade, obtained a land grant of the Rancho Carne Humana in Napa Valley, where he went in 1843. In 1846, he built the pictured grist and sawmill, the second in Napa County, and lived there until his death in 1849. Much of the neighboring towns of Calistoga and St. Helena were built by lumber processed at the mill. (Author's collection.)

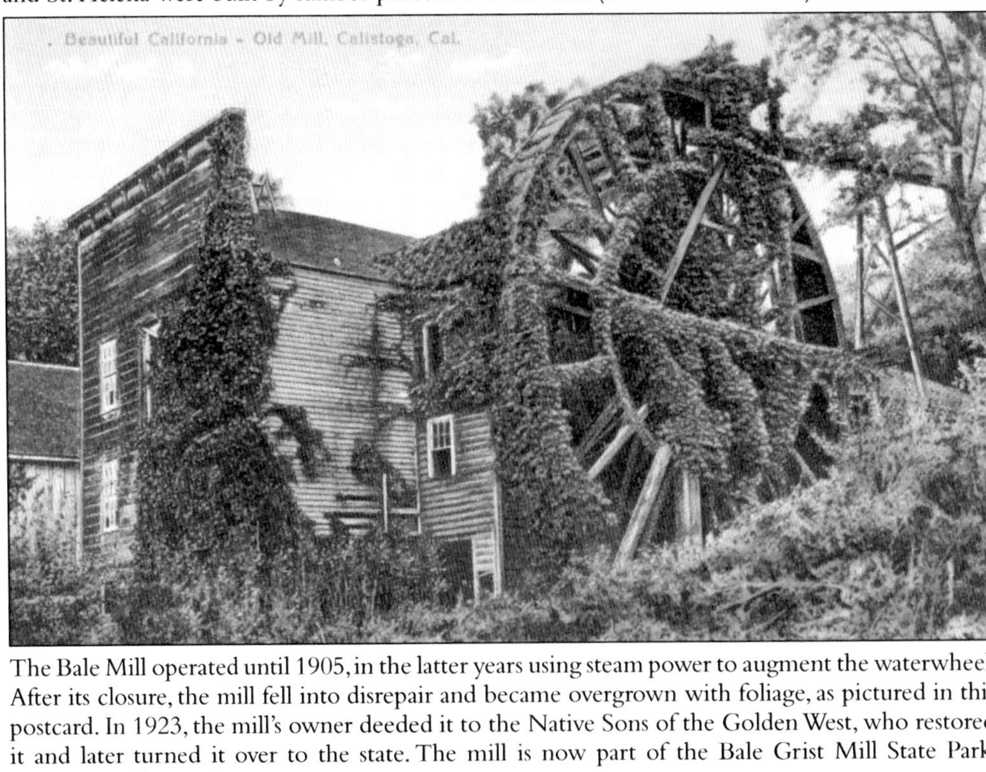

The Bale Mill operated until 1905, in the latter years using steam power to augment the waterwheel. After its closure, the mill fell into disrepair and became overgrown with foliage, as pictured in this postcard. In 1923, the mill's owner deeded it to the Native Sons of the Golden West, who restored it and later turned it over to the state. The mill is now part of the Bale Grist Mill State Park. (Author's collection.)

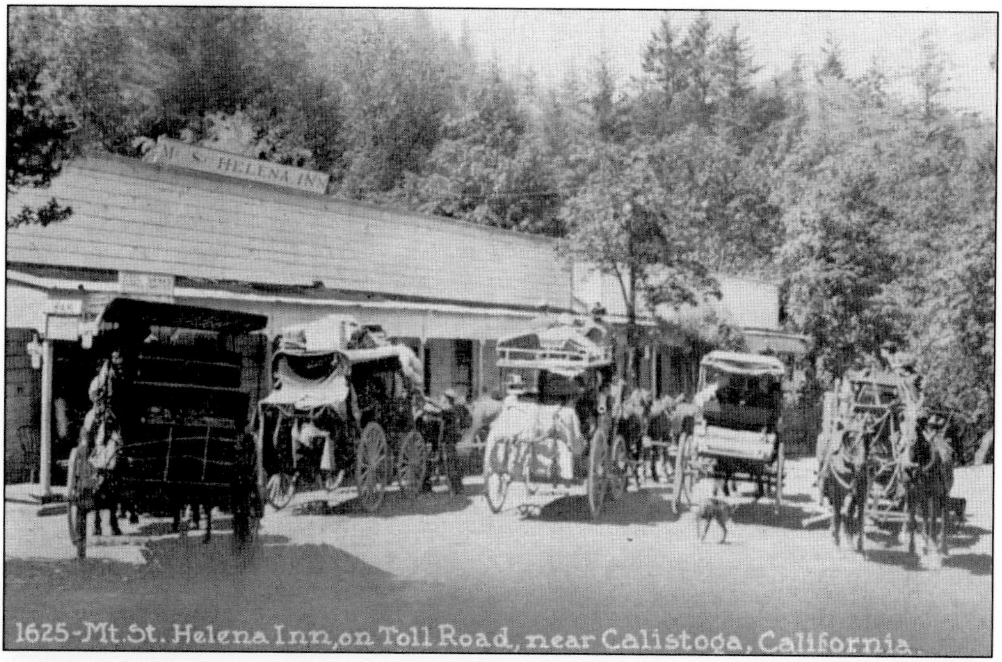

In 1866, John Lawley completed a toll road that stretched over Mount St. Helena into Lake County. He built an inn adjacent to the tollgate. This early 20th century postcard shows the many stages that made the trek between Calistoga and Lake County. The original building burned to the ground in 1883. (Courtesy of the Napa County Historical Society.)

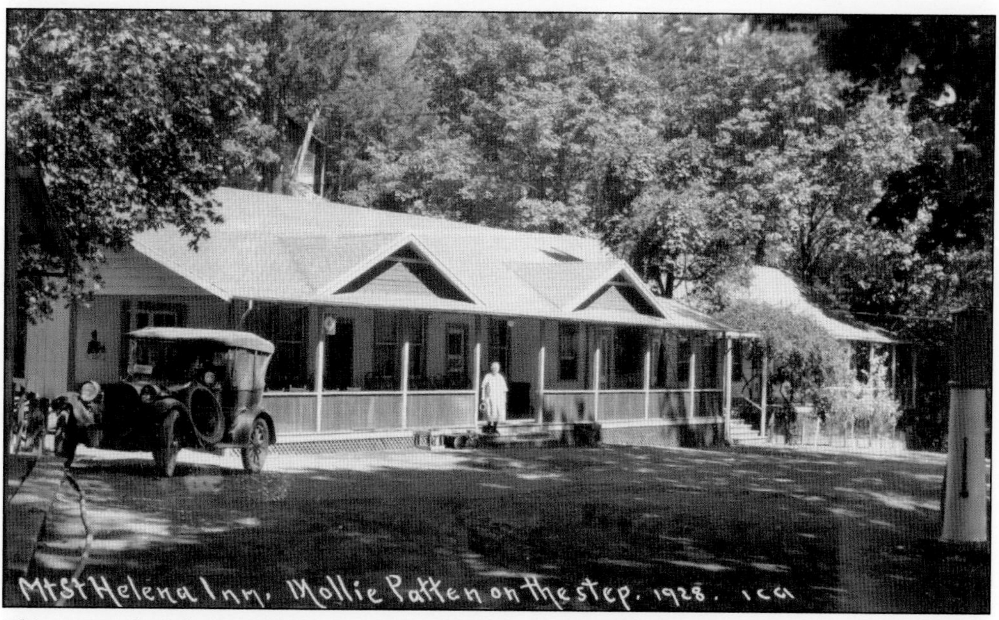

This postcard of the St. Helena Inn and toll road *c.* 1928 shows Mollie Lawley Patten in front of the inn; Mollie was John Lawley's daughter. The toll road was bought by the state in 1922 and became part of Highway 29. Later this area became part of the Robert Louis Stevenson State Park. The old tollhouse, which had fallen into disrepair, was torn down in 1953. (Courtesy of the Napa County Historical Society.)

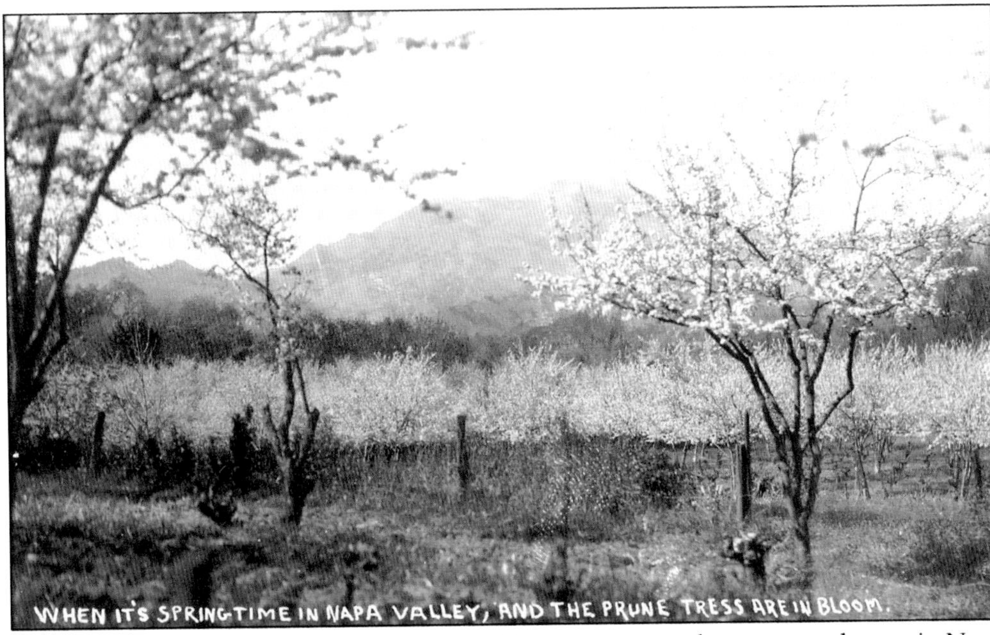

The image shows a Napa County prune orchard in bloom. Prunes became a staple crop in Napa County as a way to combat the phylloxera epidemic, which swept through the vineyards around the turn of the century. (Courtesy of the Sharpsteen Museum of Calistoga History.)

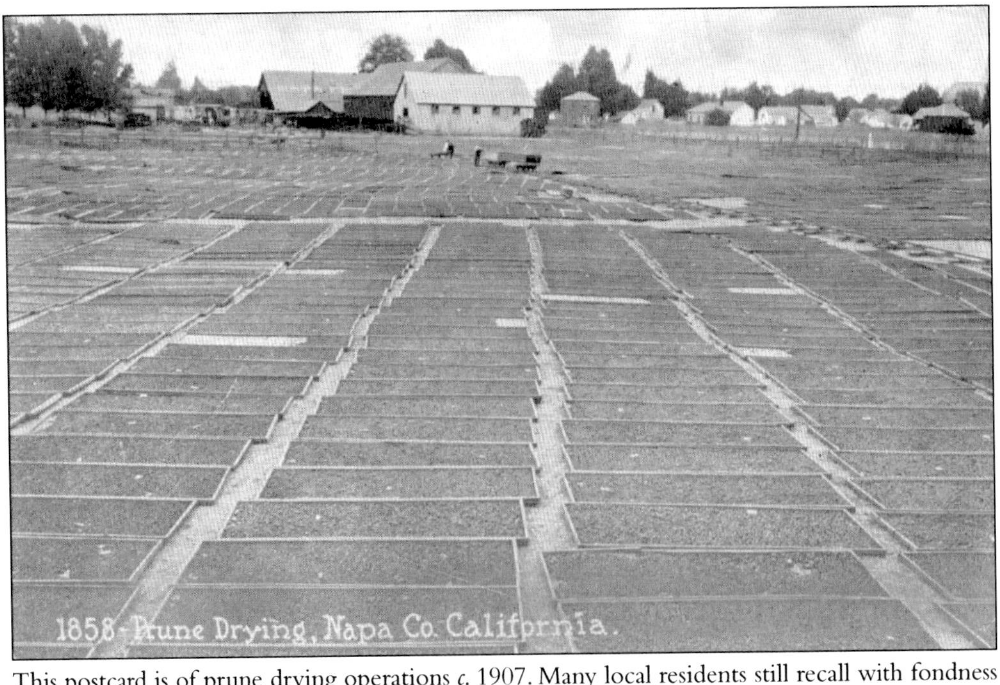

This postcard is of prune drying operations *c.* 1907. Many local residents still recall with fondness spending their summers as children picking the fruit for spending change. Much of the prune production, or dried plums as they are now known, in Northern California is now centralized in Sutter and Yuba Counties. (Author's collection.)

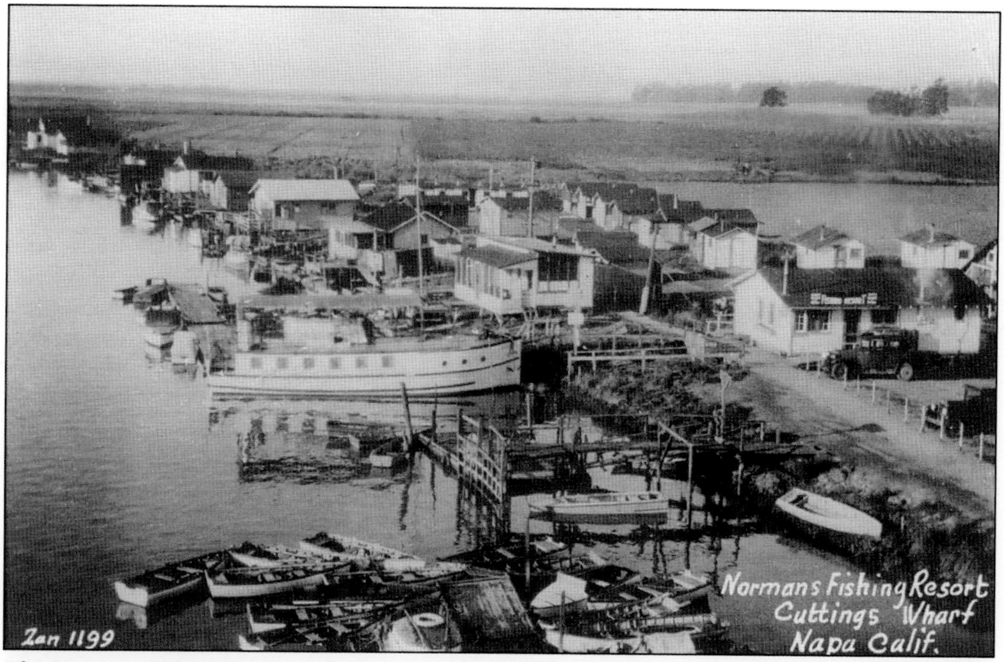

The Norman Fishing Resort is located at Cuttings Wharf in southwestern Napa County. The area was originally developed in 1893 by Francis Cutting as a docking site where ships could pick up fruit grown in Napa as part of the Cutting Fruit Packing Company. Napa County bought the site in 1924; there are currently public boat ramps that allow amateur anglers and pleasure-seekers access to the Napa River. (Author's collection.)

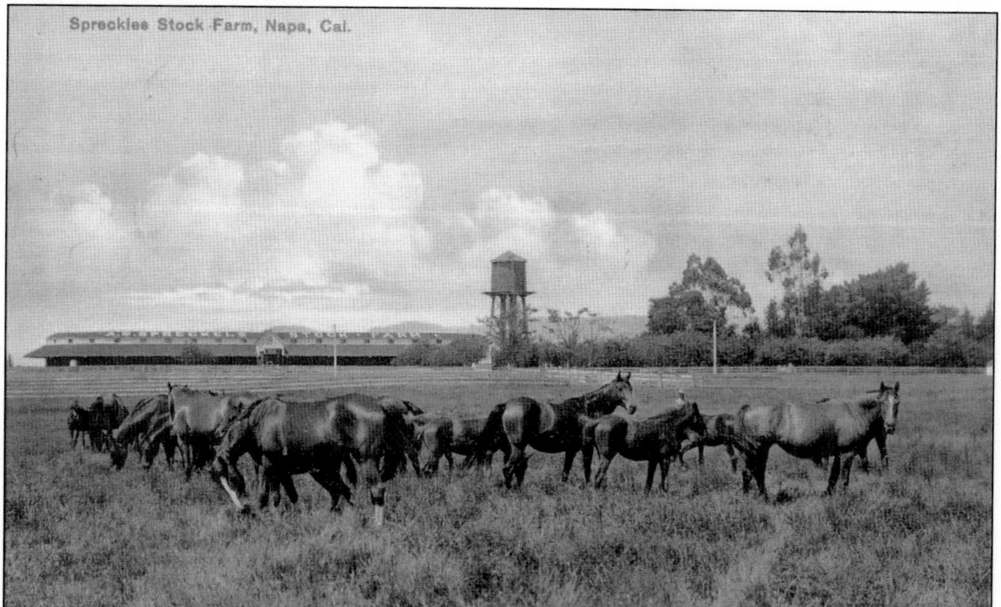

Adolph Spreckels's stock farm was located just south of Napa. The world-famous racehorse Seabiscuit was sired at the farm as well as Morvich; in 1922, Morvich became the first California-born horse to win the Kentucky Derby. Adolph's fortune came from the family business, the Spreckels Sugar Company. (Courtesy of the Napa County Historical Society.)

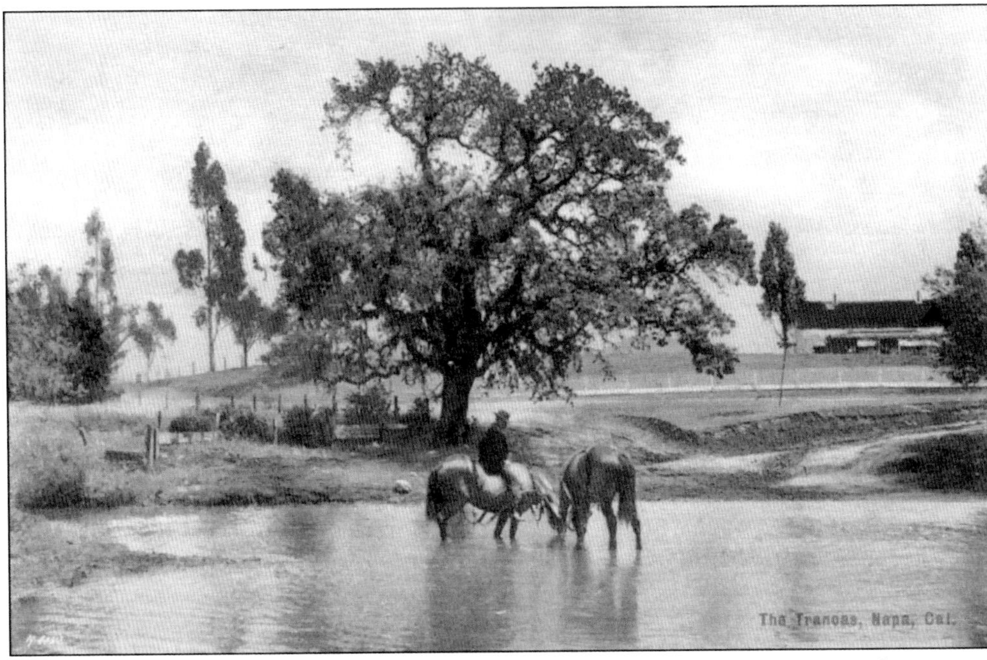

This postcard shows the Trancas Crossing at the Napa River as it appeared *c.* 1900. The area was originally named Trance by Salvador Vallejo, meaning "beam" or "crossbar" in Spanish. The Trancas was the most southerly area where cattle could cross the river, even at high tide; Vallejo placed a 30-foot-long fence at the area to prevent cattle crossings. The Trancas became a popular landmark and crossing point for those traversing the valley. (Author's collection.)

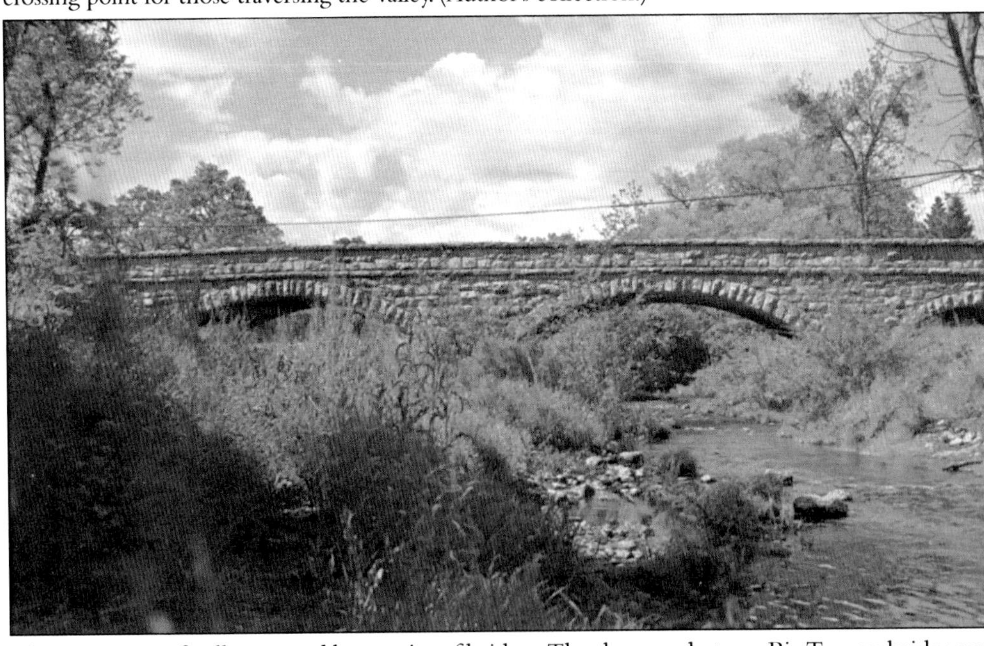

The Trancas was finally spanned by a series of bridges. The three-arch stone Big Trancas bridge was constructed in 1913. At the same time a smaller stone bridge, pictured in this postcard, and known as the Little Trancas was built to the east, spanning Milliken Creek. Both bridges still stand today. (Author's collection.)

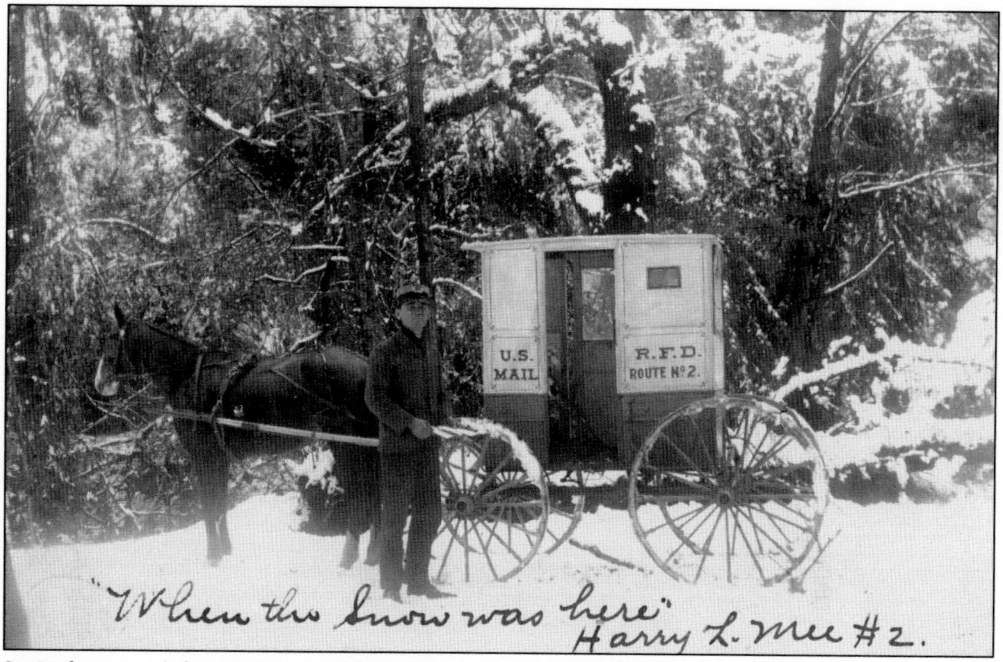

St. Helena rural free delivery mailman Harry L. Mee stands with his mail wagon in this 1907 photographic postcard, which he sent to his fellow Yountville mailman, C. W. Johnson. Mee appeared excited to show Johnson a rare snowfall, which he braved while following the postal service creed. (Courtesy of the Napa County Historical Society.)

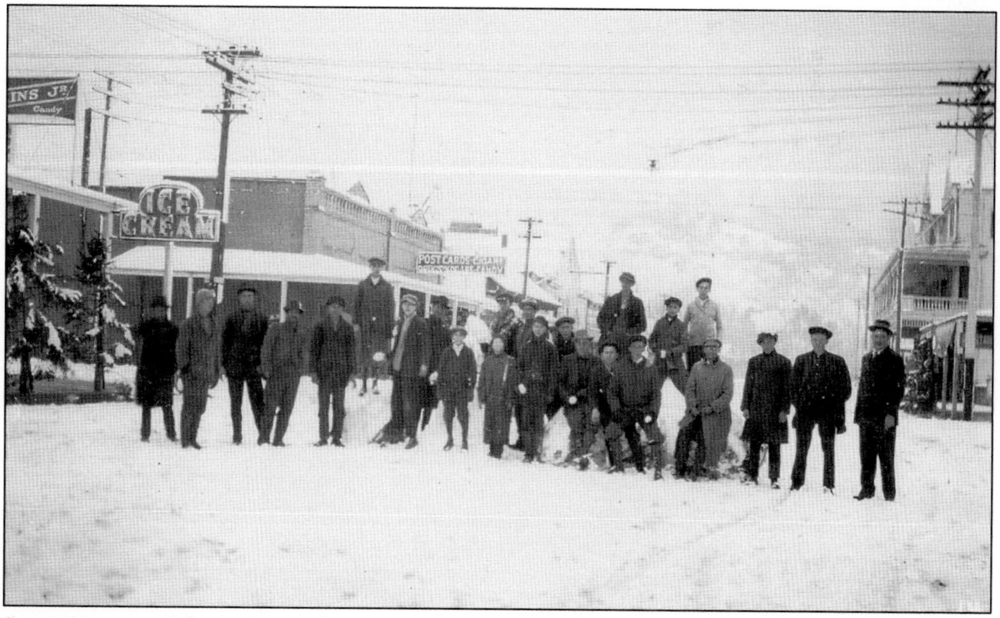

Snow is a rare sight in Napa County; the area's generally mild climate allows its agriculture to flourish. A snowstorm *c.* 1910 was cause for a group picture in the middle of Lincoln Avenue in Calistoga. (Courtesy of the Sharpsteen Museum of Calistoga History.)

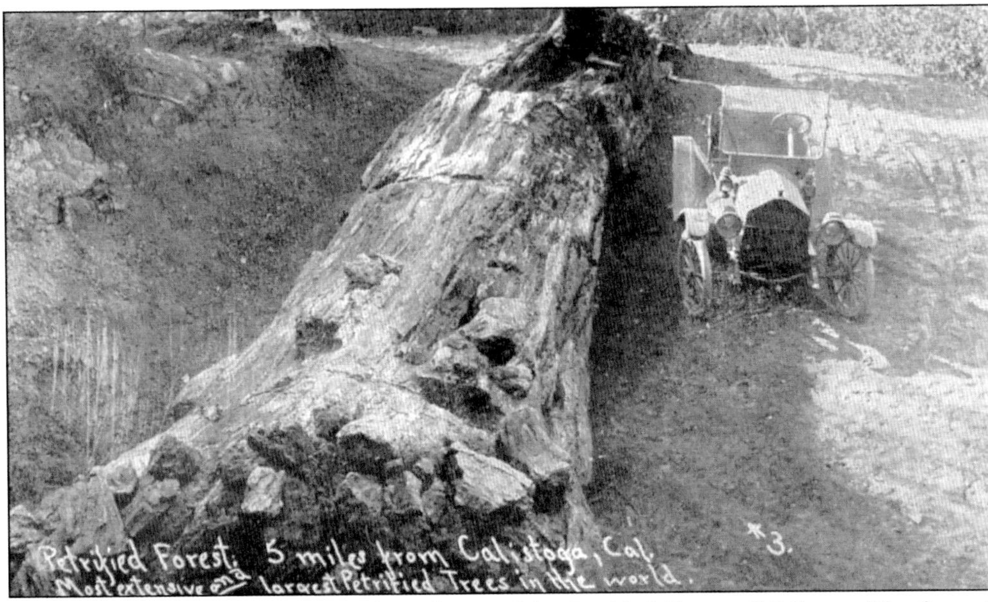

Pictured here is the "queen of the forest," part of the Petrified Forest of Calistoga. The forest is located about 5 miles west of Calistoga in the Mayacamas Mountains. William Travis originally discovered it in 1857. It was owned by "Petrified Charlie" Denison in 1879 when author Robert Louis Stevenson visited; in his book *Silverado Squatters*, he described Charlie as a "brave old white-faced Swede [having] had wandered this way . . . And taken up his acres . . . All alone, bent double with sciatica." (Author's collection.)

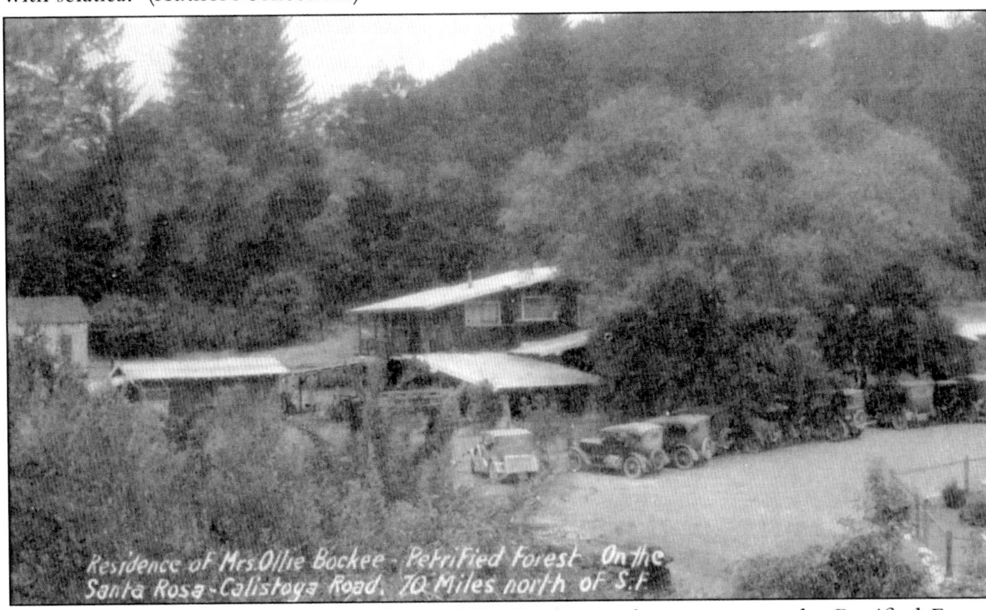

This postcard shows the residence of Mrs. Ollie Bockee at the entrance to the Petrified Forest. Bockee bought the forest in 1914 and began a 25-year excavation and promotion effort. Her son built the house, which also included a gift shop. Bockee was constantly looking for publicity; her efforts included giving a petrified tree to New York City and exhibiting one at the 1915 Pan-American Exposition. Bockee passed away in 1950. The forest is now owned by her sister's grandchildren. (Author's collection.)

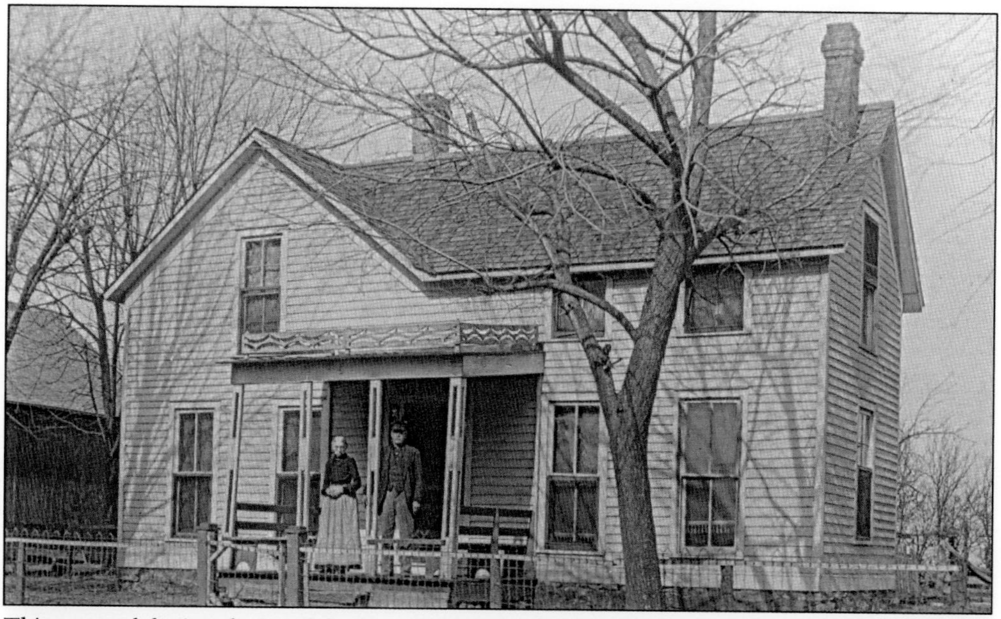

This postcard depicts the Laird family and their homestead in the town of Monticello. Monticello was located in the area now known as Lake Berryessa. It was first settled in the late 1860s. Monticello's population peaked at about 500 and had declined to about 125 by the 1950s. The Monticello Dam construction began in 1953, damming up Putah Creek and inundating Monticello to form Lake Berryessa, the second largest lake in California. The lake provides water and electricity for portions of Northern California. (Author's collection.)

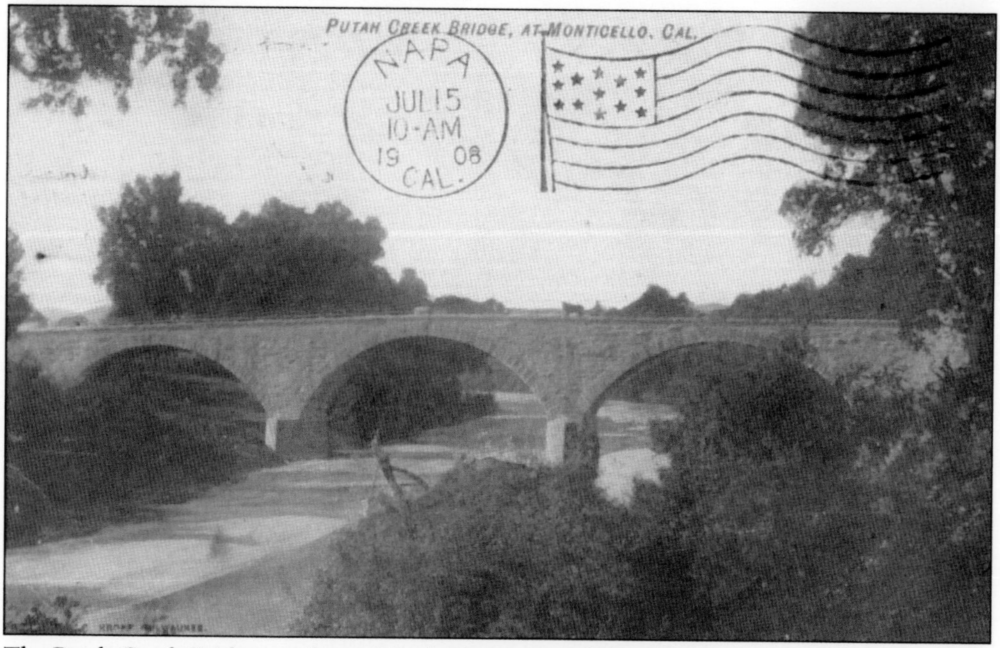

The Putah Creek Bridge was located in the Berryessa Valley near the town of Monticello. At the time of this postcard, in 1908, it was the largest masonry bridge west of the Rockies. The bridge, whose nickname was "Queen of the Bridges," is now submerged under Lake Berryessa like the rest of the Berryessa Valley. (Courtesy of Mike Vanwormer.)

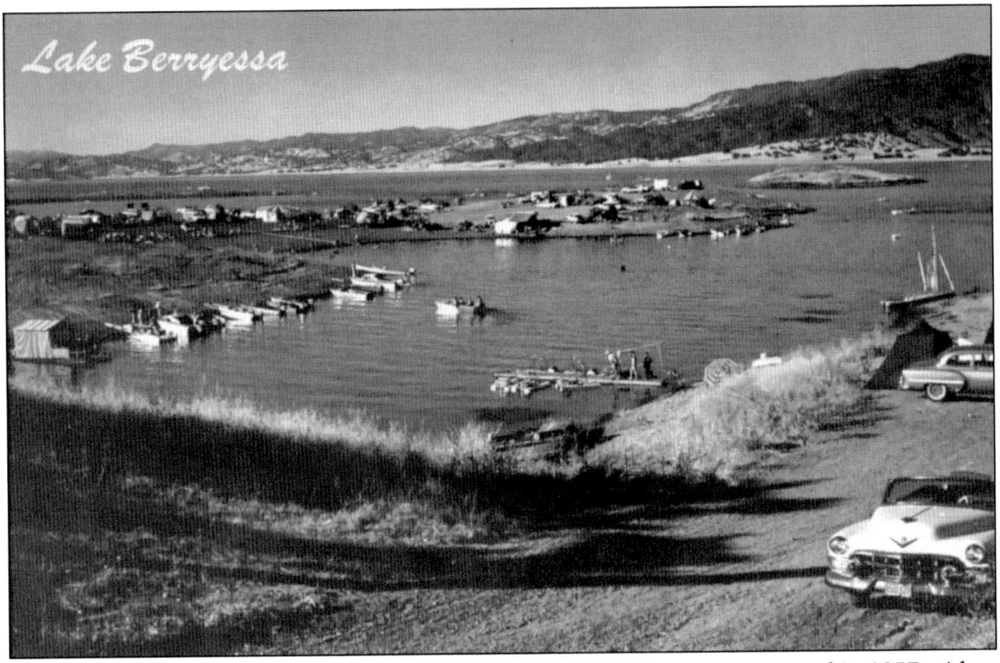

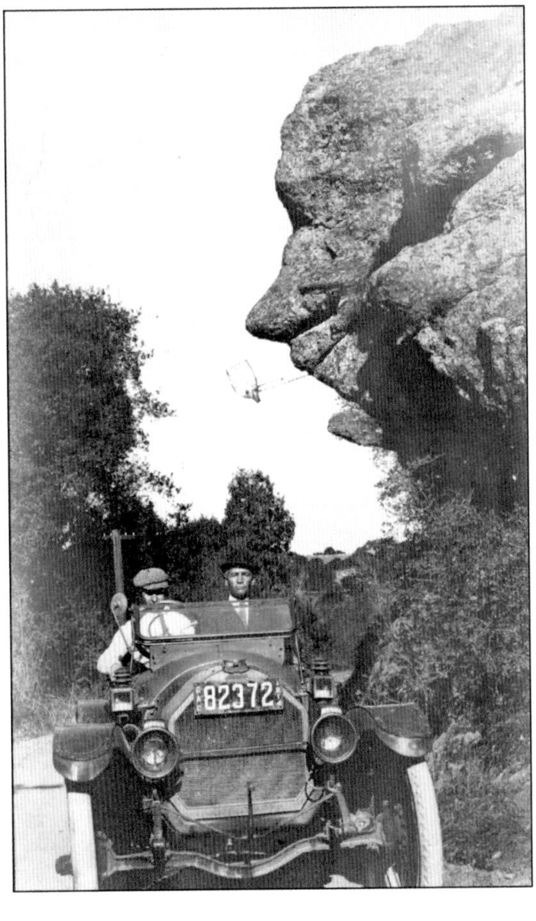

Lake Berryessa was created in 1957 with the damming of Putah Creek. Lake Berryessa is managed by the Federal Bureau of Reclamation. It offers camping, restaurants, and marinas. Until 2008, the lake had seven resorts that were managed by private concessions under contract with the federal government. These contracts are being renegotiated to allow for more day and short-term use. An estimated 1.5 million people visit Lake Berryessa every year. (Author's collection.)

The "Old Irishman" or "Man with the Pipe" is a natural rock formation etched into the side of a mountain east of Napa. It has delighted travelers along Monticello Road for years. In 1911, the distinctive pipe was added to the formation. (Courtesy of the Napa County Historical Society.)

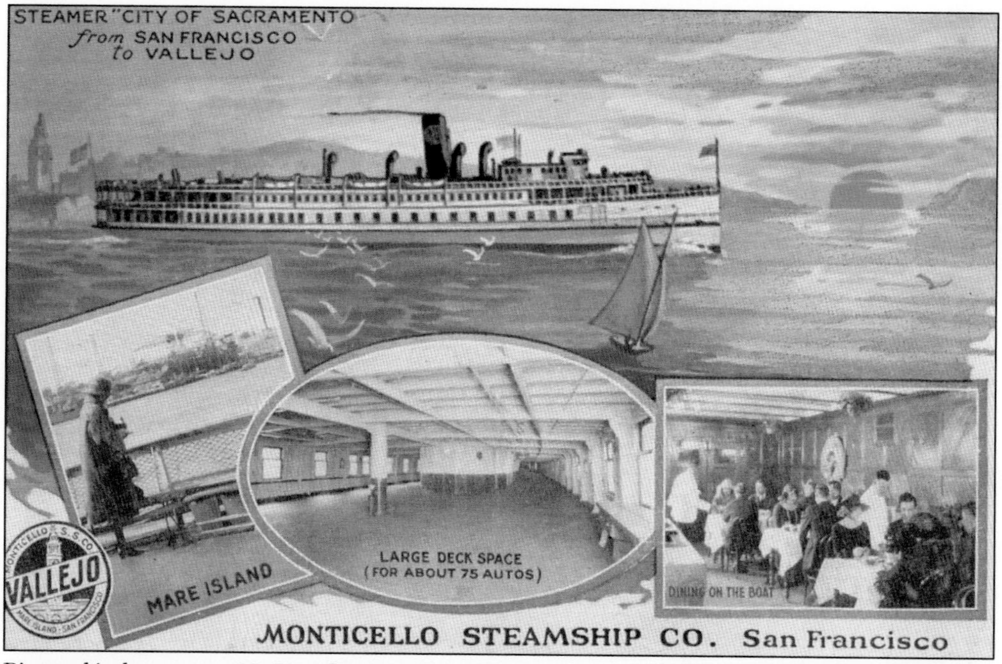

Pictured is the steamer SS *City of Sacramento* as she appeared in 1925. She was part of the Monticello Steamship Line, a vital link for people traveling to Napa County from San Francisco. Passengers boarded at the ferry building for the trip across the bay to Vallejo. From there, they would catch either the Southern Pacific (SP) train or the electric railroad for the final leg of the journey to Napa. The entire trip took two and a half hours. (Author's collection.)

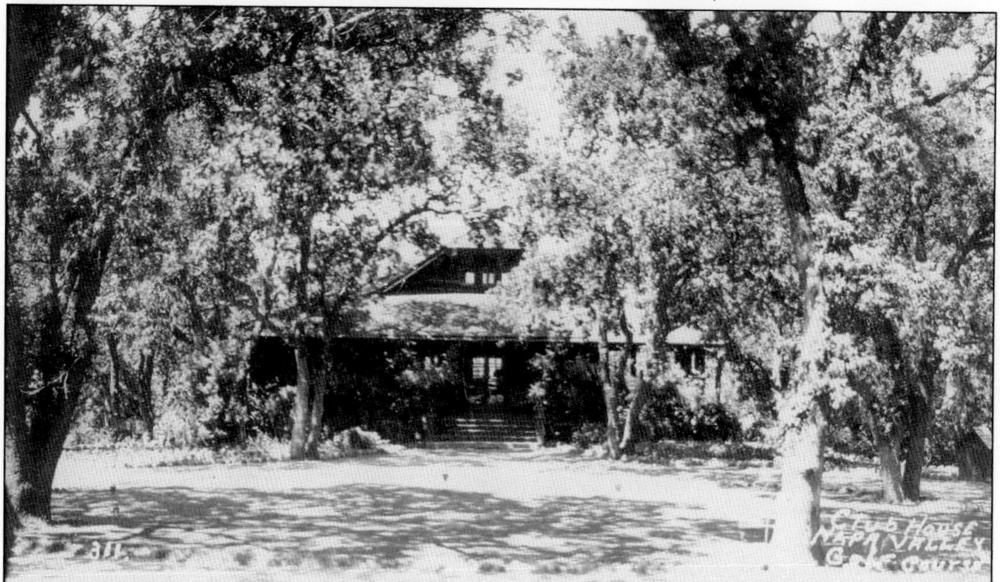

The Napa Valley Country Club is located on Hagen Road in the Coombsville area east of Napa. It was founded in 1915 by several prominent Napans, including Charles Trower, E. G. Manasse, James Migliavacca, and Frank Noyes. The clubhouse pictured amongst the trees was constructed in 1924. The course contained only nine holes until 1986, when the back nine were added. (Author's collection.)

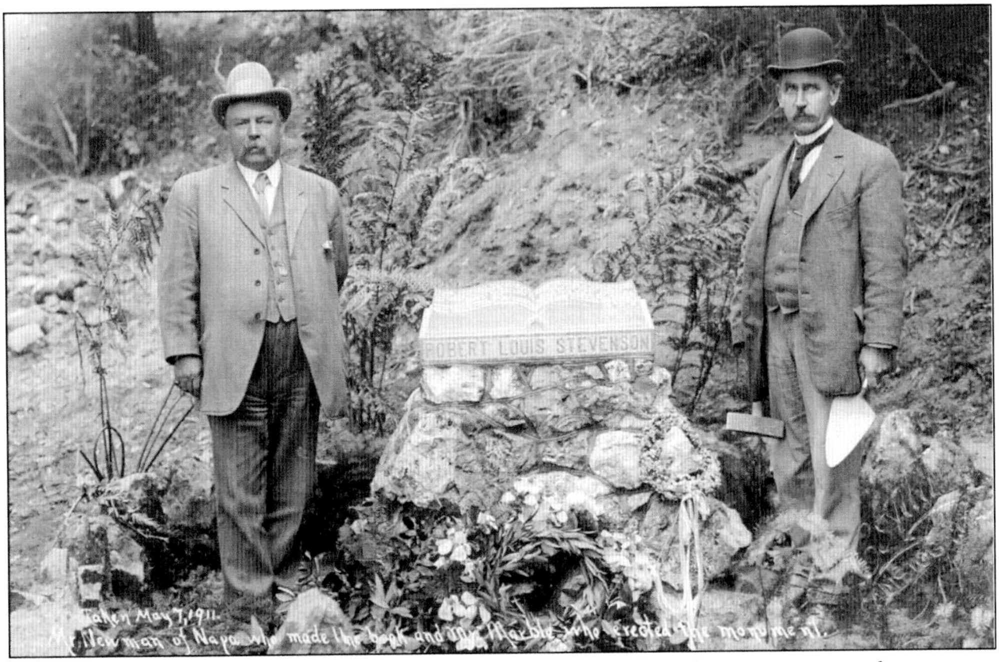

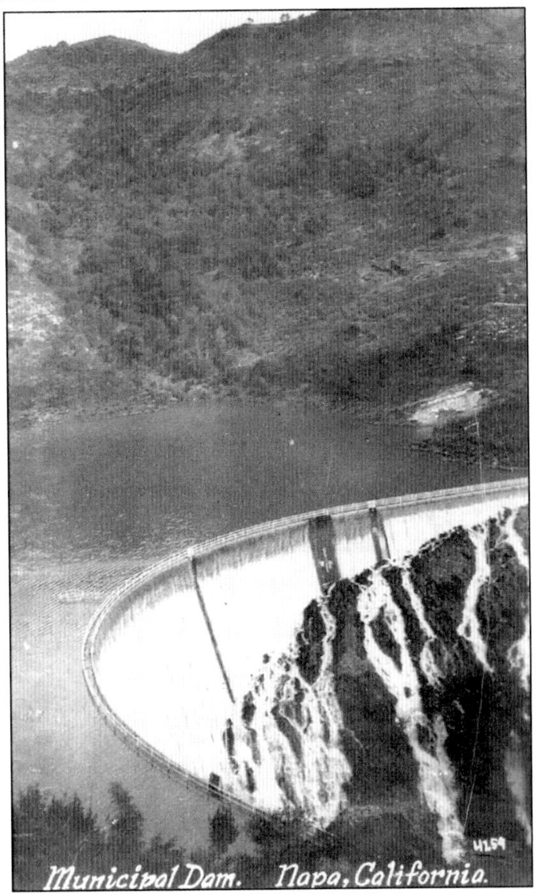

This postcard commemorates the dedication of a historical marker in honor of the author Robert Louis Stevenson. It was the first marker placed in Napa County, dedicated in 1911 by the Federated Women's Clubs of Napa County on the site of the abandoned miner's cabin where Stevenson honeymooned and wrote *Silverado Squatters*. (Courtesy of the Sharpsteen Museum of Calistoga History.)

The Conn Dam is noted on this postcard as the municipal dam. It was conceived during World War II as a way to add much needed capacity to Napa's water supply. The dam was completed in 1948. The reservoir it created was named Lake Hennessey in 1951, in honor of retiring Napa city council member Edwin Hennessey. The dam and reservoir area are located just east of the town of Rutherford. (Author's collection.)

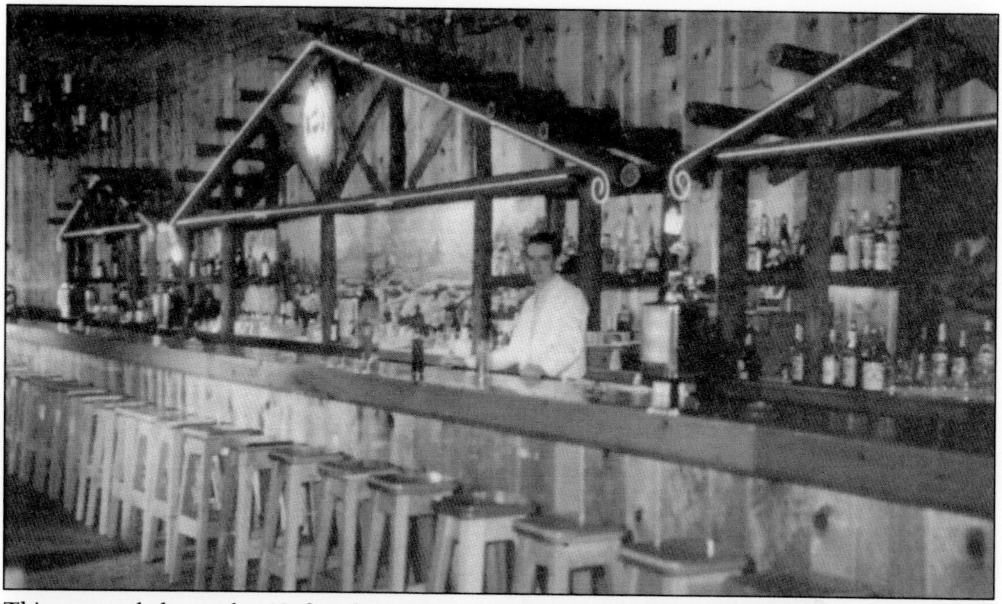

This postcard shows the 12-foot-long bar inside Bothe's Paradise Park. Bothe's was located on Highway 29 just south of Calistoga. It featured cabins, a swimming pool, bar, and roadhouse, and even had its own small airstrip. It was on land that was once the home to Lille Coit, the heiress whose affinity for the San Francisco Fire Department is visible in the landmark Coit Tower. In 1960, the area became Bothe Napa Valley State Park. (Author's collection.)

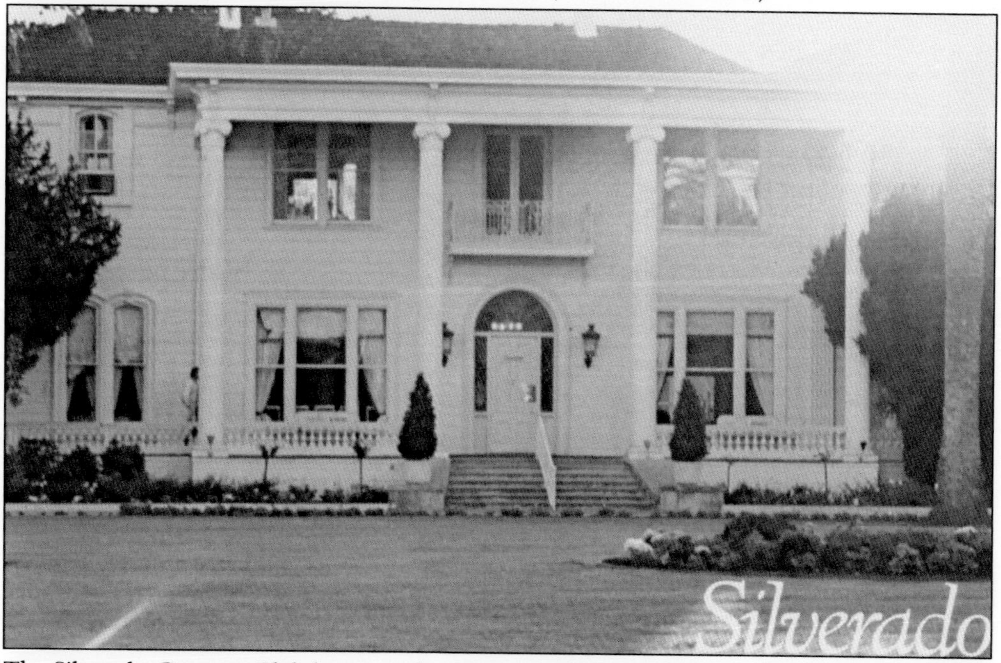

The Silverado Country Club began as the private residence of Civil War veteran John F. Miller. The mansion was built in the 1870s; he named it La Verge after a battle in which he fought. The mansion became the clubhouse of the partially private golf course in 1953. The resort was expanded to include a hotel in 1966. Today the Silverado Resort is the centerpiece of a gated community of multimillion-dollar homes. (Courtesy of the Napa County Historical Society.)

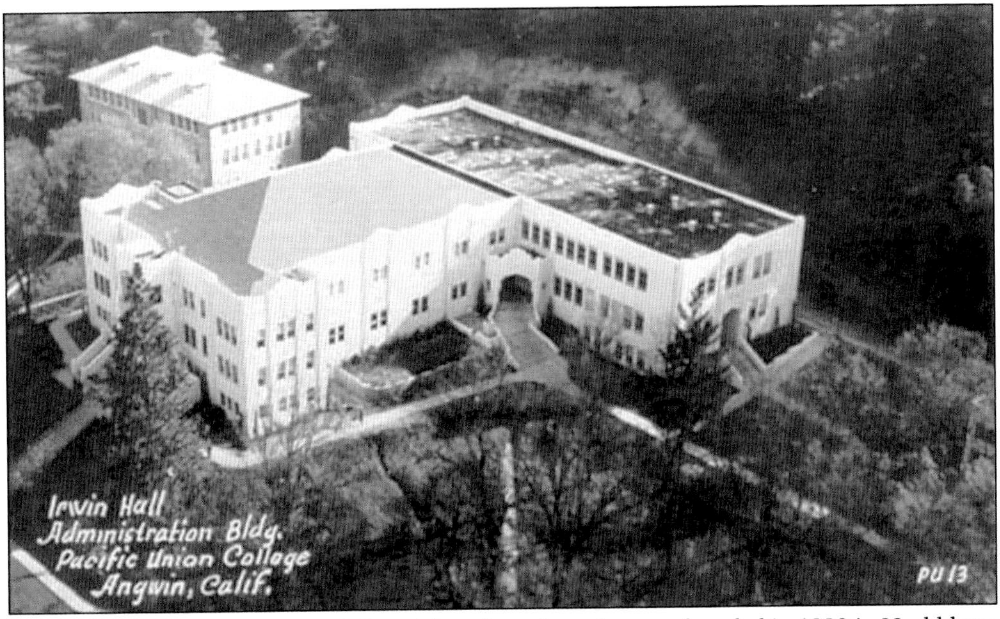

Pacific Union College is a Seventh Day Adventist college that was founded in 1882 in Healdsburg (in neighboring Sonoma County). The college purchased the Angwin Resort on Howell Mountain in Napa County in 1909. Many of the dorms and classrooms were converted from resort buildings or built by students and faculty. (Author's collection.)

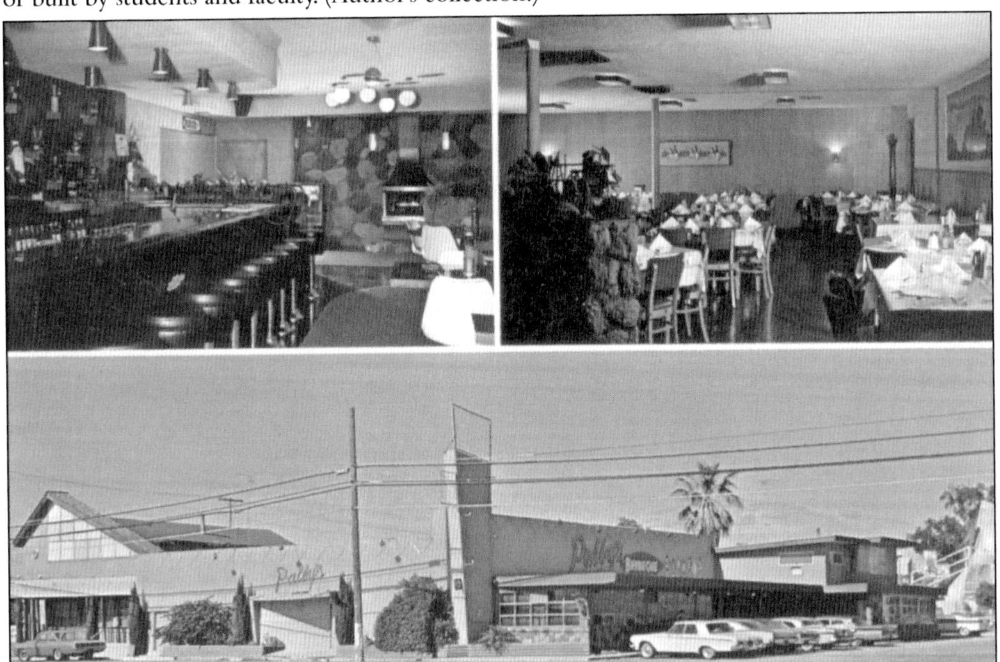

Palby's Restaurant was a fixture along Highway 29 for many years, predating the young city of American Canyon that grew up around it. Its name was a contracted combination of its owner's names, Pete and Alba Freskan. Originally opened by the Freskans in 1924 as a small grocery store, it became a nightclub and finally the restaurant. The site was sold in 2003 and redeveloped into a business park known as Palby's Junction. (Author's collection.)

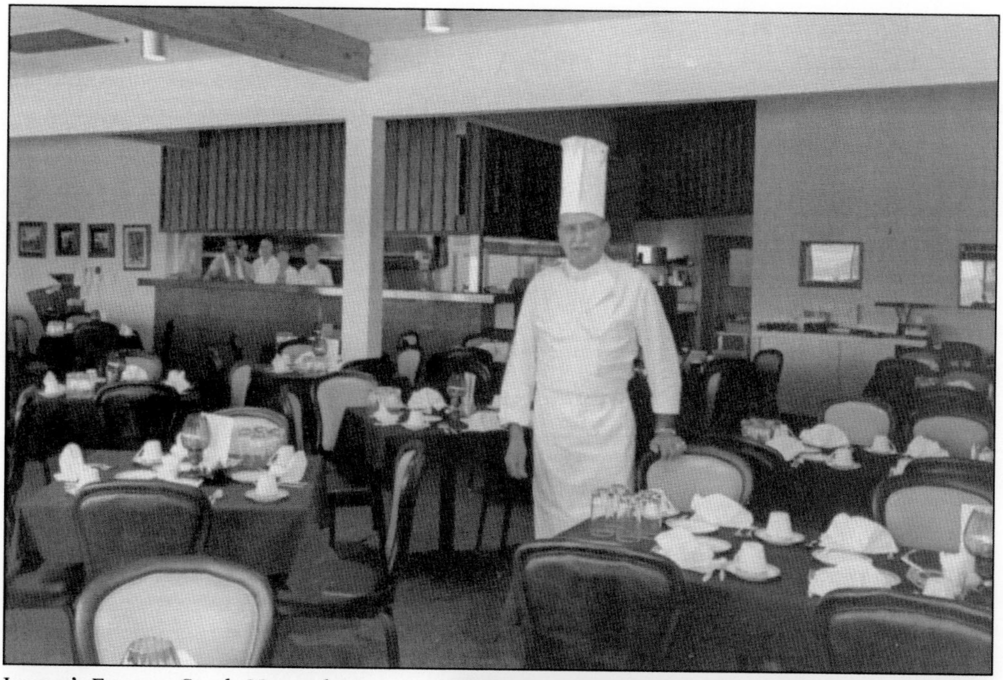

Jonesy's Famous Steak House has been a staple of Napa County diners since 1946. Located at the Napa County Airport, it offers a wall of windows from which patrons can watch the comings and goings of the private planes, corporate jets, and the pilots-in-training from the nearby Japan Airlines facility. Jonesy's was extensively remodeled in 2005. (Author's collection.)

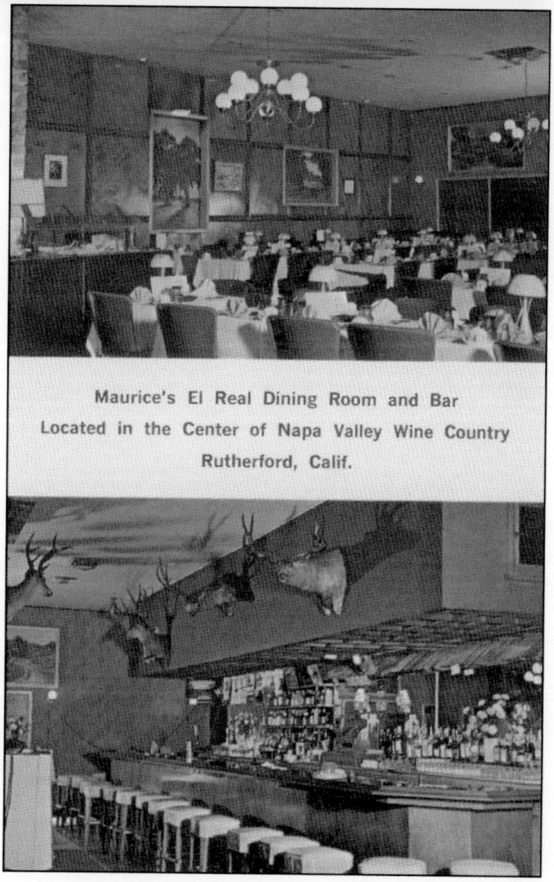

The El Real Restaurant was a fixture in the tiny town of Rutherford for many years. It was located on Rutherford Road just east of Highway 29. Owners Maurice and Frances Autenrieth dished up Italian fare from 1946 until 1971, when the building burned down. It was an important meeting place for local community groups, families, workers, and tourists alike. (Author's collection.)

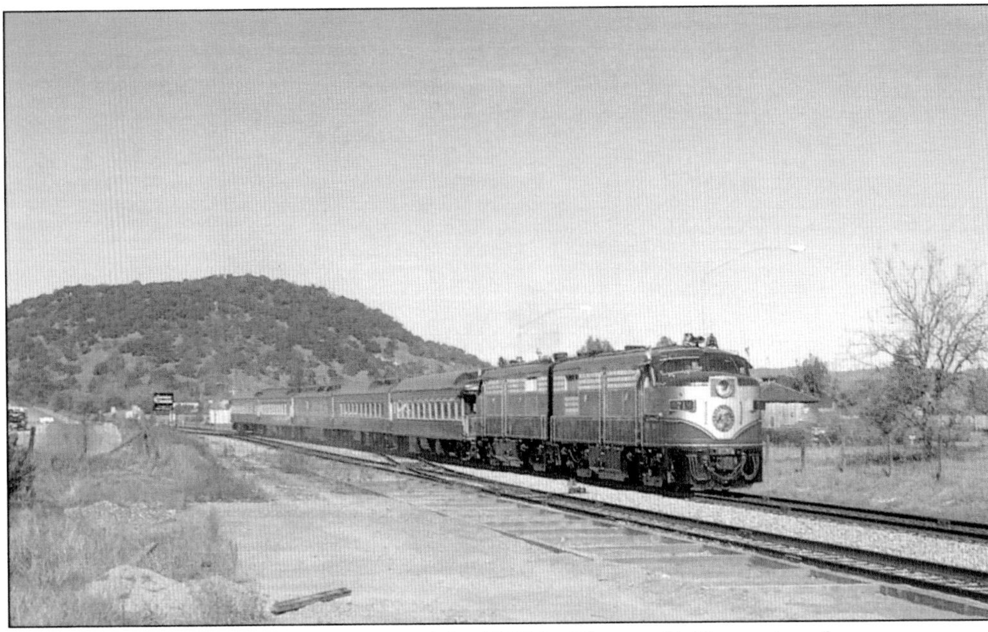

The Napa Valley Wine Train was created in 1987 by Vincent DeDomenico, former owner of the Golden Grain and Ghirardelli Chocolate Companies. The tourist train runs from Napa to St. Helena on the same tracks first laid down by entrepreneur Sam Brannan in the 1860s. The train uses restored Pullman and observation cars to take tourists on lunch or dinner excursions, sometimes stopping along the way for wine tasting. (Author's collection.)

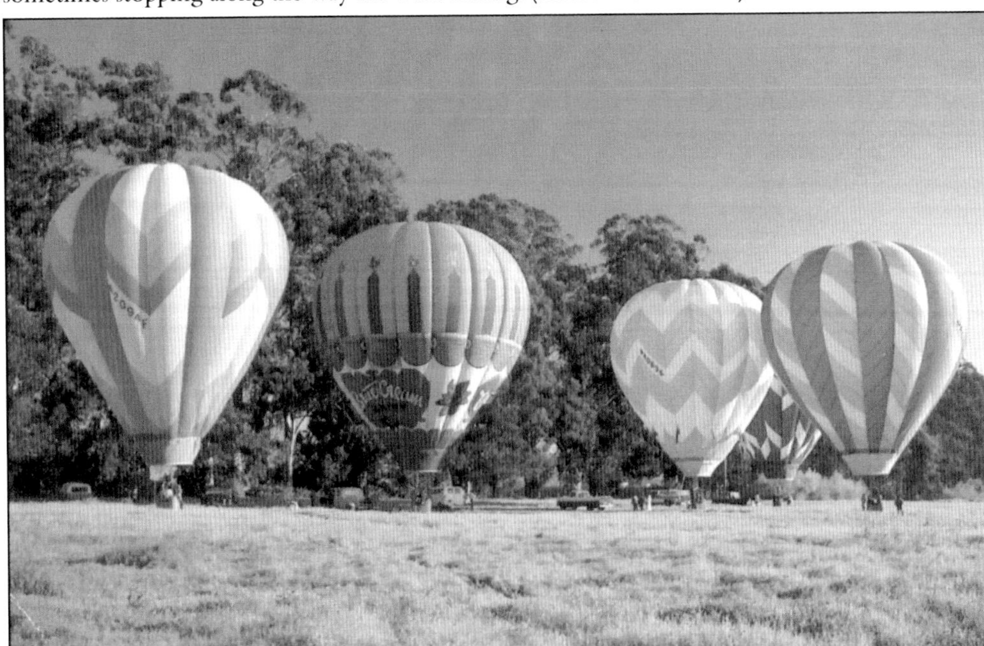

Hot air ballooning has become a popular pastime for tourists visiting Napa County. They typically launch at sunrise from sites mid-valley and drift either north or south as the wind takes them. Over the years, more people have taken balloon rides over the Napa Valley than any other flight corridor in the world. (Author's collection.)

Two

Mind and Body

From the early days of white settlement in the area, Napa County has been recognized as a destination for those seeking relief for the ailments of their minds and bodies. The area's mineral hot springs were harnessed and provided bottled elixirs and baths for the weary. Napa County enjoyed a boom period for these resorts from the late 1800s through the first decade of the 1900s. They dotted the valley and surrounding mountains. The advent of the automobile and air travel allowed bay area residents to take vacations farther from home, spelling the end of the destination resort era.

The area also attracted the medical community that was eager to treat those with mental and physical illnesses. The first hospital was the Napa County Infirmary, erected in 1869 west of Napa on a 12-acre site.

The St. Helena Sanitarium and Napa State Asylum took markedly different approaches to the treatment of mental illness. While patients at St. Helena were mostly self-admitted, seeking a cleansing of their bodies and minds, those at the state asylum were frequently prisoners of their psychological illnesses.

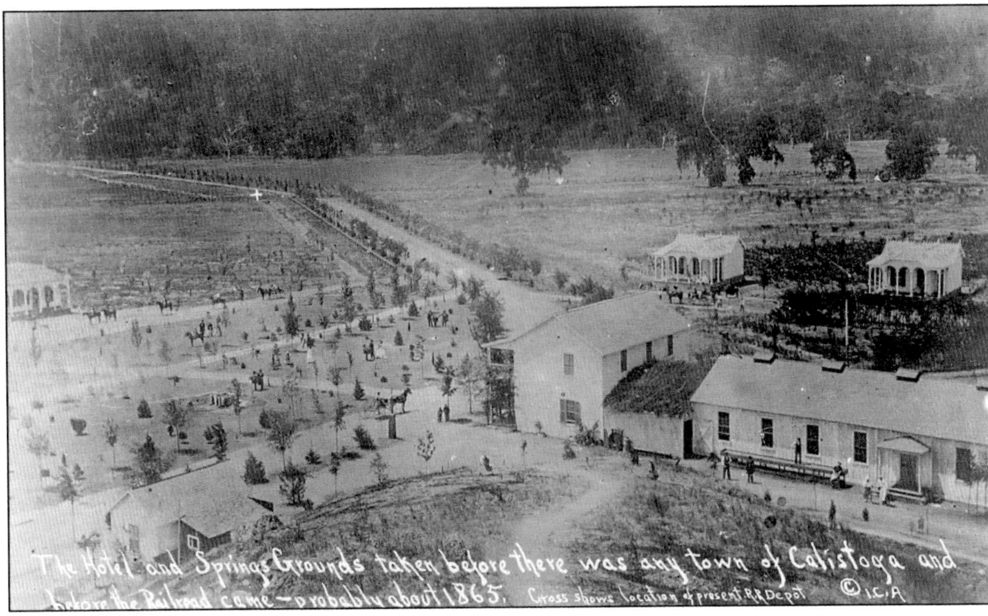

Entrepreneur Sam Brannan was the father of Calistoga. In 1862, he opened his Calistoga Hot Springs Resort by chartering a steamship to bring guests to Napa, shuttling them via stagecoach to the resort. Brannan's resort included a hotel, observatory, racetrack, skating rink, swimming pool, and sulphur and mud baths. The postcard shows an overview of the resort as it appeared around 1865. (Courtesy of the Sharpsteen Museum of Calistoga History.)

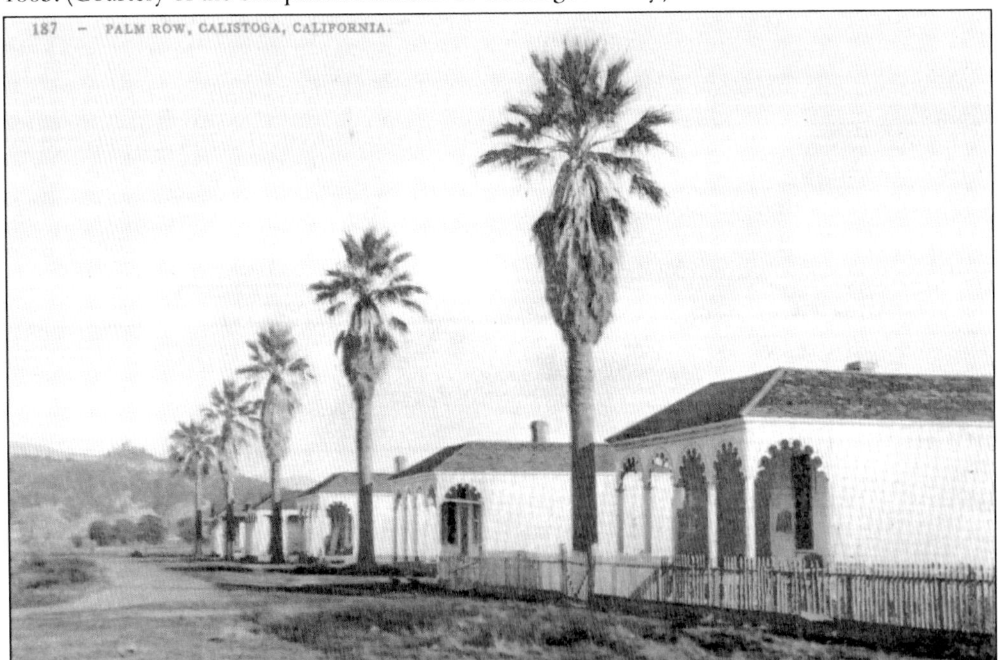

These distinctive cottages were built by Brannan as a means of attracting VIP clientele. Each five-room cottage had a palm tree planted with it. One of the last surviving cottages is currently part of the Sharpsteen Museum of Calistoga History and has been fully restored. (Courtesy of the Sharpsteen Museum of Calistoga History.)

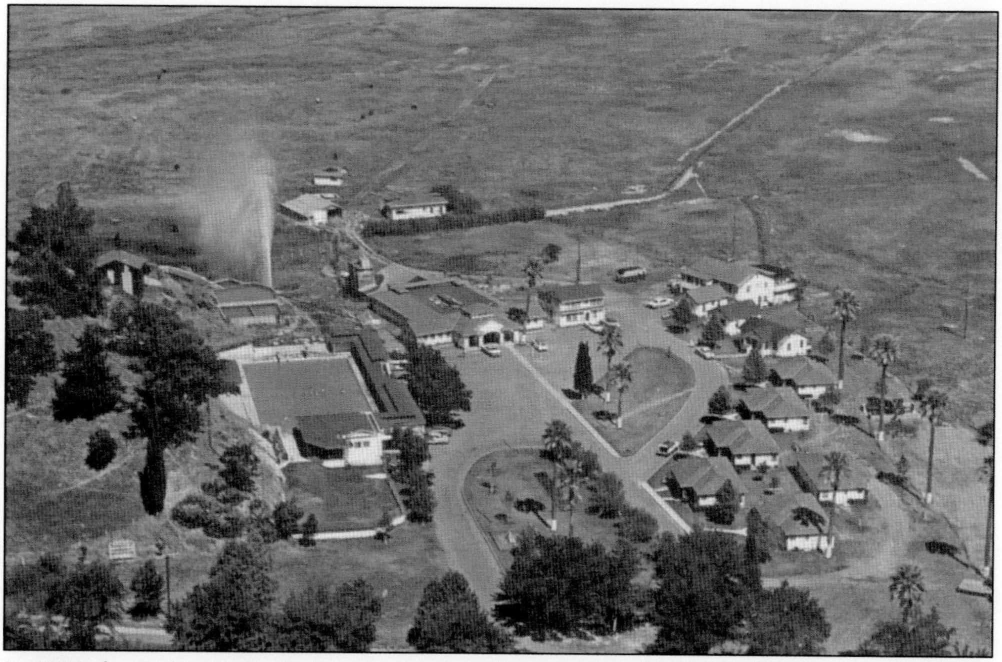

In 1905, the Pacheteau family bought the site of the former resort owned by Sam Brannan. They constructed the main building, visible at the center of this postcard, and renamed the resort the Pacheteau Baths. Eventually the Pacheteau would have several swimming pools, cottages, and a trailer park. In 1988, the Pacheteau was sold again and renamed Indian Springs. (Author's collection.)

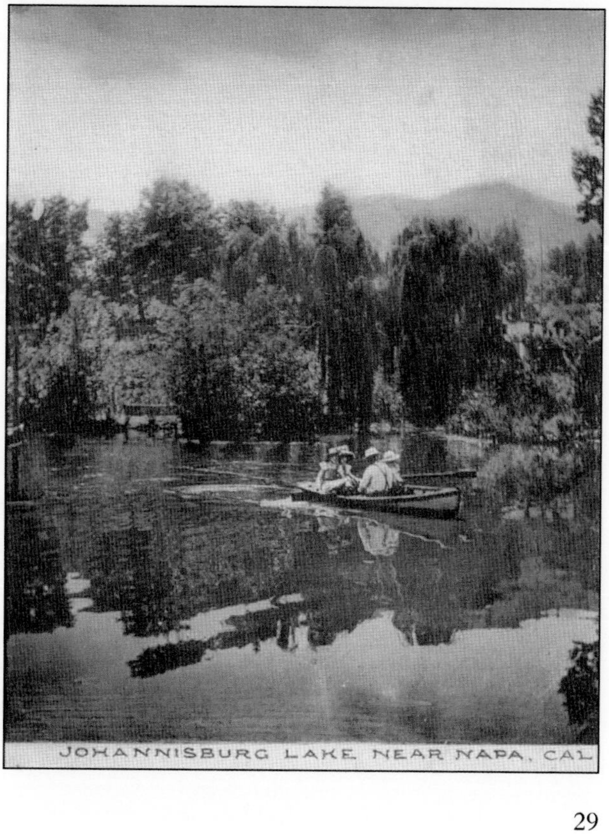

The Johannisberg Resort, the brainchild of Theodore Blanckenburg, was a seasonal retreat located on 300 acres in the redwoods of Mount Veeder. It featured the pictured lake, rose gardens, vineyards, lawn tennis, and a bowling alley. Guests would take the train or electric railroad to the Oakville Depot and then board stagecoaches for the 7-mile ride up to the resort. (Author's collection.)

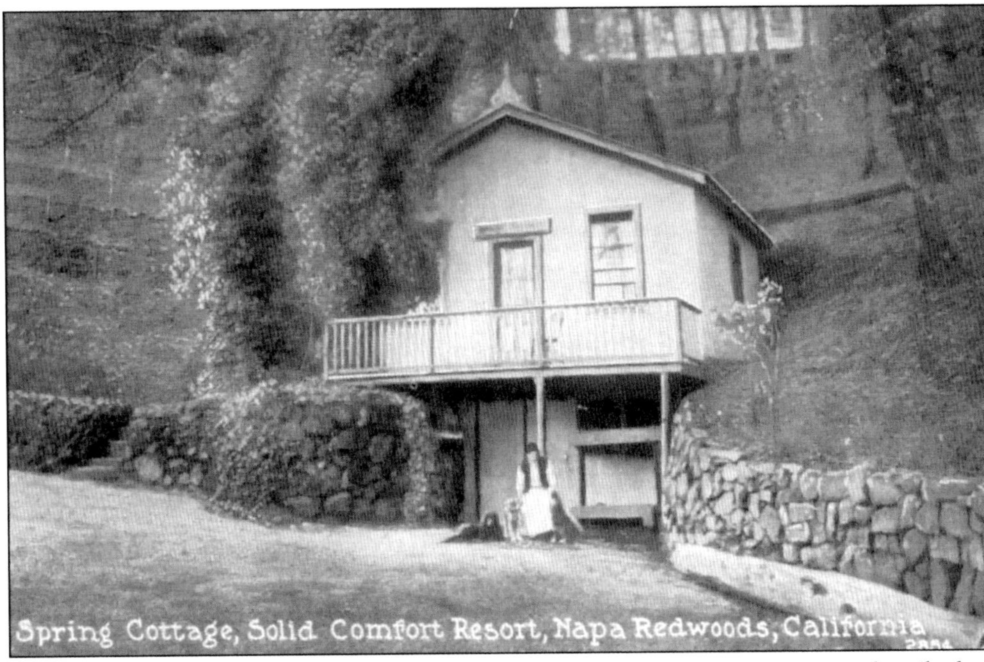

The Solid Comfort Resort was located about 9 miles northwest of Napa in an area described on this postcard as being the Napa Redwoods on Mount Veeder. This same area later became the Lokoya Mountain Lodge. (Author's collection.)

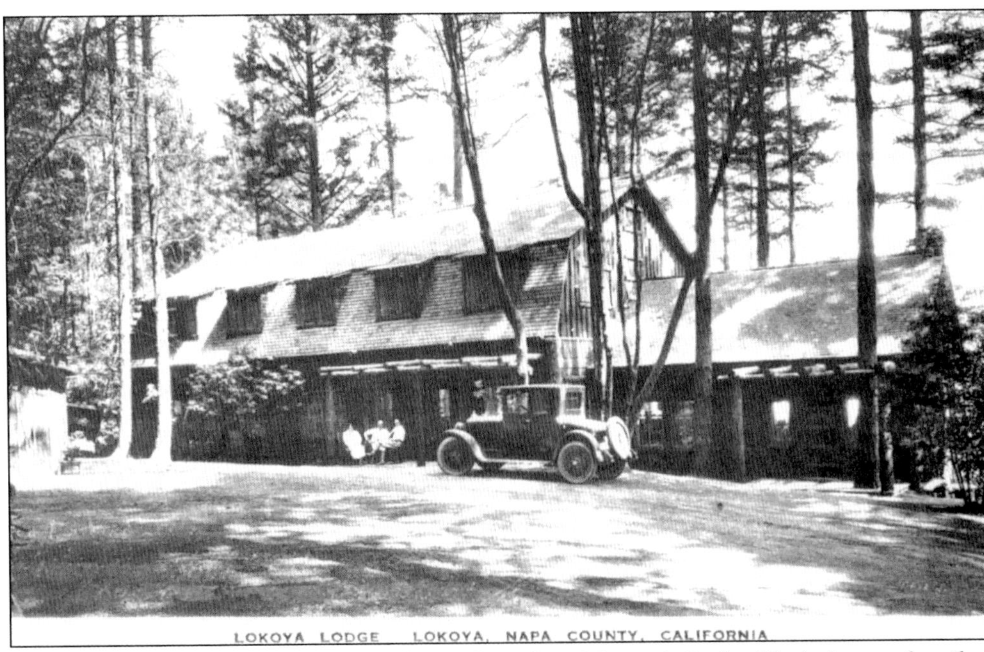

This postcard shows the main lodge building at the Lokoya Mountain Lodge. The lodge was described as being at the "top o' the world" and included a main lodge, pool, and rustic cottages. The Lokoya also ran separate boy and girl's camps. (Courtesy of the Napa County Historical Society.)

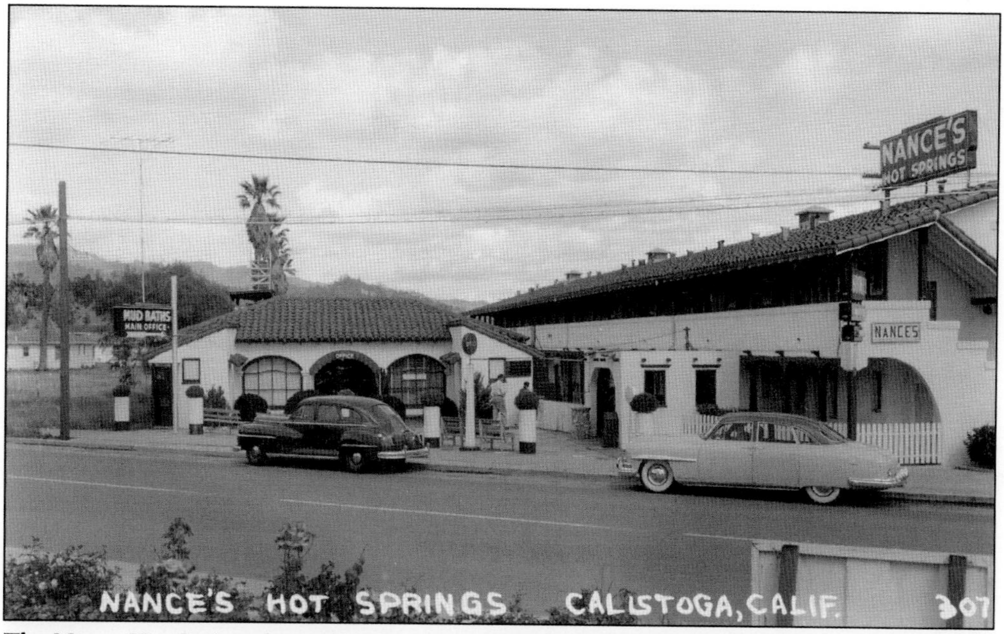

The Nance Hot Springs, located at 1614 Lincoln Avenue, was also known as Nance's Sanitarium. Founded in the early 1920s by Charles Nance, a former employee of the Pacheteau Resort, the resort featured sulphur baths, volcanic ash mud baths, physiotherapy, and colonic irrigations. In 2004, the owners of the adjoining Indian Springs Report bought Nance's and extensively renovated it; the original Nance's building is now known as the Lodge. (Author's collection.)

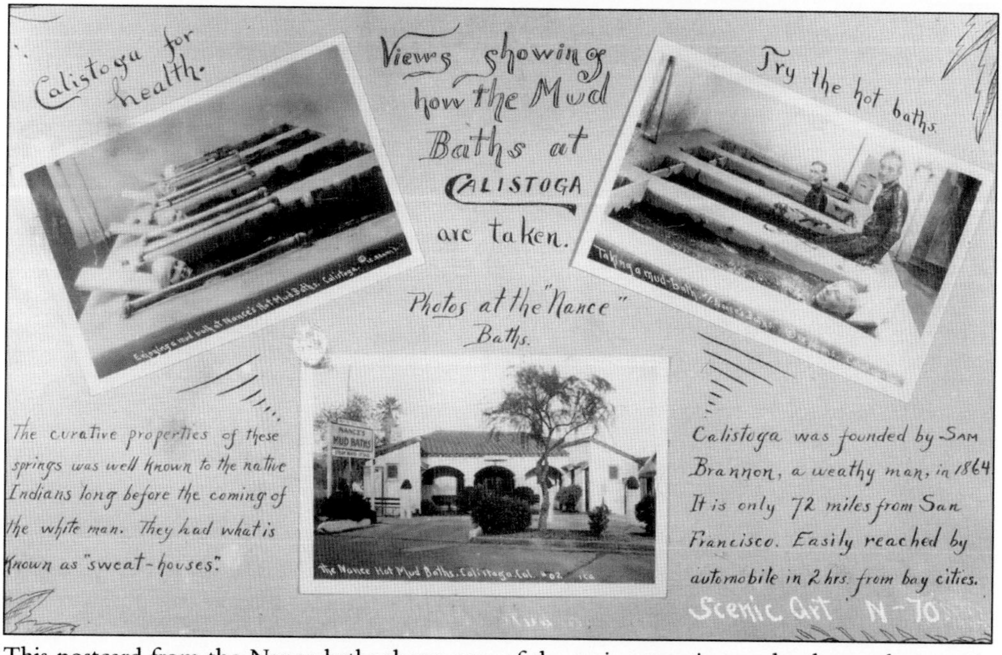

This postcard from the Nance baths shows one of the main attractions at local spas: therapeutic mud baths. The baths contained volcanic ash and peat moss, which were mixed with the natural hot springs water. (Author's collection.)

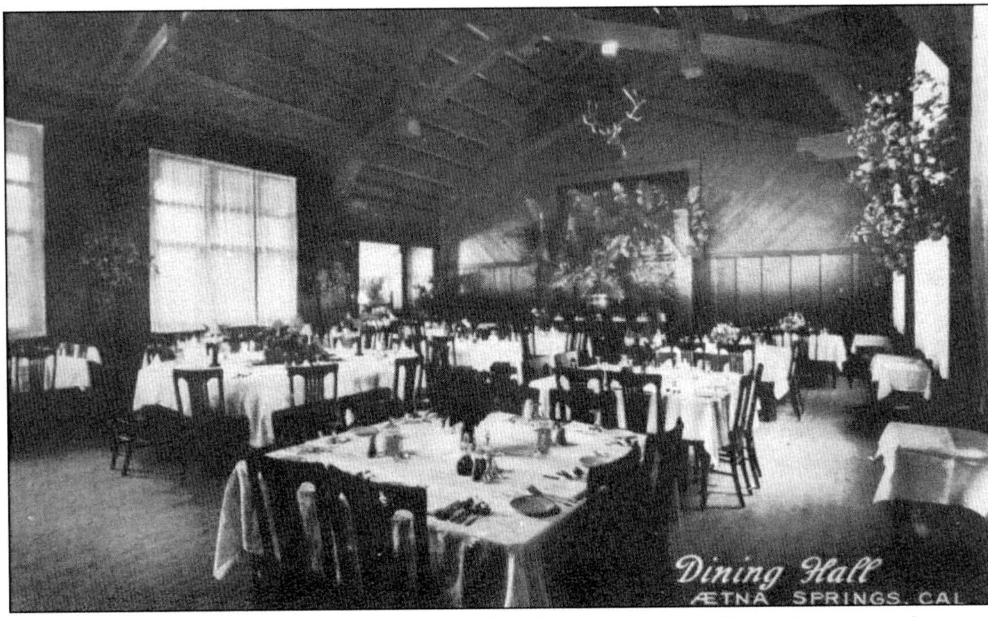

The Aetna Springs Resort, located in Pope Valley, began as a quicksilver mine. Once the mine played out, the resort was developed by Chancellor Hartson and opened in 1873. It featured elaborate wood structures, including the pictured dining hall, a lodge building, and guest cabins. Aetna installed a golf course in 1893, which is still in operation today. It is believed to be the oldest continuously operated golf course west of the Mississippi. (Author's collection.)

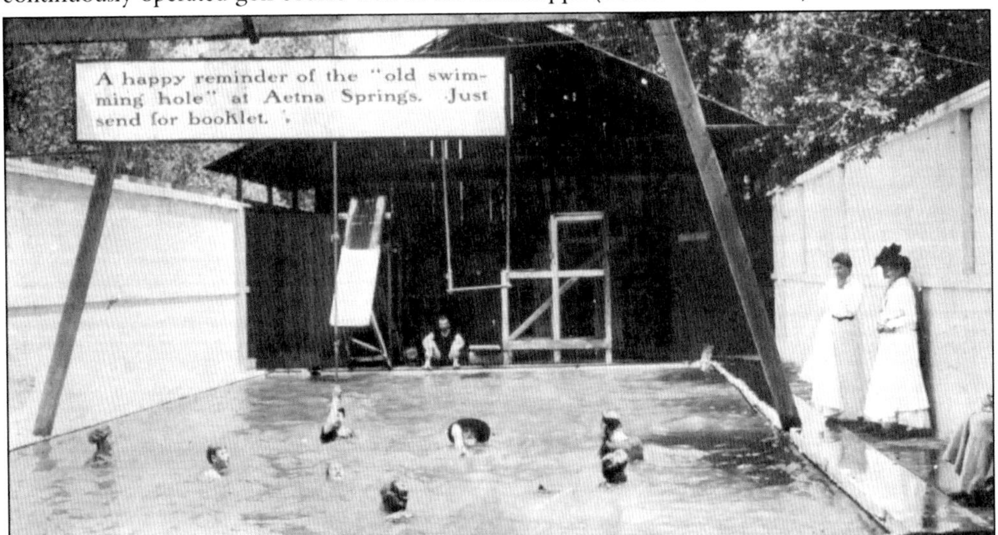

The mineral water of Aetna Springs was thought to have curative powers. It was touted to be a cure for bronchitis, stomach catarrhs, and laryngitis. It was also thought to open pores, allowing unhealthy secretions to exit, and was said to be charged with electricity. This early 1900s postcard shows a group of guests taking the waters in the resort's pool. (Courtesy of the Napa County Historical Society.)

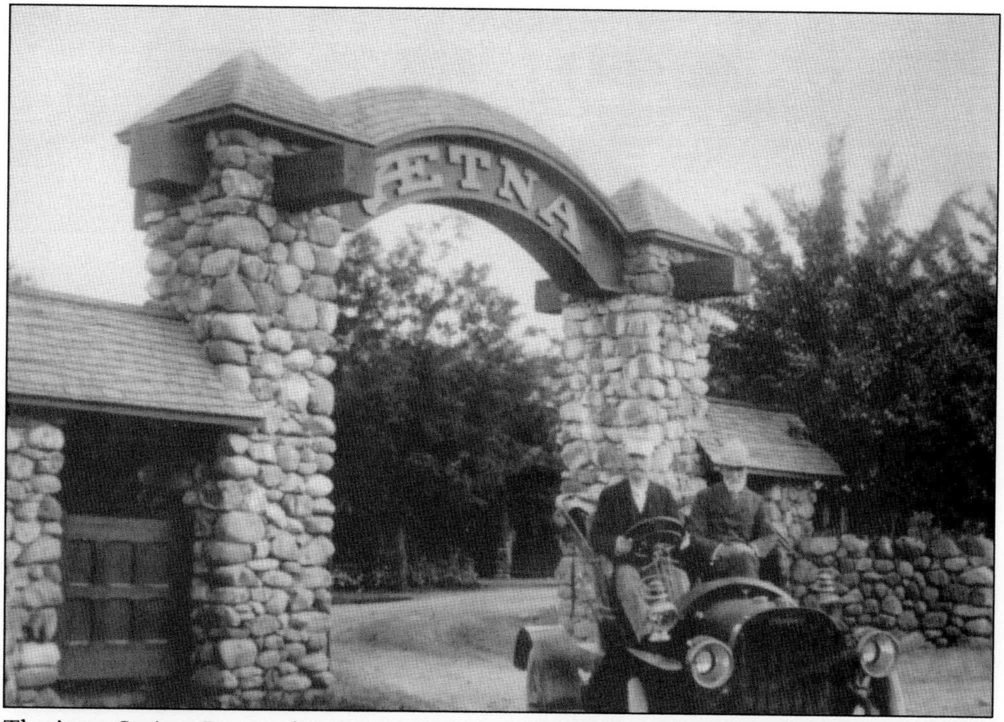

The Aetna Springs Resort closed as a public resort in 1973. After a failed attempt to convert the resort into condominiums, it was sold to the Rev. Sun Myung Moon's Unification Church, who used it as church retreat. The resort was sold to a developer in 2003, and plans call for it to be divided into luxury homesites and a destination resort. This imposing gateway arch remains today. (Courtesy of Stan France.)

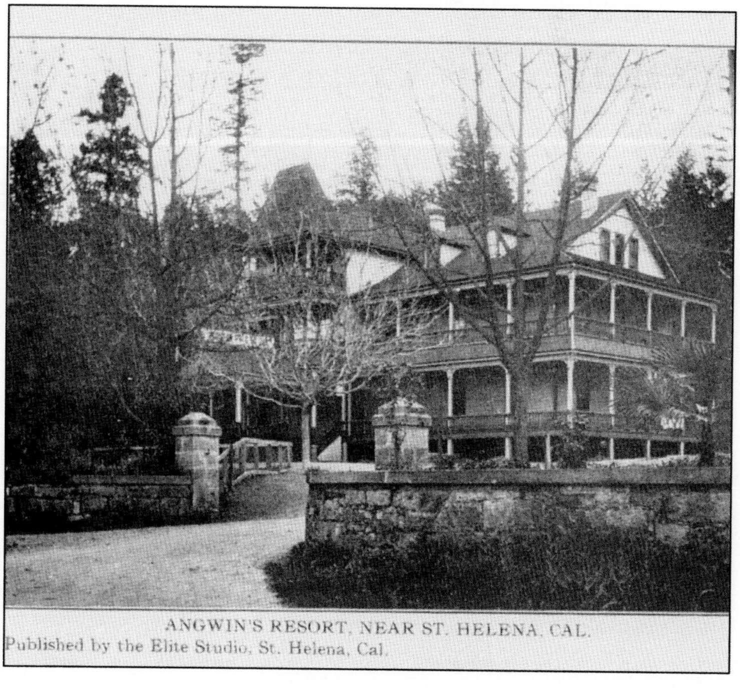

Angwin's Summer Resort began as the ranch of Edwin Angwin. One early patron was Civil War author and chronic asthmatic Ambrose Bierce. It was linked to civilization via the Pope Valley and Aetna Springs Stage Line, which traveled to and from St. Helena. Angwin sold the resort to the Seventh Day Adventist Church in 1909; it became the site for the present-day Pacific Union College. (Courtesy of the Napa County Historical Society.)

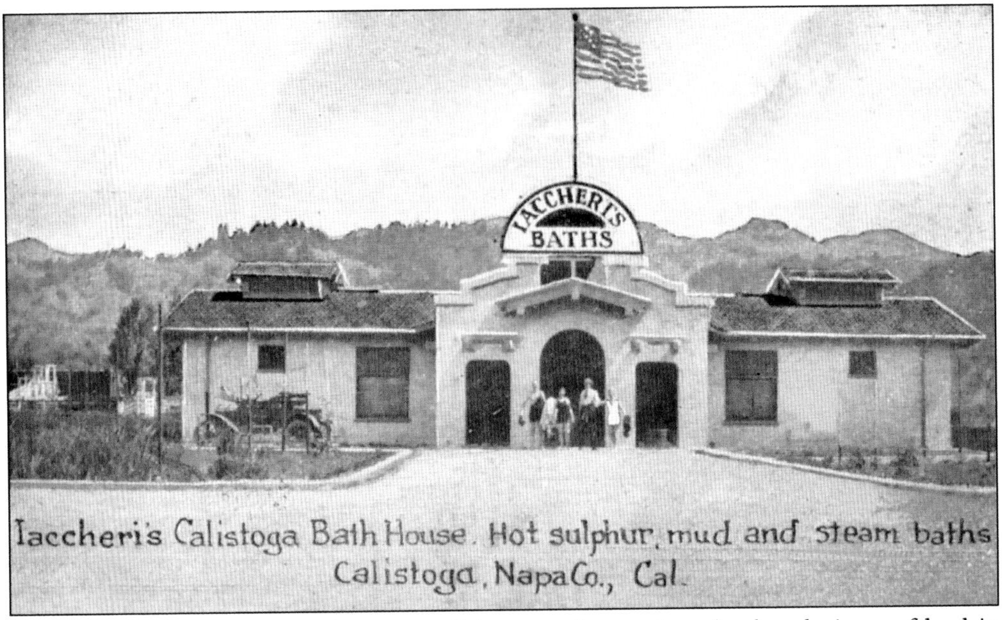

The Iaccheri Baths was located on one of the most frequently redeveloped pieces of land in downtown Calistoga. The site originally held Sam Brannan's distillery, which produced Calistoga Cognac. It was later the site of the Lathrop Baths before Garibaldo Iaccheri took over. Since that time, it has been Dr. Aalder's Hot Springs Resort and is now the Calistoga Spa Hot Springs. (Courtesy of the Napa County Historical Society.)

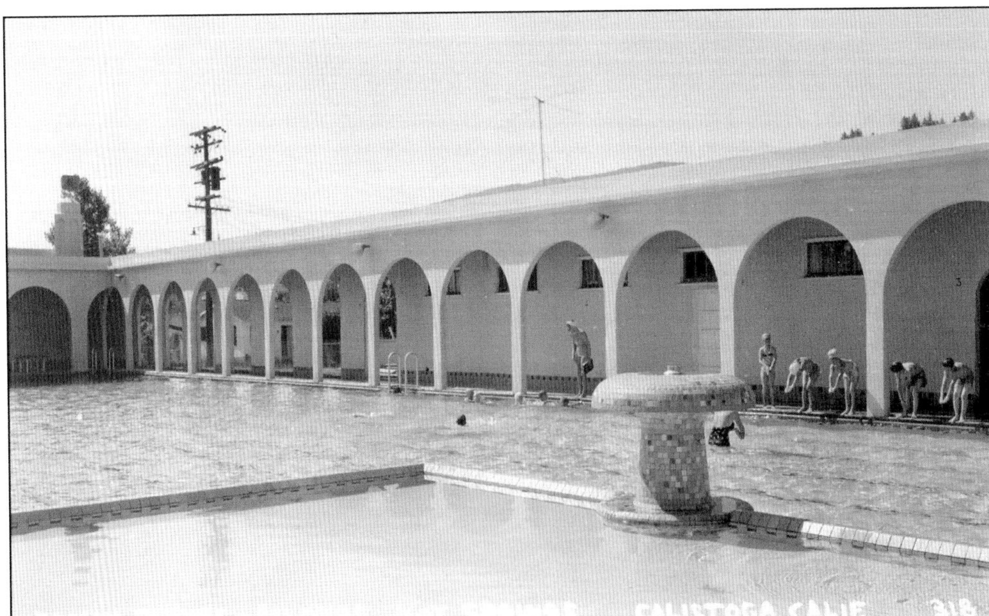

Dr. Aalder's Hot Springs Resort was located on Washington Street between Lincoln Avenue and Gerard Street. It featured mud baths and a large "Roman Plunge" swimming pool. The site is currently called the Calistoga Spa Hot Springs. (Author's collection.)

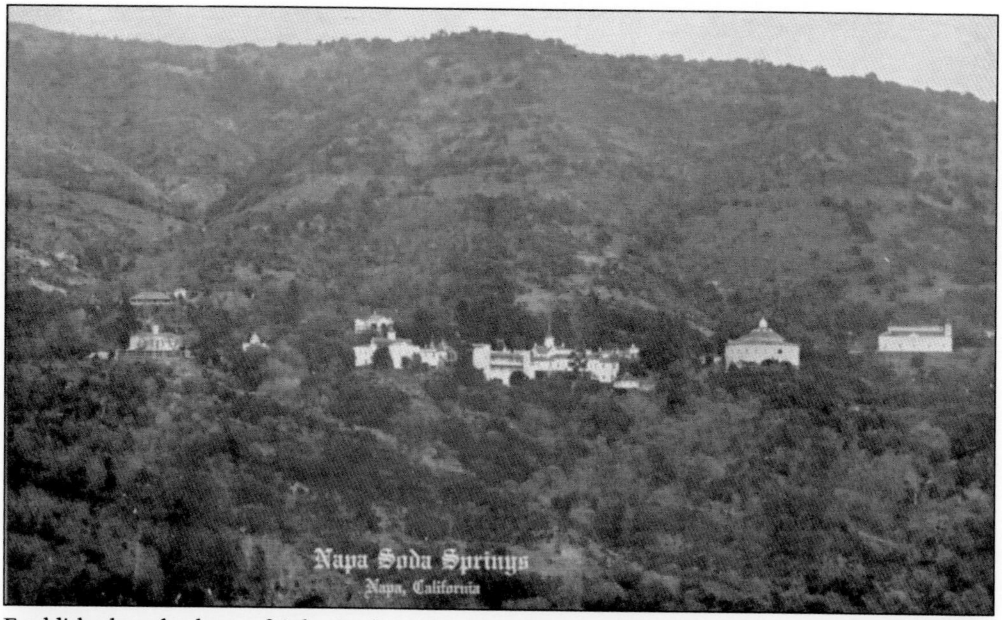

Established at the base of Atlas Peak in the late 1850s by Amos Buckman, Napa Soda Springs was the most luxurious and exclusive resort in all of Napa Valley. It began as a bottling facility for the native spring water, bottled as Napa Soda. Many influential people went on to visit the Soda Springs, including the 23rd president, Benjamin Harrison, in 1894. The Soda Springs fell victim to fire in 1944. (Author's collection.)

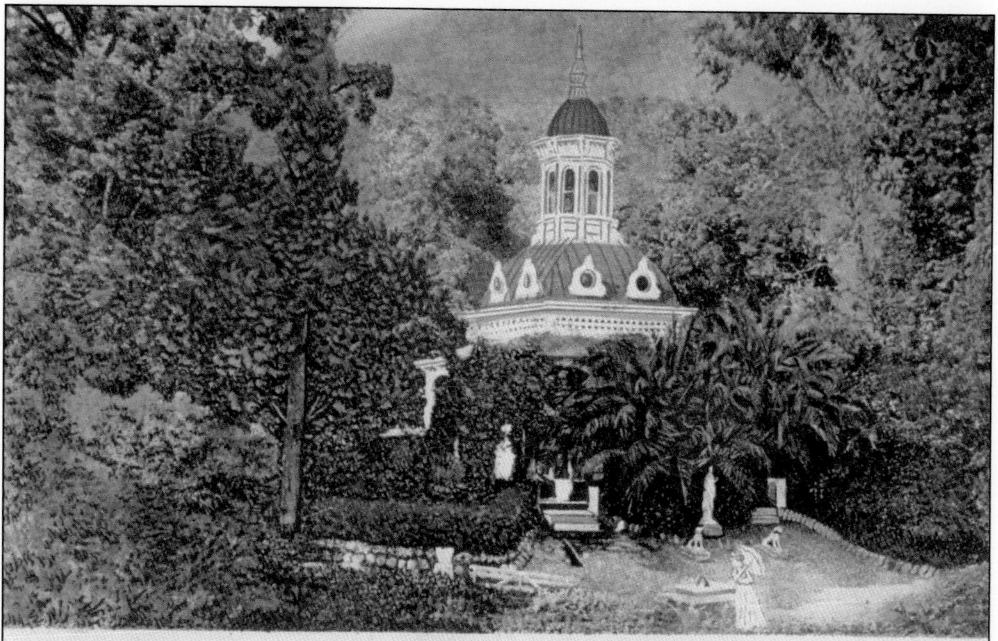

The pagoda was built over one of the 27 natural springs at the Napa Soda Springs. The Soda Springs also had a 50-foot-by-200-foot natural swimming pool cut out of solid rock, as well as a covered and steam-heated man-made pool. The Soda Springs are located off of Soda Canyon Road north of Napa. The area is currently used as a private hunting club. (Author's collection.)

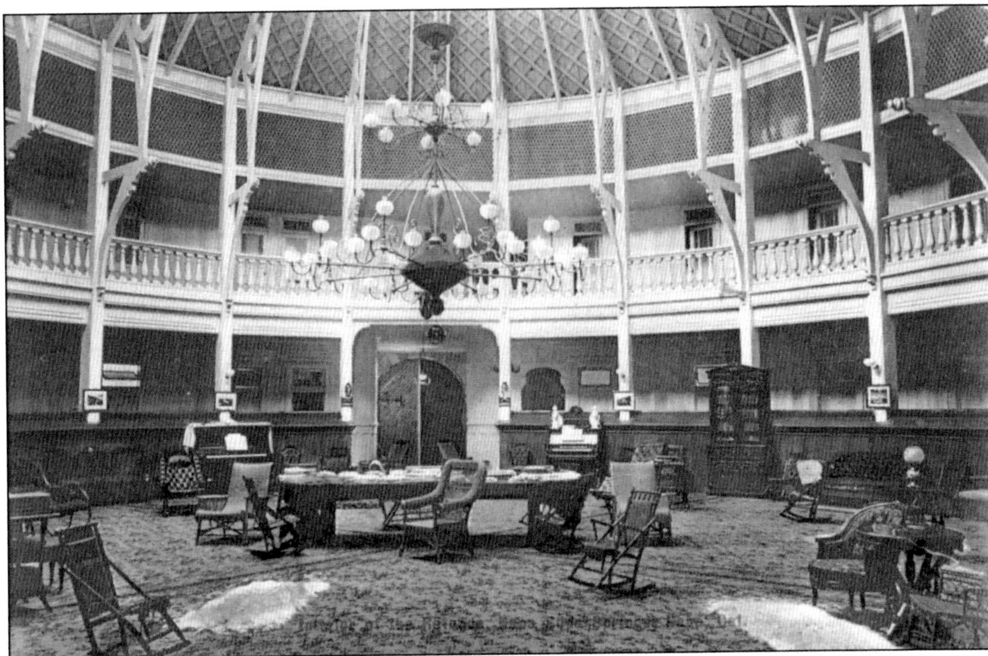

The postcard shows the interior of the rotunda building at the Napa Soda Springs. The circular building was 75 feet tall and capped with a glass cupola. The rotunda featured a post office, reception area, and grand parlor, all lighted by a huge gas chandelier of 32 lights. Guest rooms were built around the entire second floor promenade. (Author's collection.)

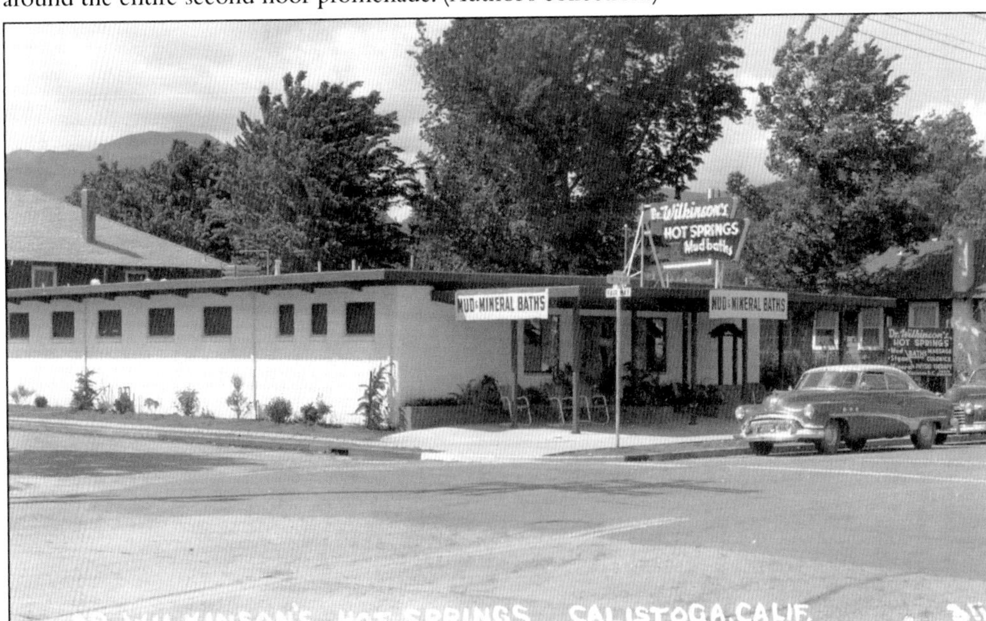

Dr. Wilkinson's Hot Springs Resort is located at 1507 Lincoln Avenue. It was opened in 1952 by John "Doc" Wilkinson, a chiropractor. The postcard shows the resort shortly after it opened. Today the original neon sign still lights up the resort, although the resort has been greatly expanded to include a motel and indoor and outdoor mineral pools. (Courtesy of the Sharpsteen Museum of Calistoga History.)

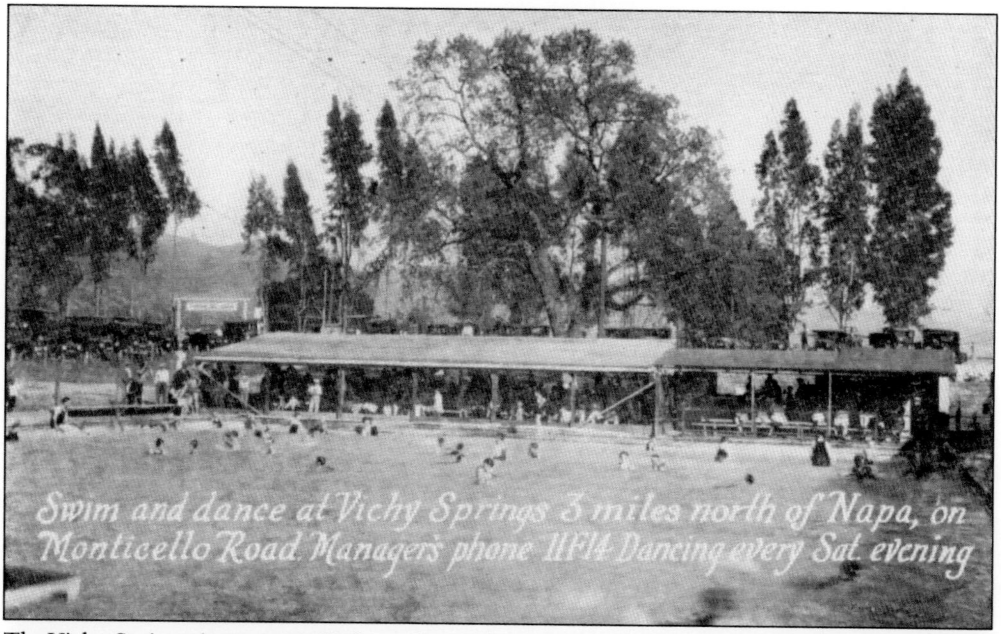

The Vichy Springs Amusement Park was located on the northwest corner of Monticello and Atlas Peak Roads east of the city of Napa. It featured a large swimming pool, pictured here in the 1920s, as well as picnic areas and a Kiddieland. Many Napans fondly remember making the trek out to Vichy Springs to take a dip on a hot summer day. (Courtesy of the Napa County Historical Society.)

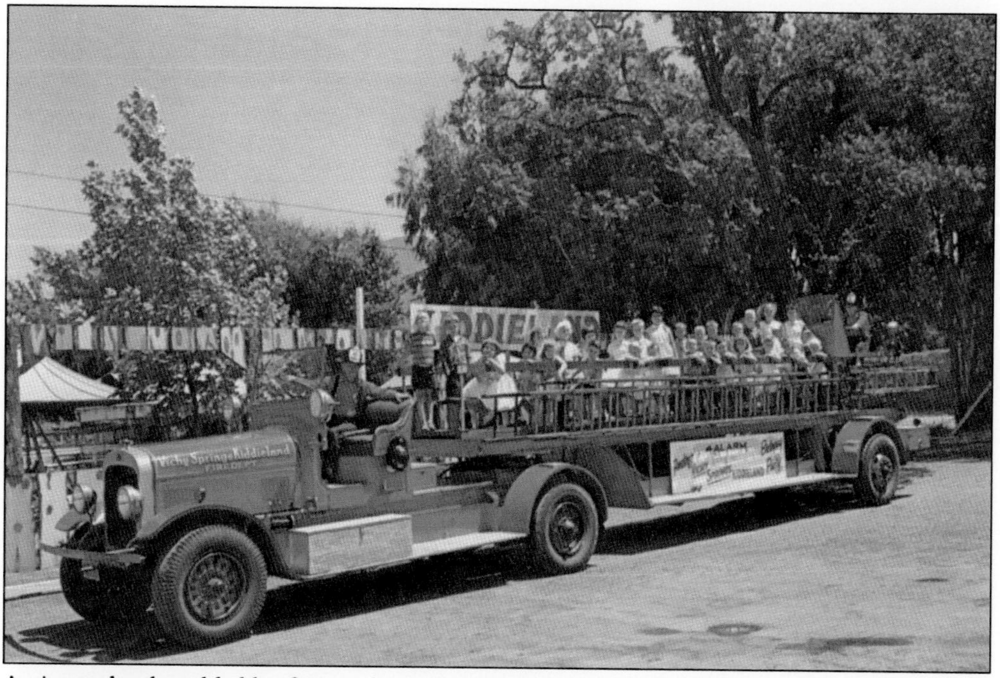

A vintage hook and ladder fire truck was one of the features of the Vichy Springs Kiddieland in the 1960s. Manning the rear driver's seat is Charlie "Bud" Rauch, a Napa firefighter who worked at the springs on the weekends. (Courtesy of Dennis Gonslin.)

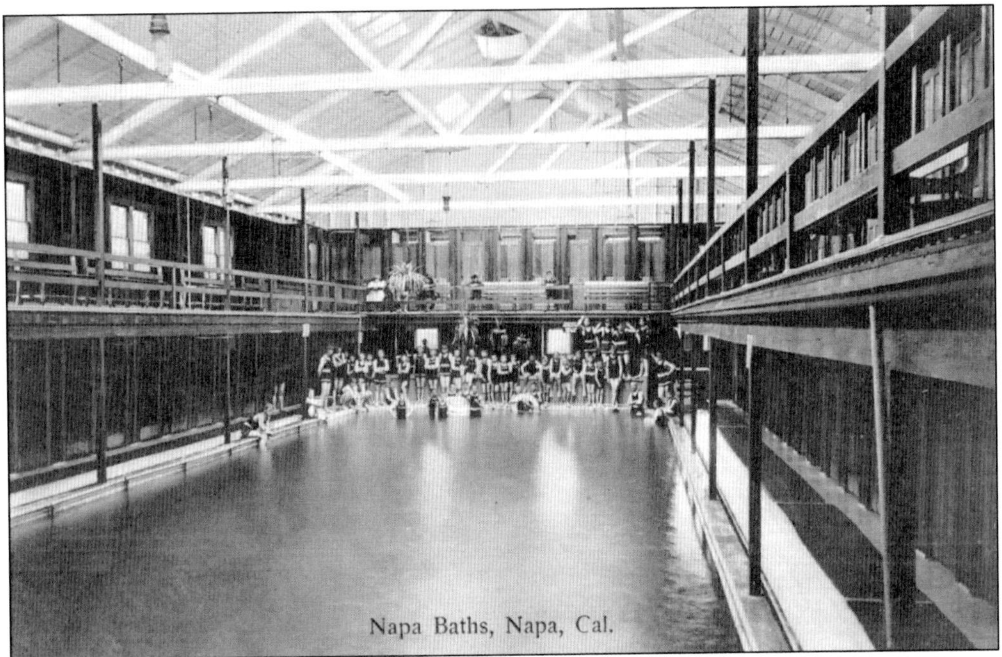

The Napa Baths, located at 715 Franklin Street, are pictured as they appeared *c.* 1910. The baths, or natatorium, were built by G.W.Young in 1905 and featured a pool that varied in depth from two to eight feet. The baths also had steam rooms available. The building was sold to the Catholic Church in 1912. The pool was concreted over, and the building was used as a school. Today it houses the Community Projects Thrift Store. (Author's collection.)

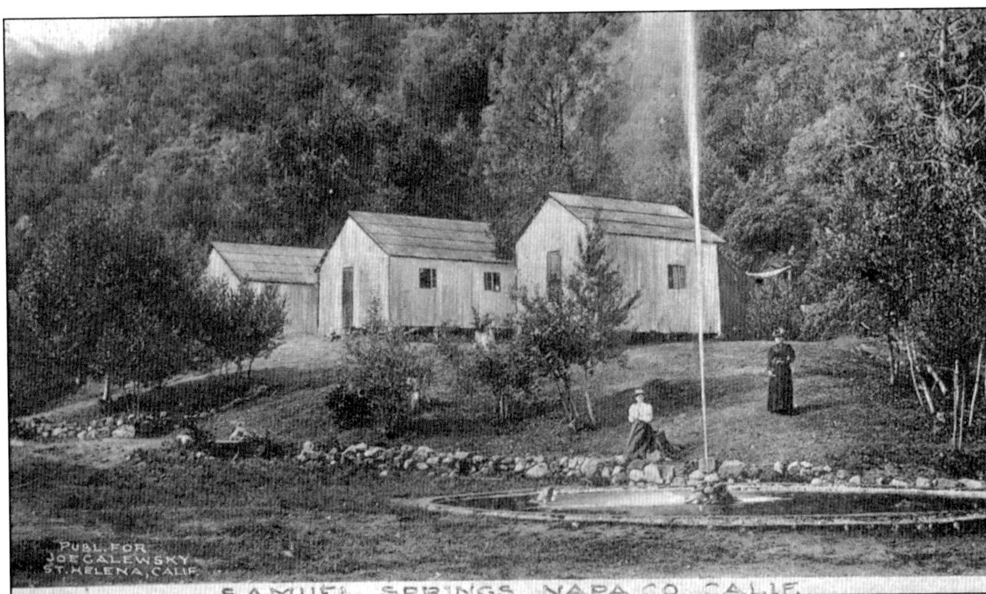

The Samuel Springs Resort was located in Chiles Valley, about 11 miles northeast of St. Helena. Originally founded in the early 1890s by E. C. Samuels, it featured the requisite soda and sulphur springs. Guests could stay at a main hotel, in tents, or in the cabins pictured in this 1907 postcard. (Author's collection.)

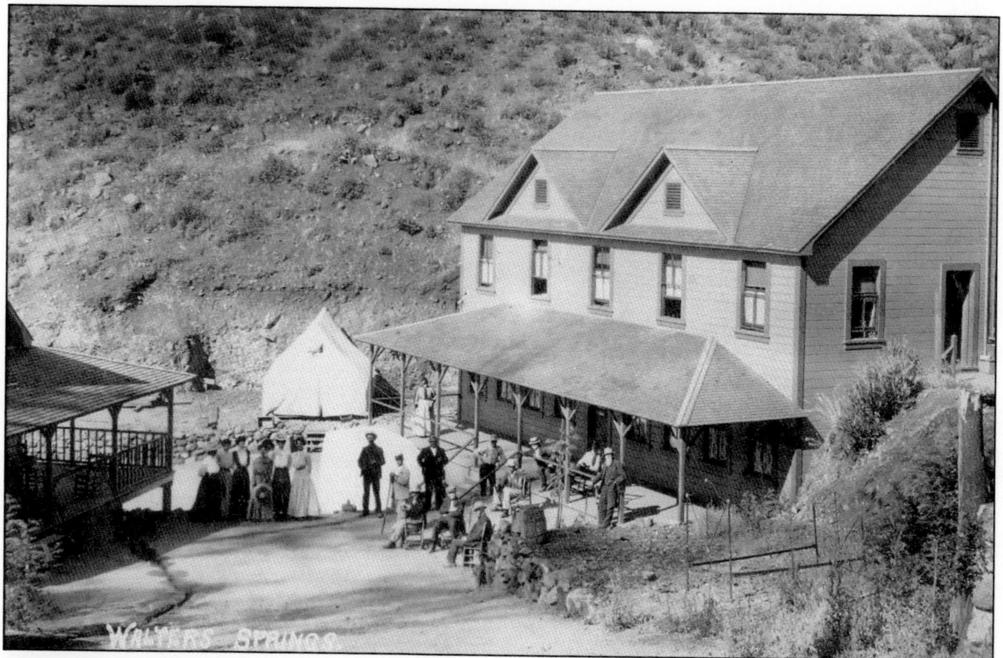

The Walters Springs Resort was located in the Pope Canyon area. Two natural springs were first discovered by J. J. Walters in 1871, although the area was not developed into a resort until 1881. The resort featured a hotel, bathhouse, dining room, and several small cottages. Local residents would also come to the resort and pitch tents in order to take advantage of the resort's curative waters. (Author's collection.)

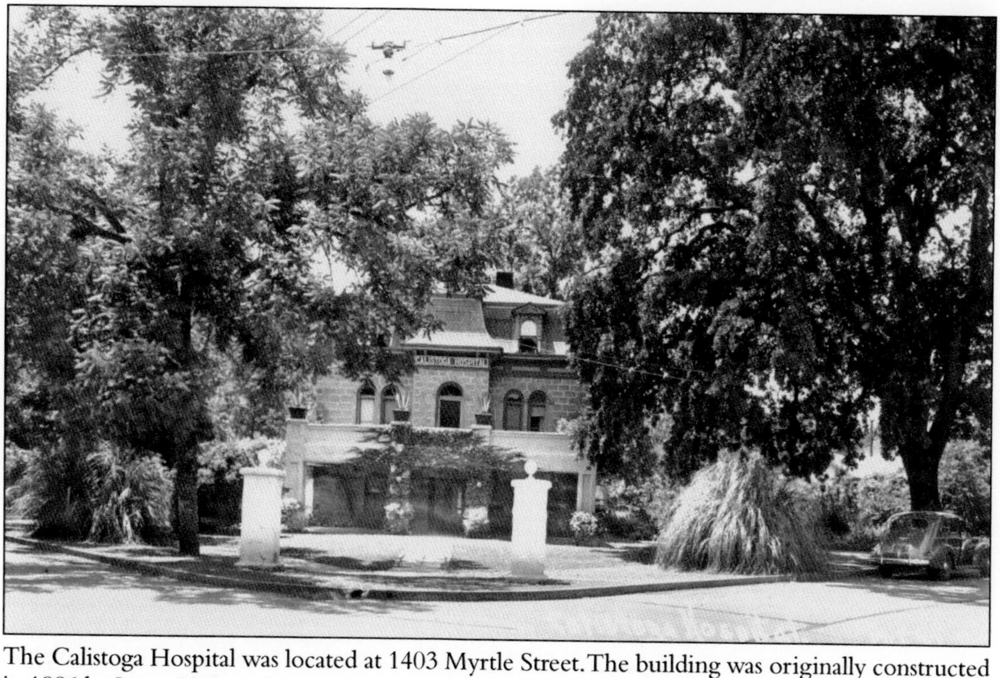

The Calistoga Hospital was located at 1403 Myrtle Street. The building was originally constructed in 1886 by James H. Francis as a private residence. It served as the city's hospital from 1918 to 1964. (Courtesy of the Napa County Historical Society.)

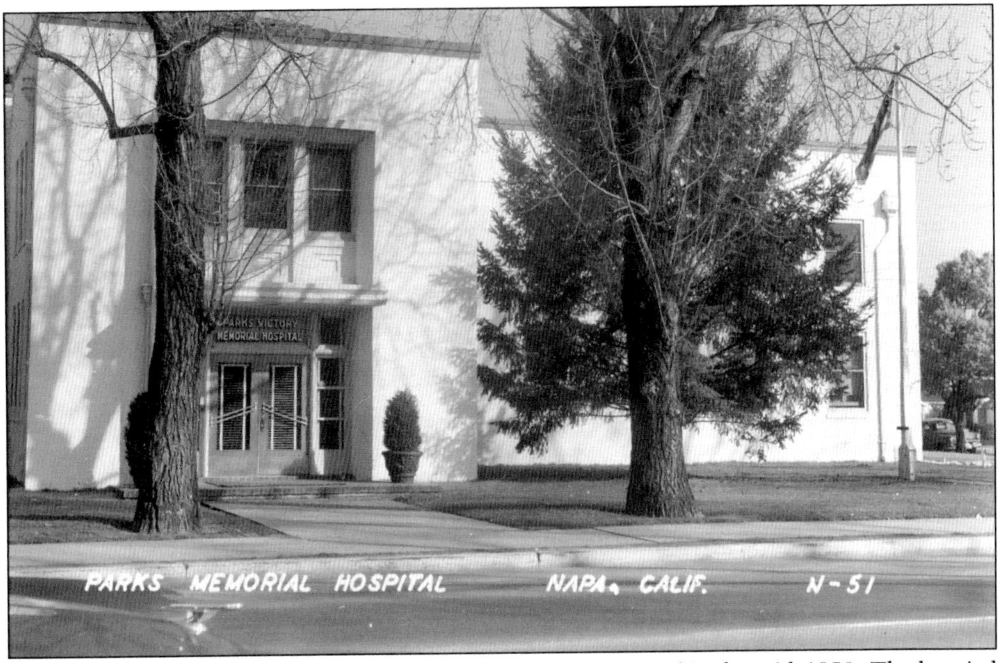

Parks Memorial Hospital, located in Napa, is pictured as it appeared in the mid-1950s. The hospital was located at Jefferson and G Streets and was officially known as Parks Victory Memorial Hospital. "Victory" denoted the victory it was when the community opened the hospital in 1929. "Parks" was in honor of the hospital's administrator, Anna Parks. The hospital's ownership transferred to the Sisters of St. Joseph in 1953. (Author's collection.)

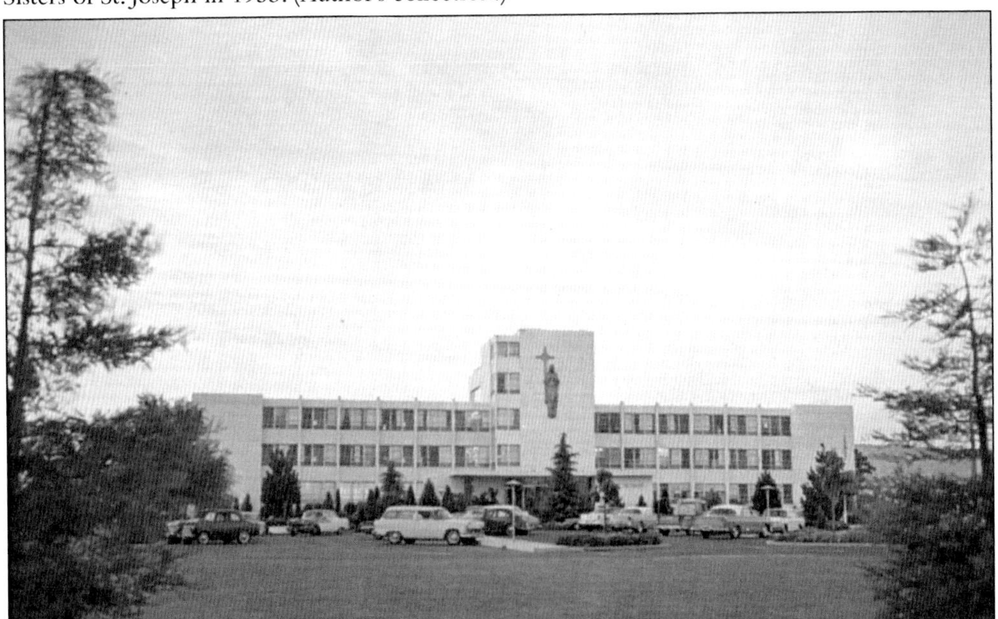
The Sisters of St. Joseph found Parks Victory Memorial Hospital to be inadequate to meet the growing community's need in Napa. In 1955, the ground was broken for the Queen of the Valley Hospital, located at 1000 Trancas Street. Queen of the Valley accepted its first patients in March 1958. (Author's collection.)

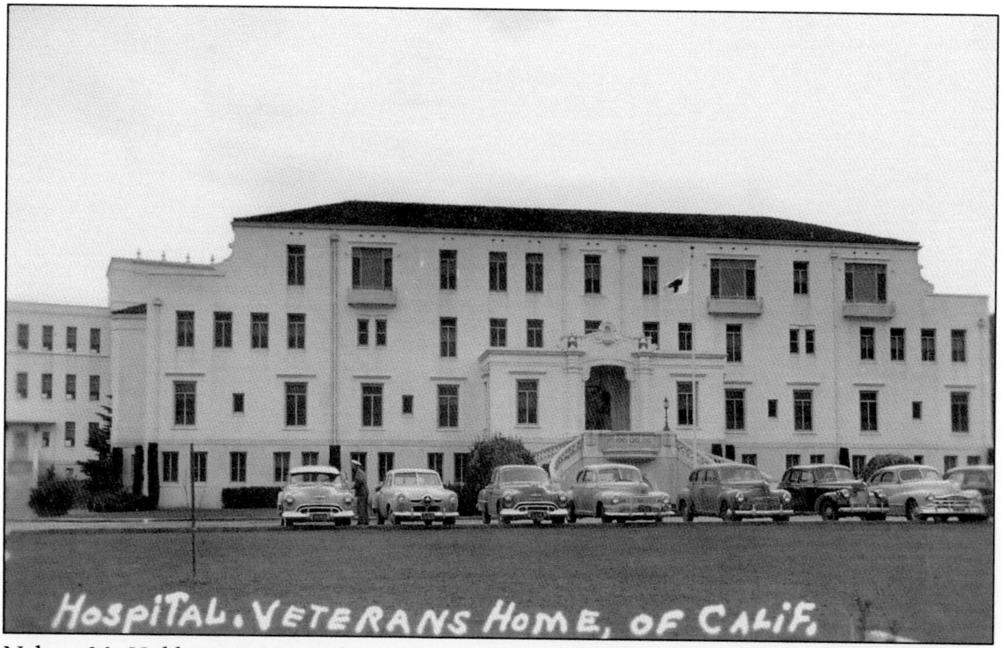

Nelson M. Holderman Hospital is on-site at the Veterans Home of Yountville and provides immediate, skilled nursing and general acute care. The hospital was named after Capt. Nelson Holderman, commander of the Lost Battalion during World War I, for which he was awarded the Medal of Honor. (Author's collection.)

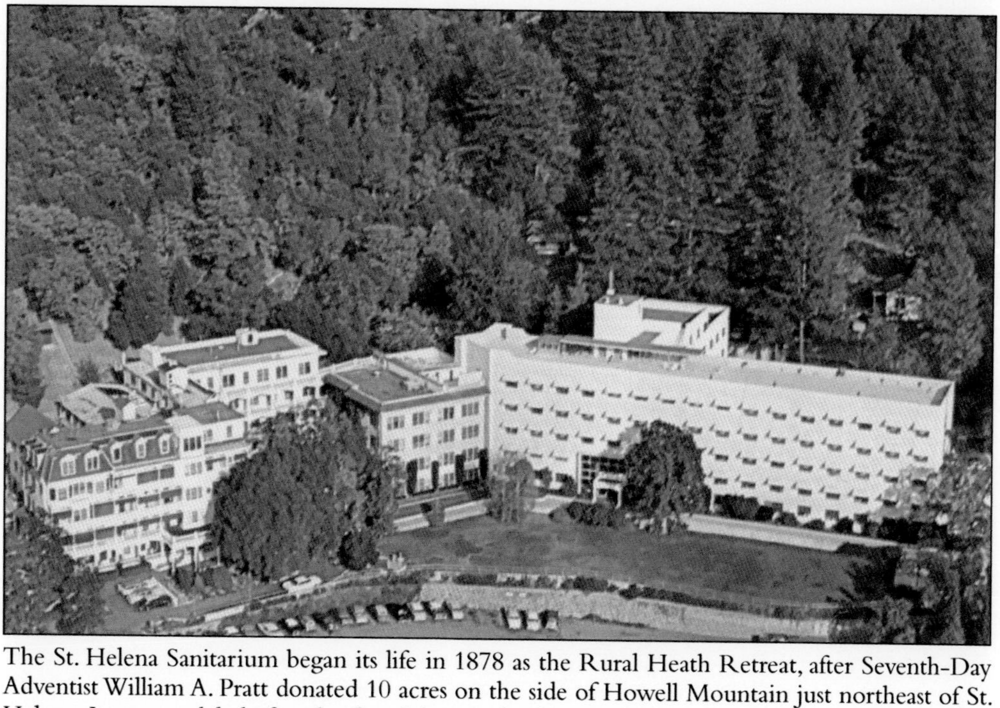

The St. Helena Sanitarium began its life in 1878 as the Rural Heath Retreat, after Seventh-Day Adventist William A. Pratt donated 10 acres on the side of Howell Mountain just northeast of St. Helena. It was modeled after the first Adventist health care facility, the Battle Creek Sanitarium in Michigan. This 1970s postcard shows the original building at the far left and a more modern hospital wing at the right. (Author's collection.)

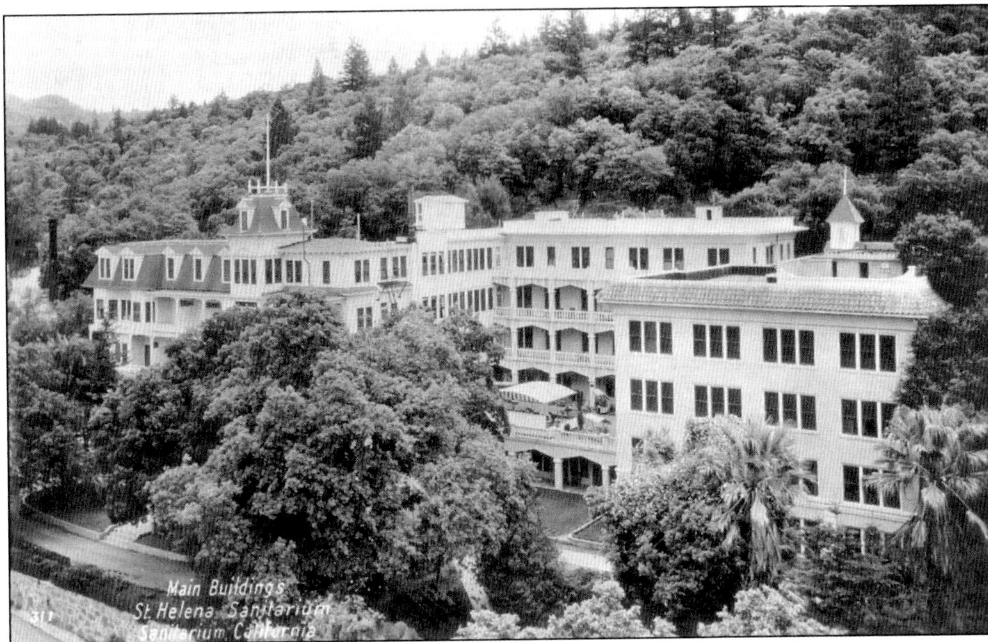

The sanitarium's first medical director was Dr. Merritt Kellogg, whose brothers started the Battle Creek Sanitarium and founded Kellogg's Cereal Company. Dr. Kellogg described the new sanitarium as follows: "I shall immediately commence to erect buildings suitable to treat patients on the hygienic system. The location is all that could be desired. The climate, location, and surroundings are not second to any other locality in California for the recovery and preservation of health." (Author's collection.)

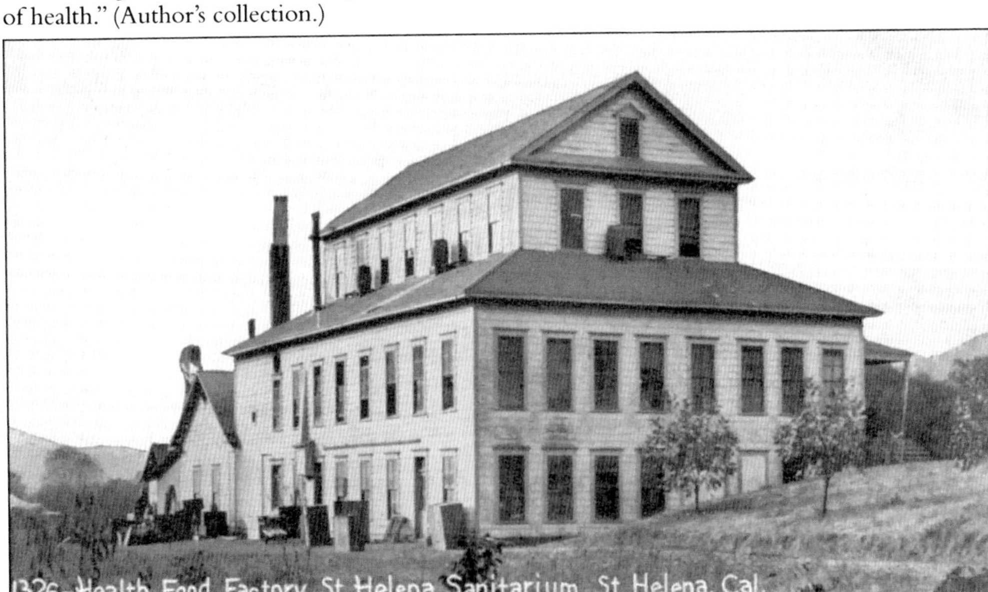

St. Helena Hospital business manager John A. Burden mimicked the work of the Kellogg brothers in Battle Creek, Michigan, when he opened a four-story factory on Sanitarium Road in 1901. The factory initially produced crackers, breads, and biscuits. It later produced a wide range of healthy foods, including granola, cereal, coffee, and vegetarian meat substitutes made from nuts. The factory was shuttered in 1920 and later torn down. (Author's collection.)

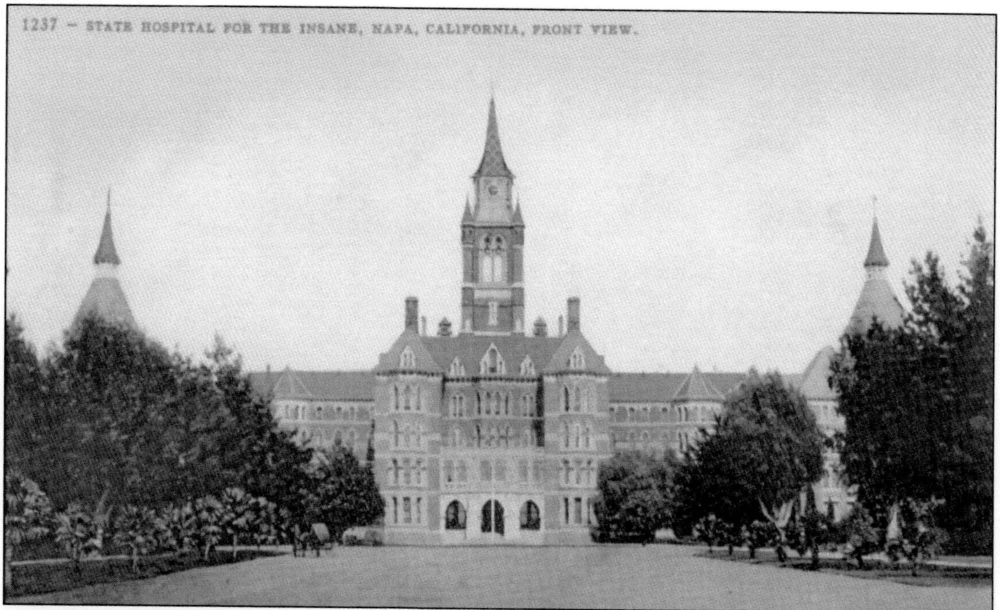

The Napa State Asylum was first authorized by the state in 1872. Dr. Edmund Wilkins toured mental institutions around the world, researching how the state's second asylum for the mentally ill should be built and operated. The 192 acres for the asylum were purchased for $11,500 from Don Cayetano Juarez. The initial 500-bed asylum opened on November 15, 1875. The main building, known as the Castle, was demolished in 1949. (Author's collection.)

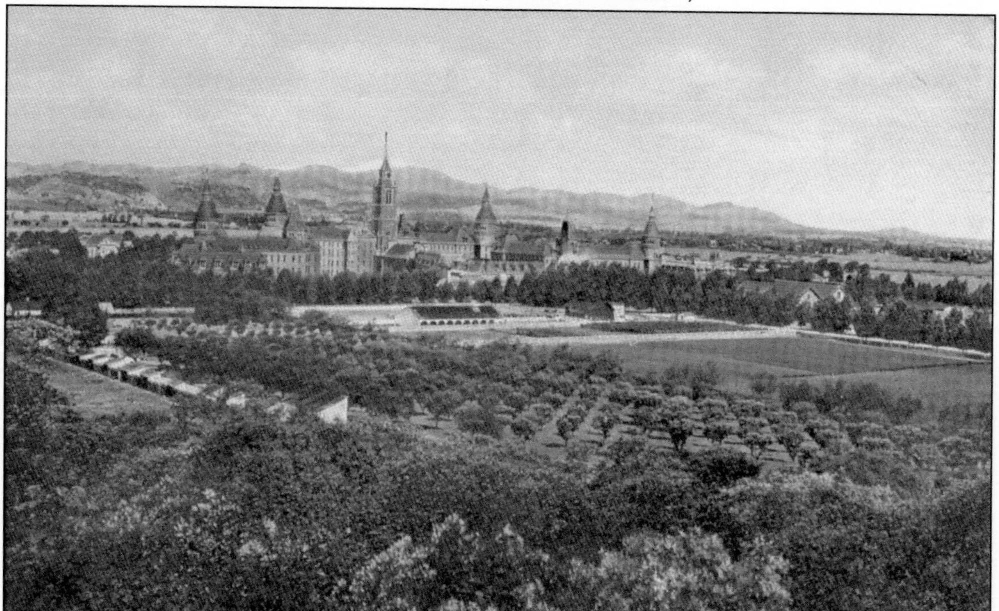

The asylum acquired more land over the years, bringing the total to over 2,000 acres. The land extended from a wharf on the Napa River to the eastern edge of present-day Skyline Park. It was nearly self-sustaining, with live-in staff, vegetable fields, orchards, cattle, a bakery, and a wharf on the Napa River to receive supplies that could not be made on-site. Napa Valley College, Kennedy Park, and Skyline Wilderness Park now occupy most of this land. (Author's collection.)

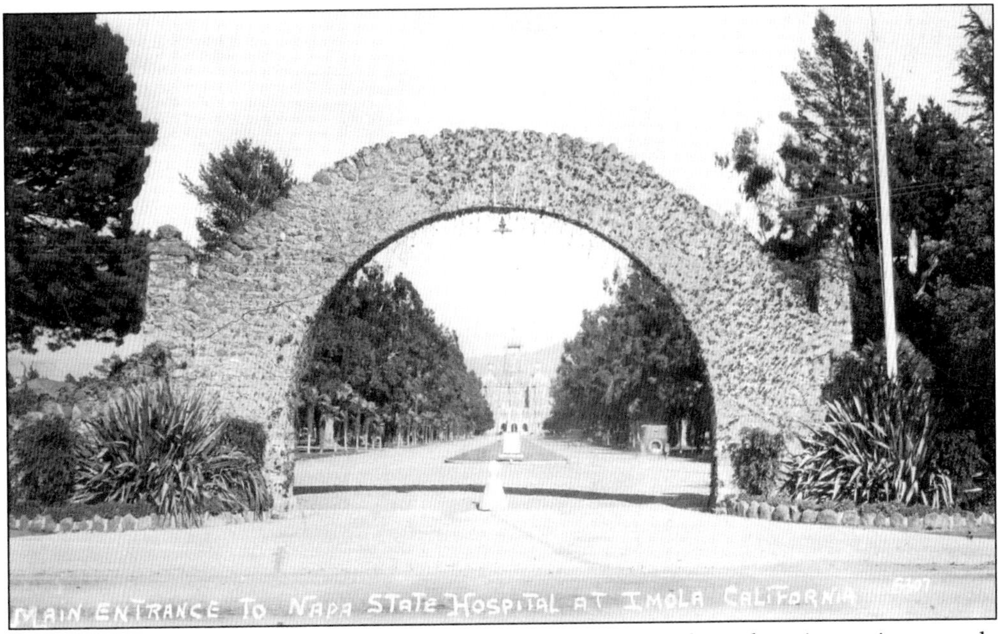

The original entrance to the Napa State Hospital would have certainly made an impression on early travelers as they passed by en route to the city of Napa. The stone archway stood for many years as the gateway to the asylum, which is visible in the background. (Author's collection.)

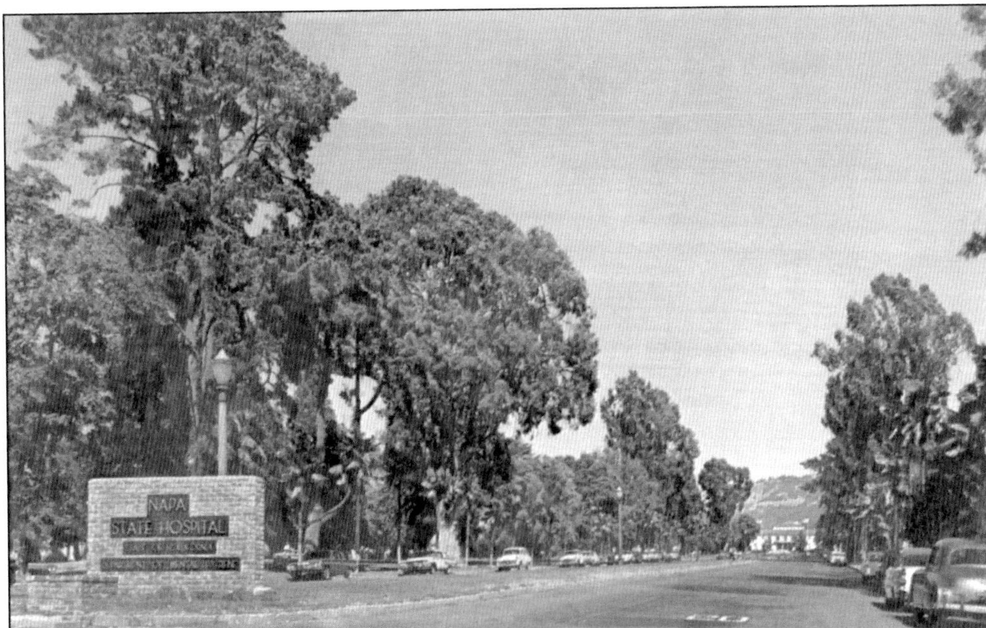

The entrance to the Napa State Hospital is pictured here as it appeared in the 1950s. The main entrance is located just south of Imola Avenue off of Highway 221. It appears nearly the same today; although the state no longer has a department of mental hygiene, the hospital is now part of the department of mental health. The administration building is visible at the end of the entrance road. (Courtesy of the Napa County Historical Society.)

Three

Wineries

The wine industry in Napa County traces its roots back to one of its first white settlers, George Yount, who planted three modest vineyards in the late 1830s.

Historians differ on whether it was John Patchett (in 1856) or Dr. George Crane (in 1858) who planted the first vines for commercial purposes. In any case, it was winemaker Charles Krug who is credited with establishing Napa Valley's first commercially viable, sustainable winery in 1861.

Historians and authors Clarence Smith and Wallace Elliot keenly made the following observations of the wine industry in Napa in 1878, "The planting of vineyards goes on steadily, and people are learning every year better where to plant, what varieties, and how to trim and manage the vines. At first every one raising vines attempted to manufacture . . . but as of late this system is being abandoned, and the small raisers sell the crops to those who have the large cellars and every appliance requisite to properly manufacture and store until suitable for sale."

By 1889, there were more than 140 wineries in operation and 35 distilleries, including Schramsberg (founded in 1862), Beringer (1876), and Inglenook (1879). Before long, however, the rapid expansion of the new wine industry saw prices plummet amidst a sea of surplus grapes, and the arrival of phylloxera dealt vintners a stunning blow, as much of the valley's vineyard acreage fell victim to the destructive root louse. Many wineries went out of business, including that of pioneer winemaker Charles Krug.

An even greater threat to Napa Valley's wine business arrived in 1920 with the enactment of Prohibition. Vineyards were abandoned, and many winemakers found other trades during the next 14 years, with a handful of wineries continuing to operate by producing sacramental wines for churches.

Today Napa Valley has more wineries per square mile than anywhere else in the world. Even though Napa County only contains four percent of California's total wine production and five percent of the total for the United States, its wines have distinguished themselves by winning awards year after year in international competitions. Almost five million people a year travel to the valley to experience the wine country.

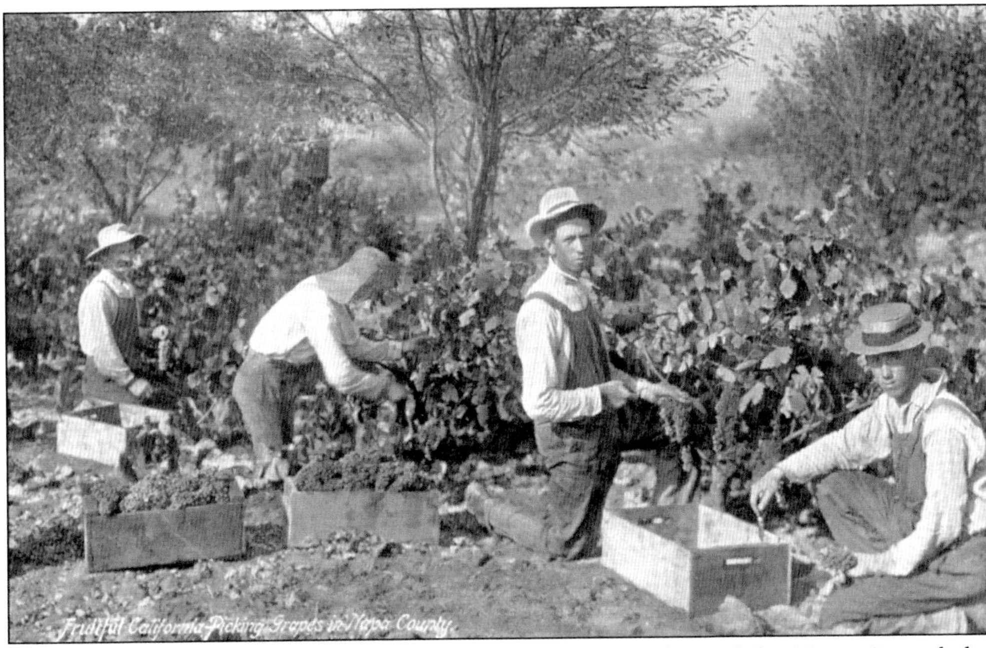

The backbreaking work of pruning and later harvesting the fruit of the Napa vineyards has remained relatively unchanged in the last 150 years. Although the fermentation and bottling of wine has become mechanized, the process still starts with skilled workers wielding pruning shears. (Courtesy of the Napa County Historical Society.)

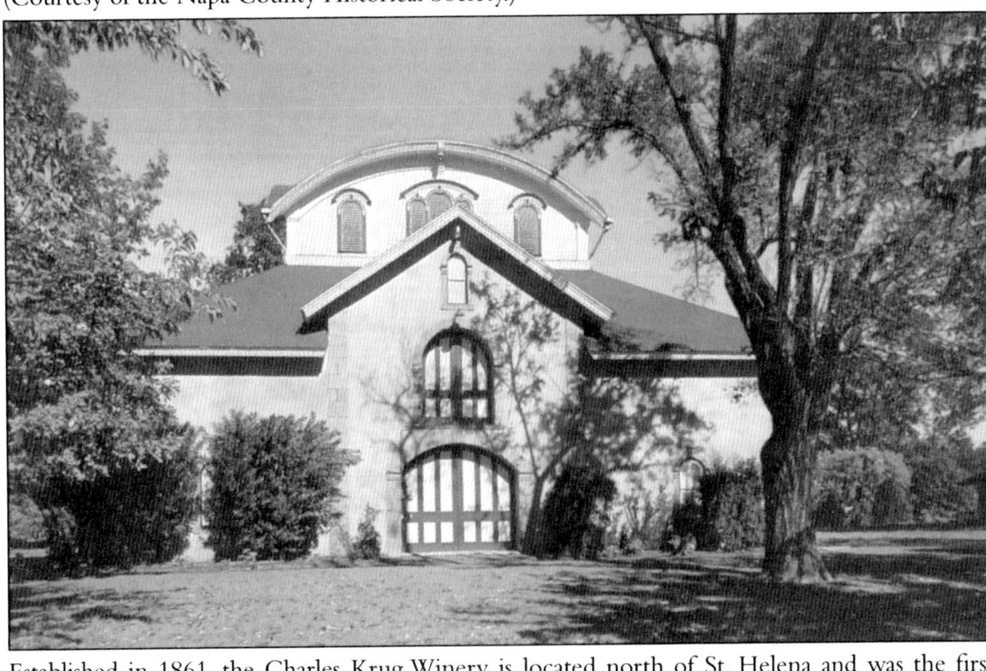

Established in 1861, the Charles Krug Winery is located north of St. Helena and was the first winery in the Napa Valley. This postcard features the Oak Room, which was originally built in 1881 by Krug as a carriage house and stable. It now houses barrel storage and a tasting room. The winery was purchased by the Mondavi family in 1943 and is now run by Peter Mondavi and his family. (Author's collection.)

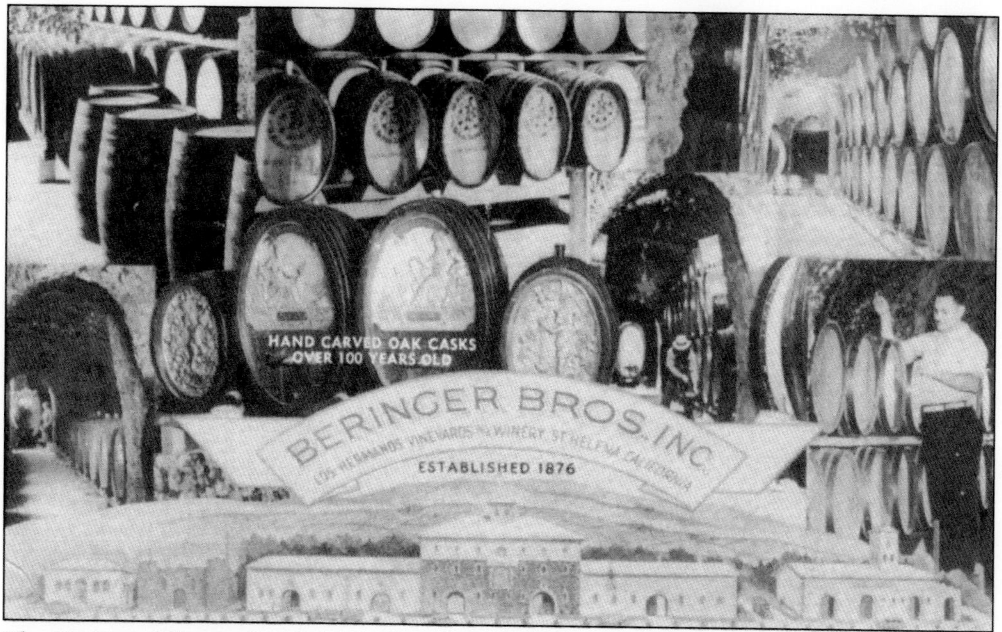

The Beringer Winery, founded in 1876, is the oldest continuously operating winery in Napa County. This postcard shows the main winery buildings, which back up to a hillside and provide access to the extensive wine caves. (Author's collection.)

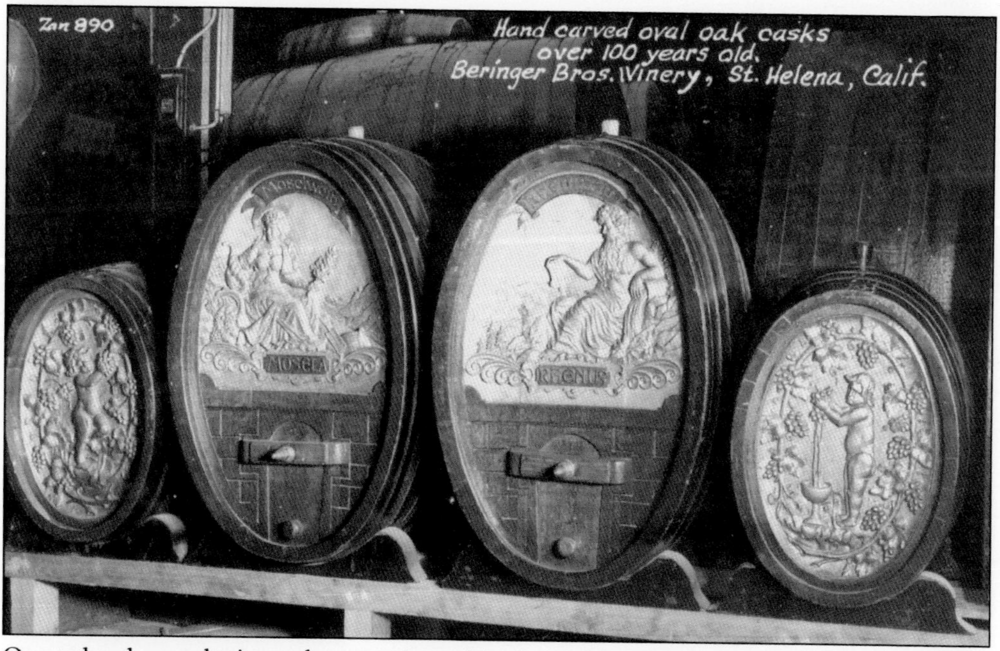

Ornate hand-carved wine casks were pictured in the Beringer Winery tunnel caves in 1948. The tunnels were hand-chiseled out of a mountainside by Chinese workers who had earlier completed the transcontinental railroad. The tunnels maintain an average temperature of 58 degrees, perfect for aging and storing wine. (Courtesy of the Napa County Historical Society.)

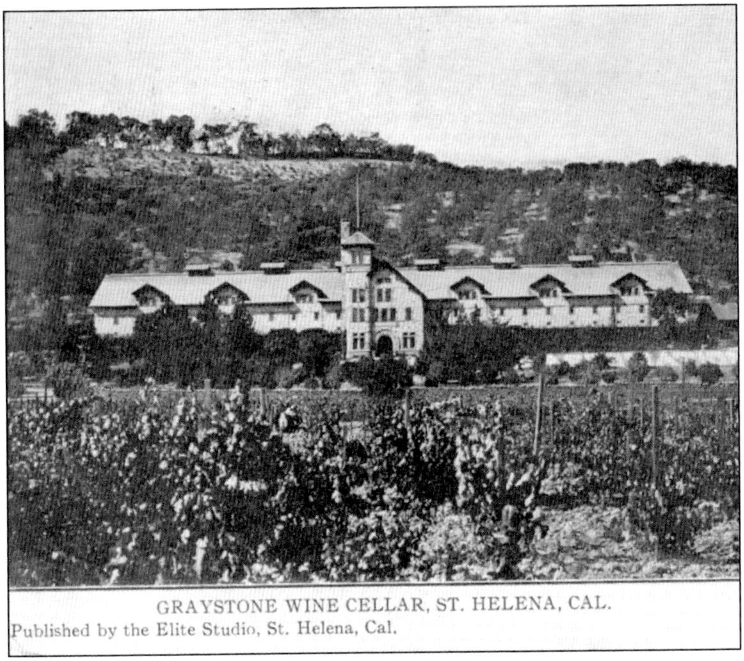

The Greystone Winery is shown here as it appeared in 1912. Built in 1882, the winery was later taken over by Christian Brothers, who ran it until 1989. Still housed in the lobby is an extensive collection of vintage corkscrews collected by Christian Brothers's master wine chemist, brother Timothy Diener. (Author's collection.)

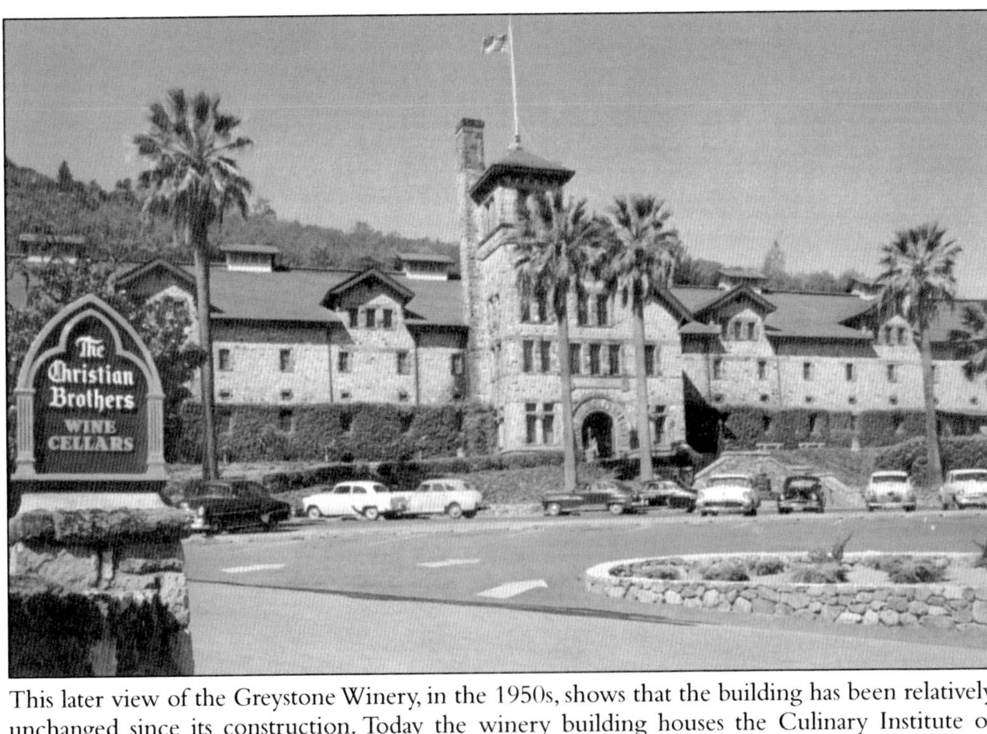

This later view of the Greystone Winery, in the 1950s, shows that the building has been relatively unchanged since its construction. Today the winery building houses the Culinary Institute of America's west coast chef's training campus. It features classrooms, a demonstration kitchen, and the Wine Spectator Greystone Restaurant. (Author's collection.)

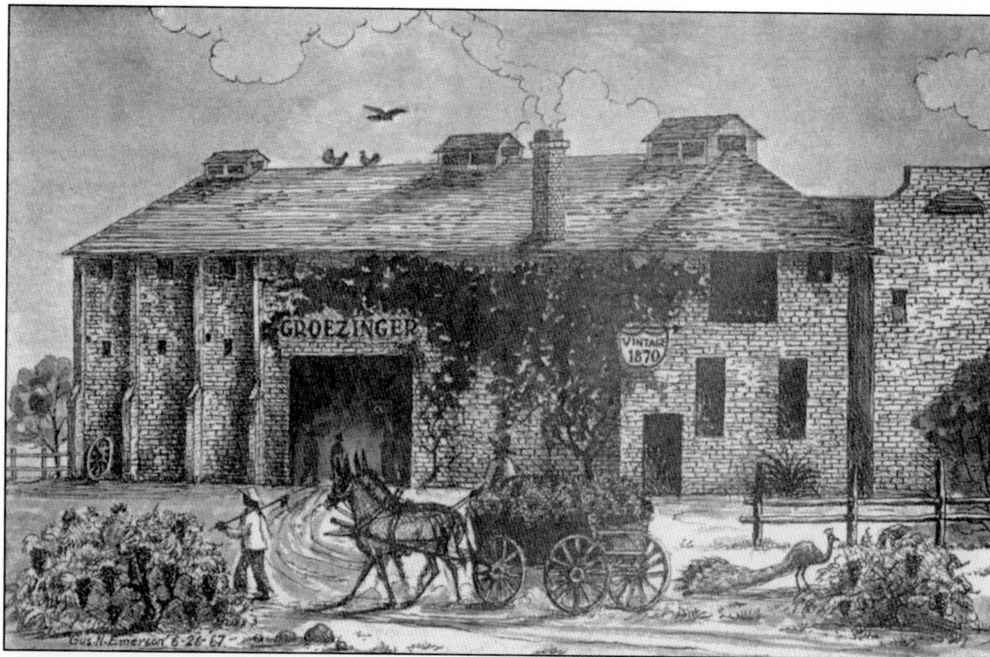

This postcard shows the Groezinger Wine Cellar as it appeared *c.* 1870. Gottlieb Groezinger purchased a portion of present-day Yountville from the estate of George Yount. He added 10 square blocks to the new city and built his wine cellar. The cellar operated under various owners until 1955. (Courtesy of Stan France.)

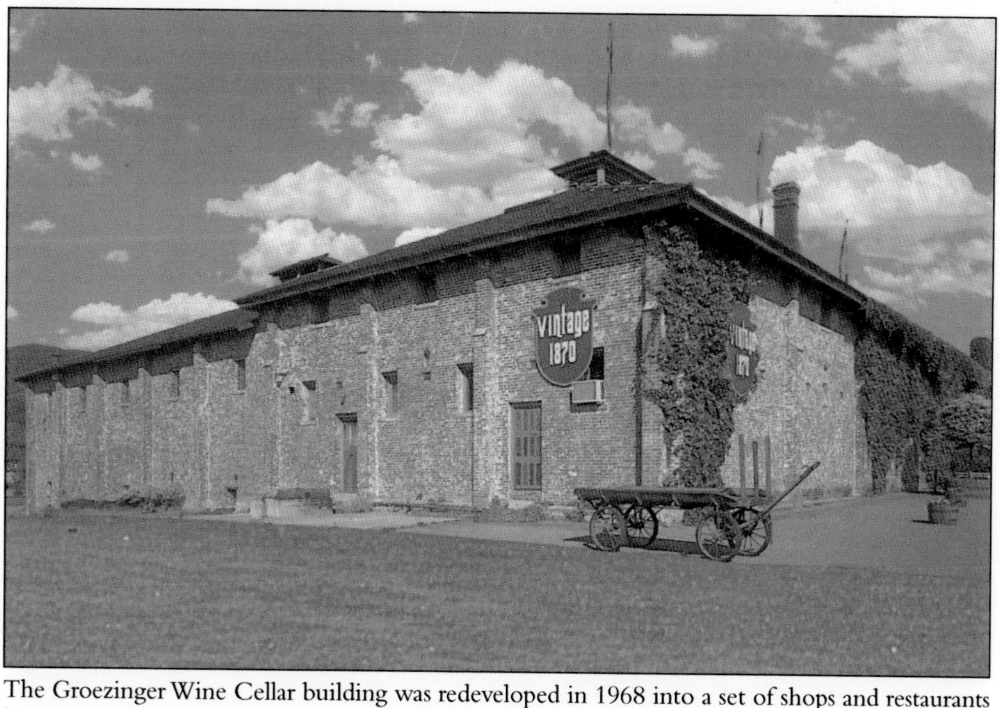

The Groezinger Wine Cellar building was redeveloped in 1968 into a set of shops and restaurants known as Vintage 1870. In 2007, the building was bought and renamed V Marketplace in keeping with the adjacent Villagio and Vintage Inns. (Author's collection.)

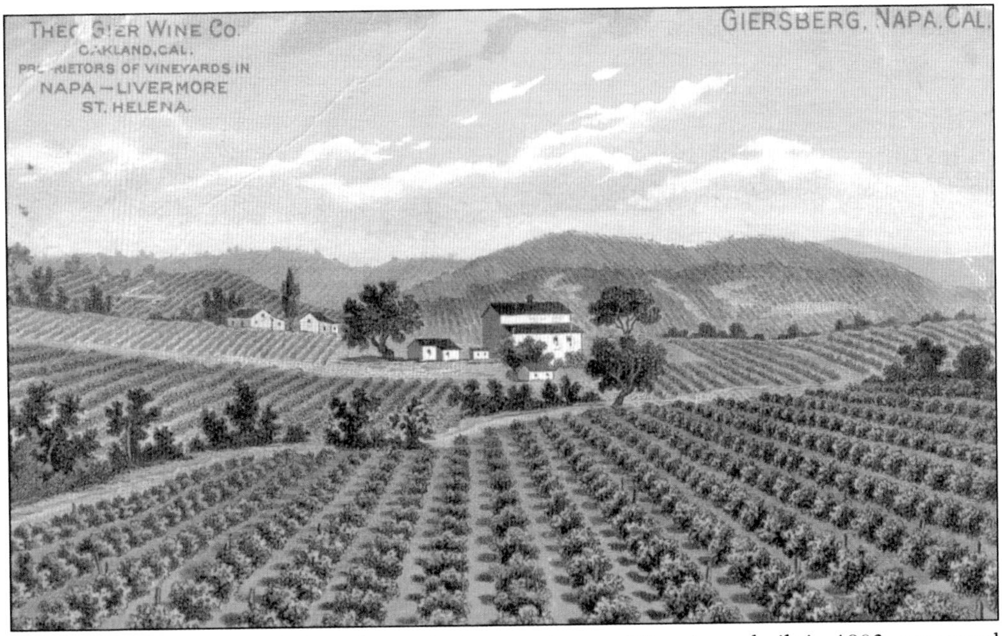

Theodore Gier was one of Napa County's pioneer vintners. His winery, built in 1903, was noted on this postcard as being in Giersberg; it was actually located on Mount Veeder. Several of Gier's wines won awards at the 1909 World's Fair. Hit hard by Prohibition, Gier sold the winery to Christian Brothers in 1930. (Author's collection.)

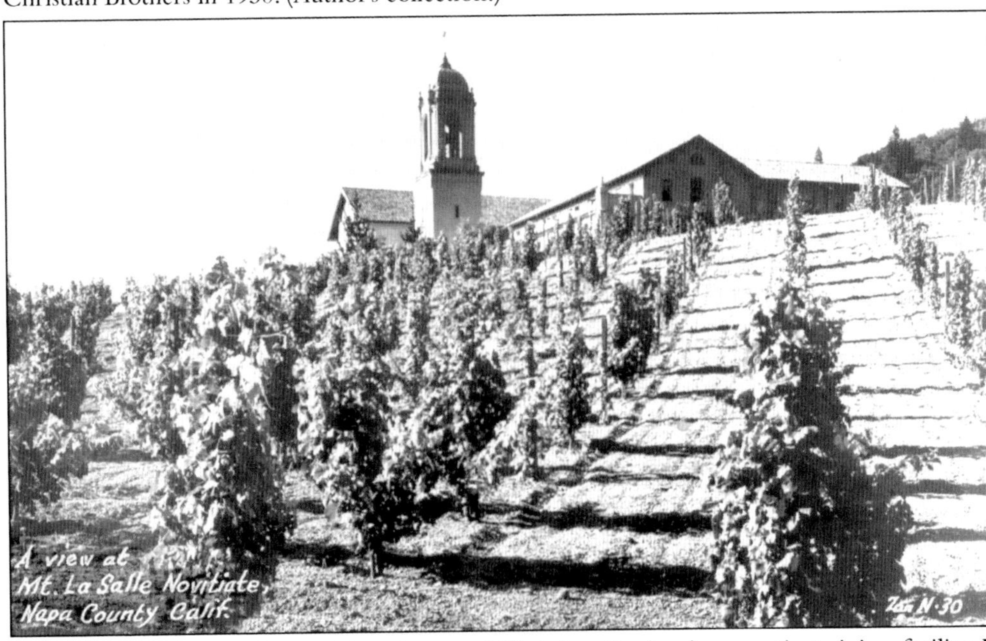

Pictured is Mont La Salle Novitiate, home of Christian Brothers's monastic training facility. It is surrounded by the vineyards originally cultivated by Theodore Gier. In 1989, the winery was bought by Heublein, which sold its Napa Valley holdings, including the historic Greystone Cellars north of St. Helena. The vineyards surrounding Mont La Salle were sold to the Hess Collection Winery. The main buildings visible now serve as a retreat and conference center for Christian Brothers. (Courtesy of the Napa County Historical Society.)

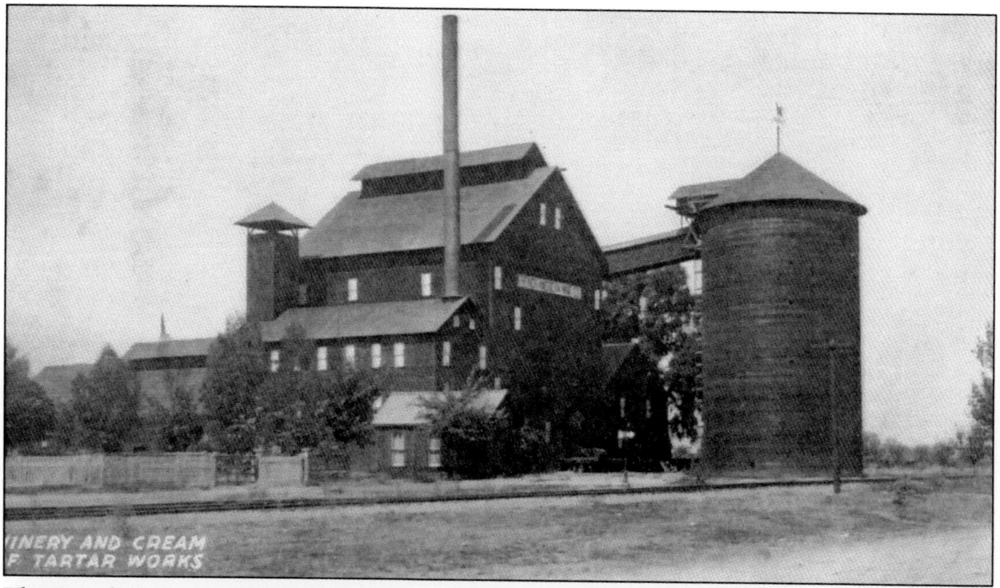

The French-American Wine Company was located in Oakville. This 1908 postcard notes that the company also produced cream of tartar. The tartar is actually potassium bitartrate that crystallizes in wine casks during the fermentation process. It is collected and purified to produce the white, odorless, acidic powder used for many culinary and other household purposes. (Courtesy of the Napa County Historical Society.)

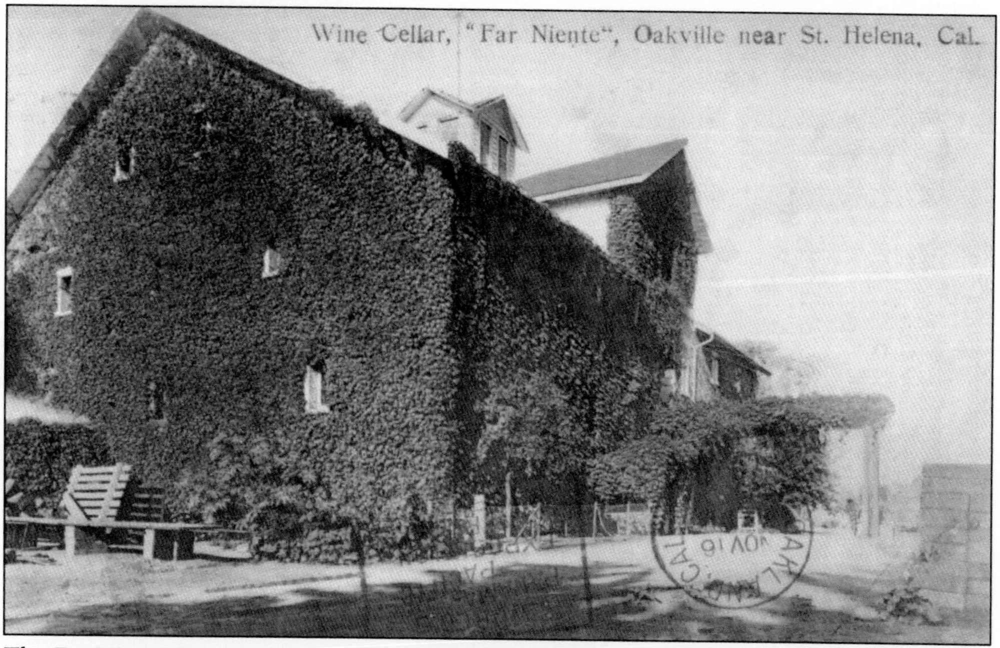

The Far Niente Winery was founded in 1885 by John Benson, the uncle of the famous painter Winslow Homer. The winery building, constructed against a hillside in western Oakville, was designed by architect Hamden McIntyre, who also designed the Greystone Winery. Far Niente prospered until Prohibition, when it was abandoned and left to fall into disrepair. Sixty years later, Gil Nickel purchased the winery and adjacent vineyard and restored the winery building. (Courtesy of Far Niente Winery.)

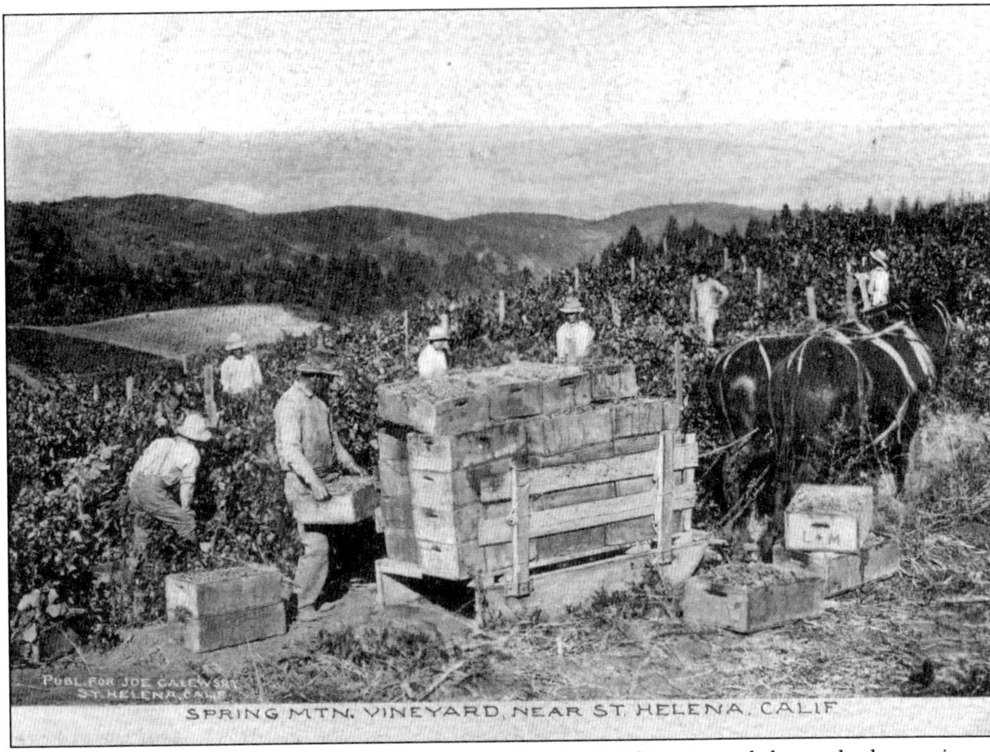

This postcard shows the harvesting of grapes at the Spring Mountain Vineyard. Native Mexican Tiburcio Parrott first planted a vineyard in the rolling hills of the area northwest of St. Helena in 1884. (Courtesy of the Napa County Historical Society.)

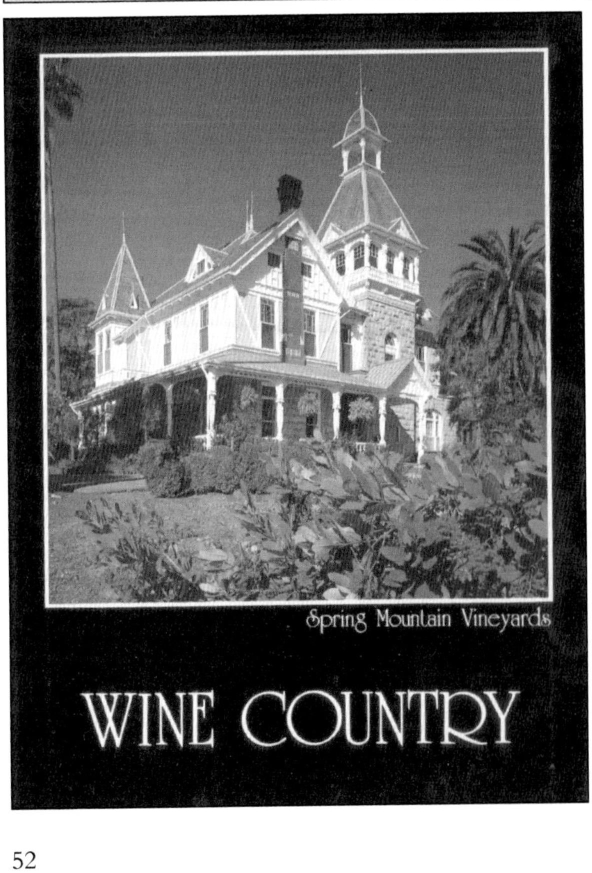

Winemaker Tiburcio Parrot built this mansion known as Miravalle, literally "look valley" in Spanish, at his Spring Mountain Vineyard. The mansion was designed by Albert Schroepfer, the same architect who built the homes of Gustave Niebaum and the Beringer brothers. In the 1980s, the mansion was used in the television show *Falcon Crest*. In the show, the mansion's distinctive stained-glass windows with parrots were misidentified as falcons. (Author's collection.)

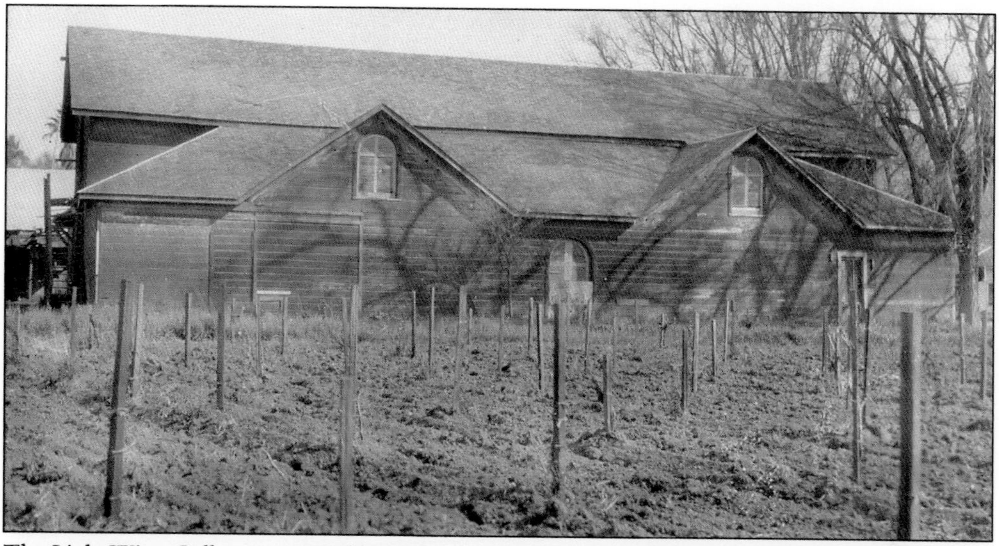

The Light Wine Cellar was owned by Ephraim Light, who would become known for digging the well that created the Old Faithful Geyser, at his farm off of Tubbs Lane north of Calistoga. The wine cellar pictured was originally built as a stable by Calistoga developer Sam Brannan. (Courtesy of the Sharpsteen Museum of Calistoga History.)

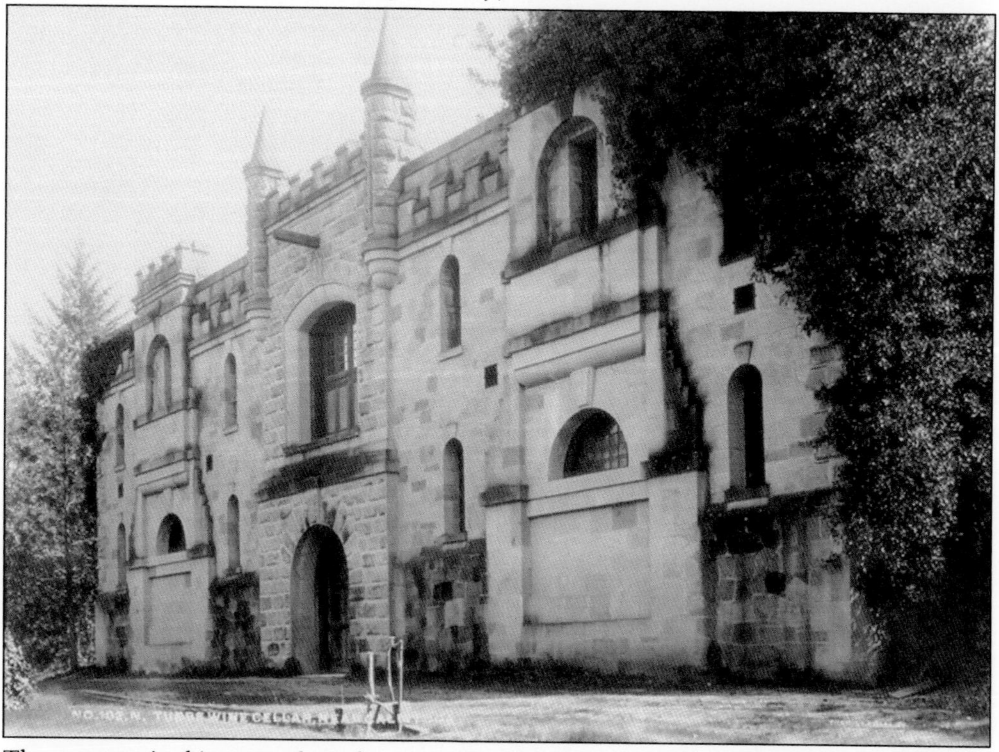

The structure in this postcard was known as the "Castle" and was the main building of Alfred C. Tubbs' Hillcrest Winery, also referred to as the Chateau Montelena (a contracted form of Mount St. Helena). The winery, which is located just north of Calistoga off of Tubbs Lane, began in 1882 and went out of business during the Prohibition era. It was reestablished by James Barrett in 1972 and continues operation today. (Courtesy of the Montelena Winery.)

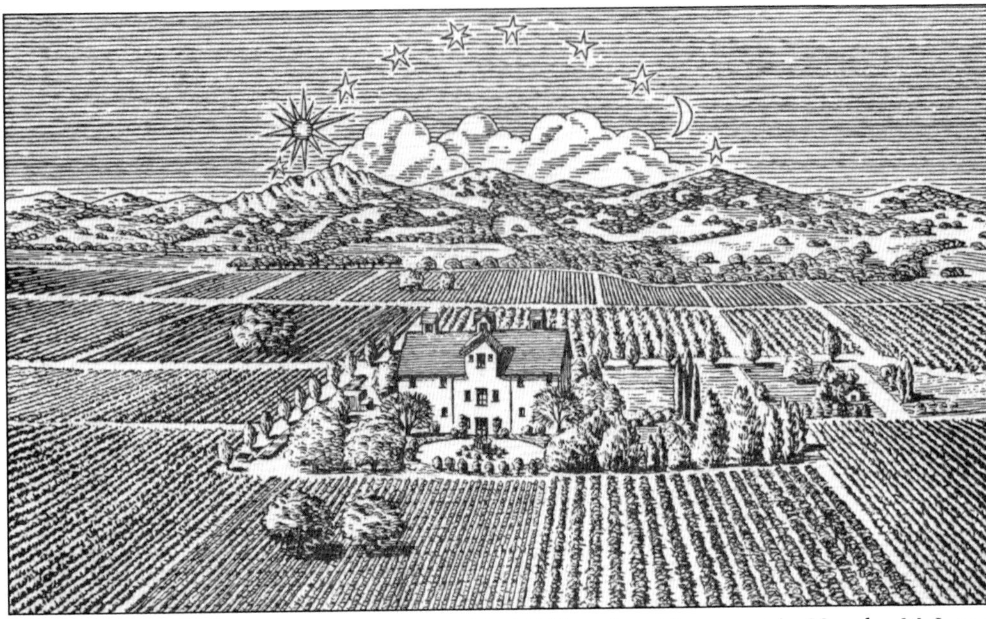

Eschols Winery's main building was constructed in 1886 by a Scottish sea captain, Hamden McIntyre. The winery employed a gravity-flow system: a horse-drawn winch brought grapes to the third floor for crushing; gravity carried the juice to the second floor for fermenting and eventually to the first floor for aging. The winery was bought by the Trefethen family in 1968 and restored to become the centerpiece of their new winery. (Courtesy of the Trefethen Family Vineyard.)

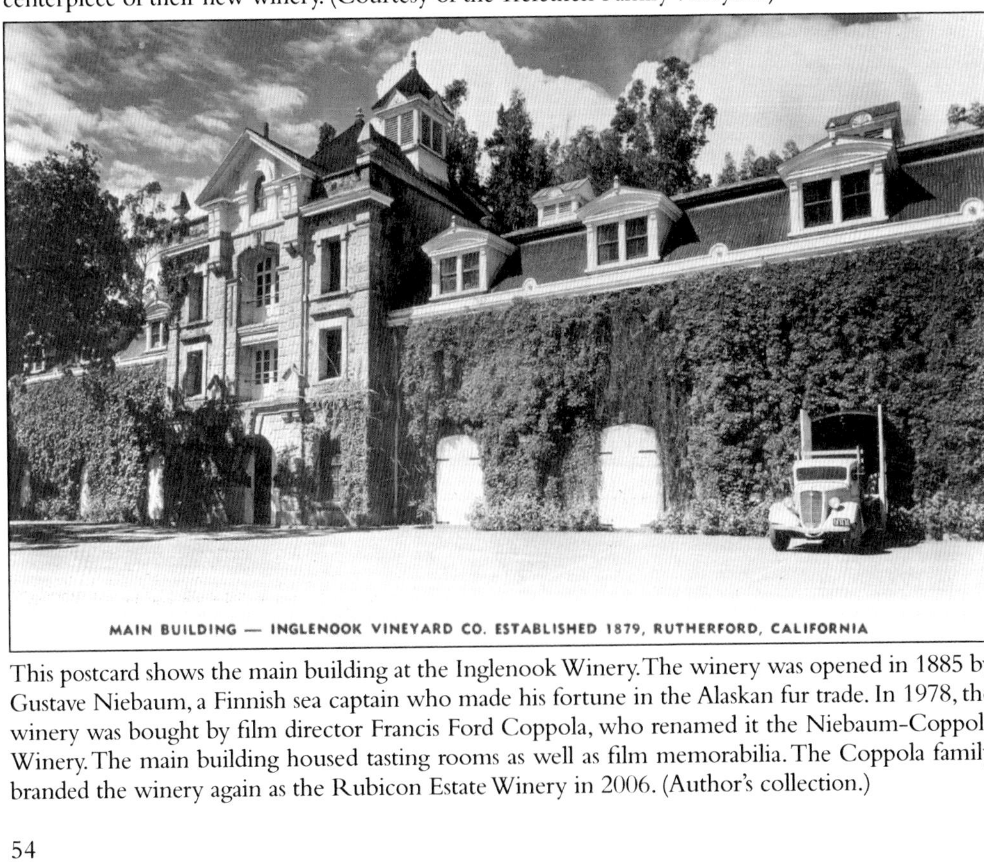

This postcard shows the main building at the Inglenook Winery. The winery was opened in 1885 by Gustave Niebaum, a Finnish sea captain who made his fortune in the Alaskan fur trade. In 1978, the winery was bought by film director Francis Ford Coppola, who renamed it the Niebaum-Coppola Winery. The main building housed tasting rooms as well as film memorabilia. The Coppola family branded the winery again as the Rubicon Estate Winery in 2006. (Author's collection.)

Beaulieu Vineyard, known by its initials BV, was founded in 1900 by Georges de Latour. It reportedly got its name when Georges' wife, Fernande, saw the area around Rutherford and exclaimed in French, "beau lieu" (beautiful place). Pictured in this postcard is the former Fred Ewer Winery building, constructed in 1885 and purchased by BV in 1923. Today it sits next to the popular Rutherford Grill Restaurant fronting Highway 29. (Courtesy of Beaulieu Vineyard.)

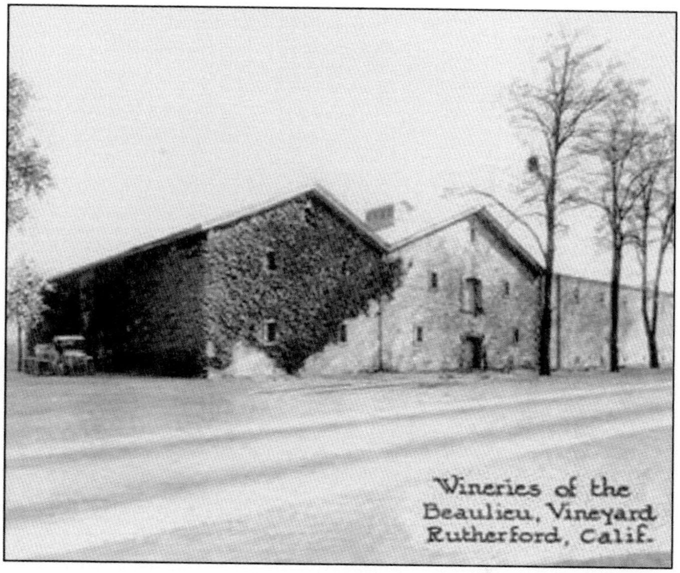

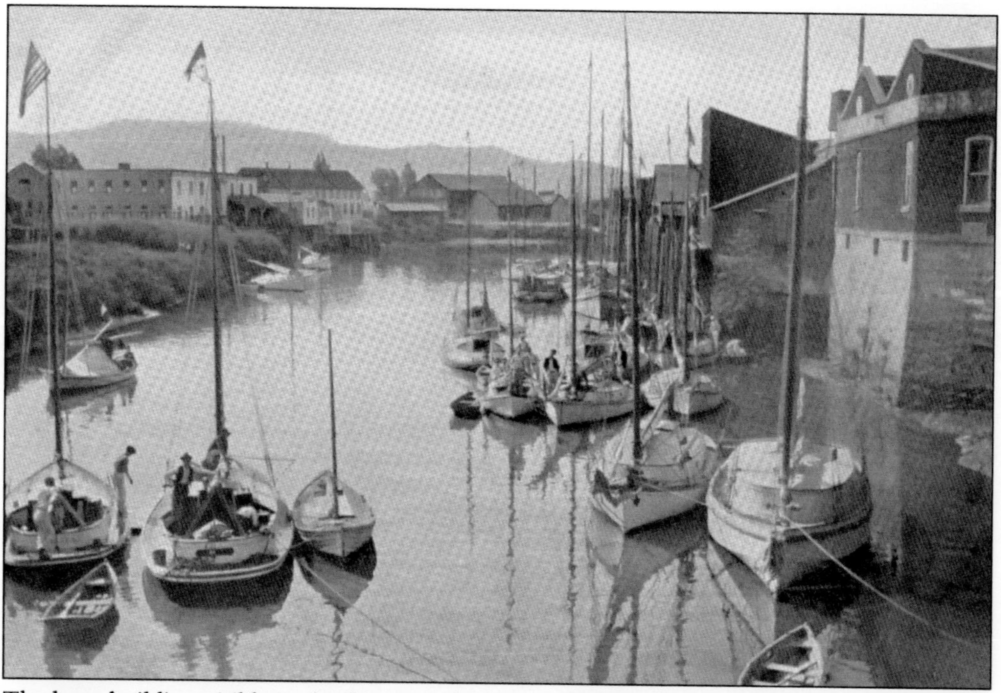

The large building visible in the foreground, on the right bank of the Napa River, is the Uncle Sam Cellar. It first began making wine in 1870; in 1872, the two-story brick building pictured above was constructed at the corner of Main and Fourth Streets. The distillery, connected with the cellar, had a capacity of 500 gallons. In 1874, a vinegar factory was added to the business. (Author's collection.)

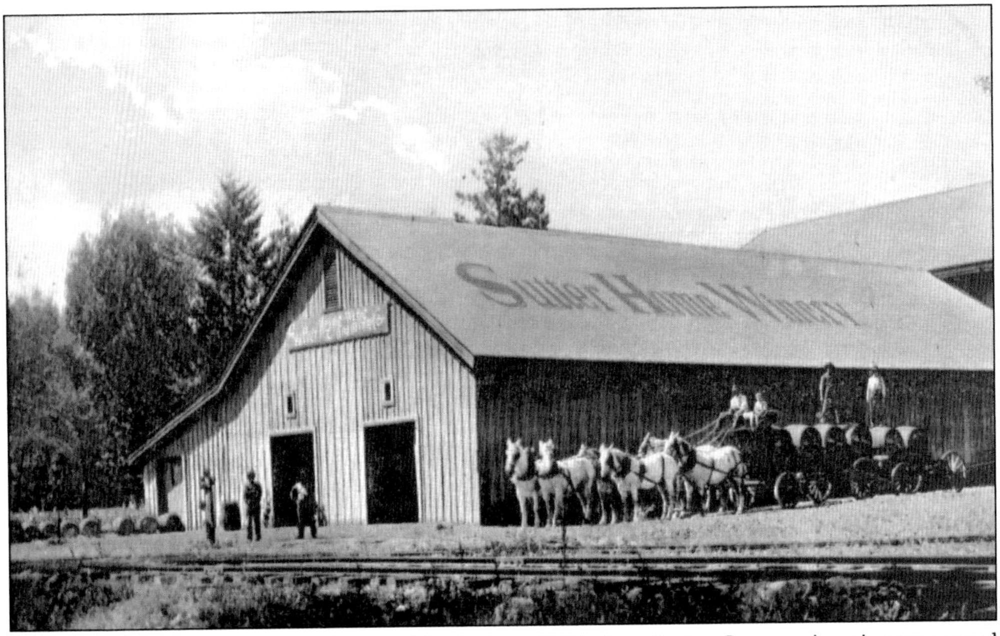

The Sutter Home Winery was founded in the late 1800s by a Swiss-German immigrant named John Thomann. It was shut down during Prohibition. In 1948, Sutter Home was resurrected by the Trinchero family, who continues to operate it today. (Courtesy of the Napa County Historical Society.)

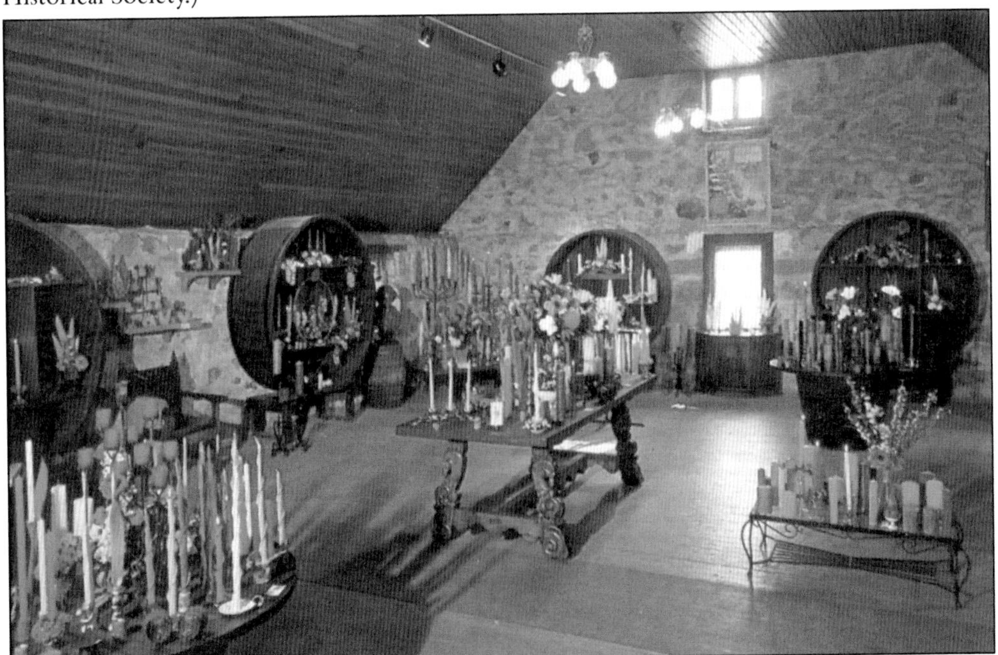

The Freemark Abbey Winery traces its roots back to 1886 when Josephine Tychson became the first woman to build and operate a winery in California. She sold the winery in 1894; it became the Lombarda Cellars until it went out of business during Prohibition. In 1939, the winery was reopened as Freemark Abbey Winery (a combination that includes a portion of each partner's name). For 37 years, the winery also housed the Hurd's Beeswax Candle Company. (Author's collection.)

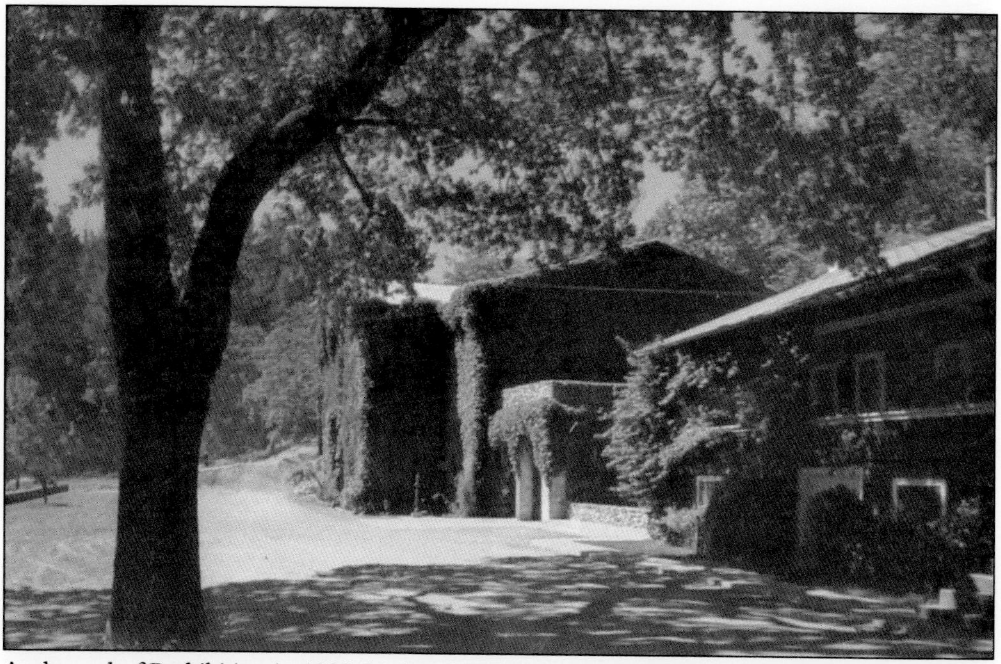

At the end of Prohibition in 1933, Louis M. Martini began building a new winery in St. Helena. Martini was a founding member of the Napa Valley Vintners Association. In 1951, Martini's son Louis P. was one of the first people to employ wind machines to combat vineyard frost. The Gallo family purchased the winery in 2002. (Author's collection.)

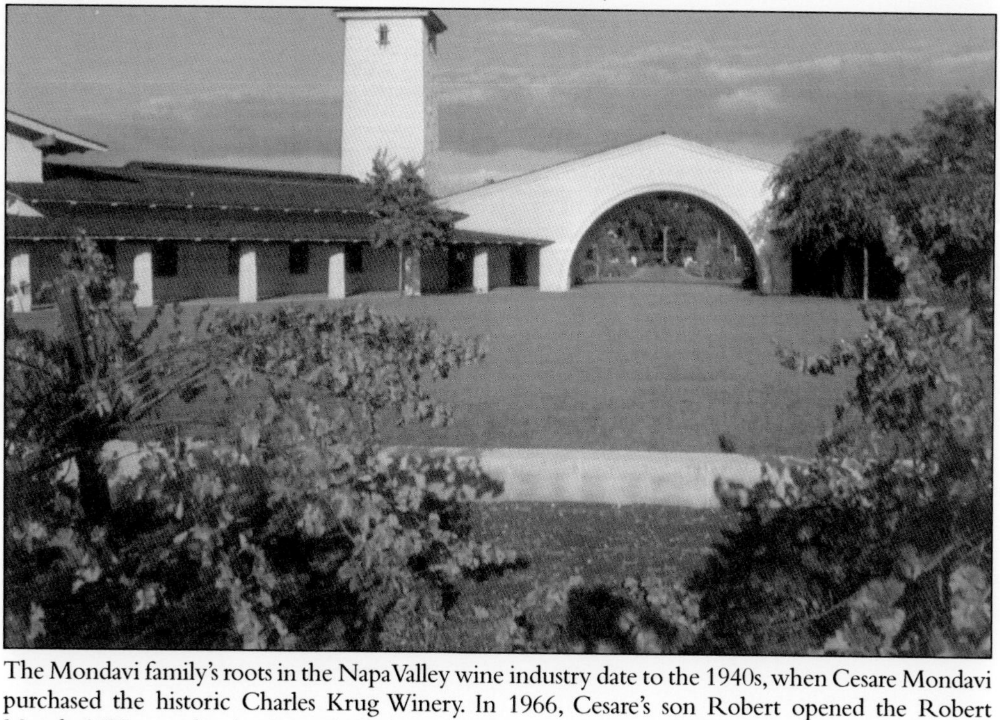

The Mondavi family's roots in the Napa Valley wine industry date to the 1940s, when Cesare Mondavi purchased the historic Charles Krug Winery. In 1966, Cesare's son Robert opened the Robert Mondavi Winery that is pictured. Robert Mondavi and his wife, Margrit, have been very visible philanthropists in Napa Valley and at the University of California at Davis. (Author's collection.)

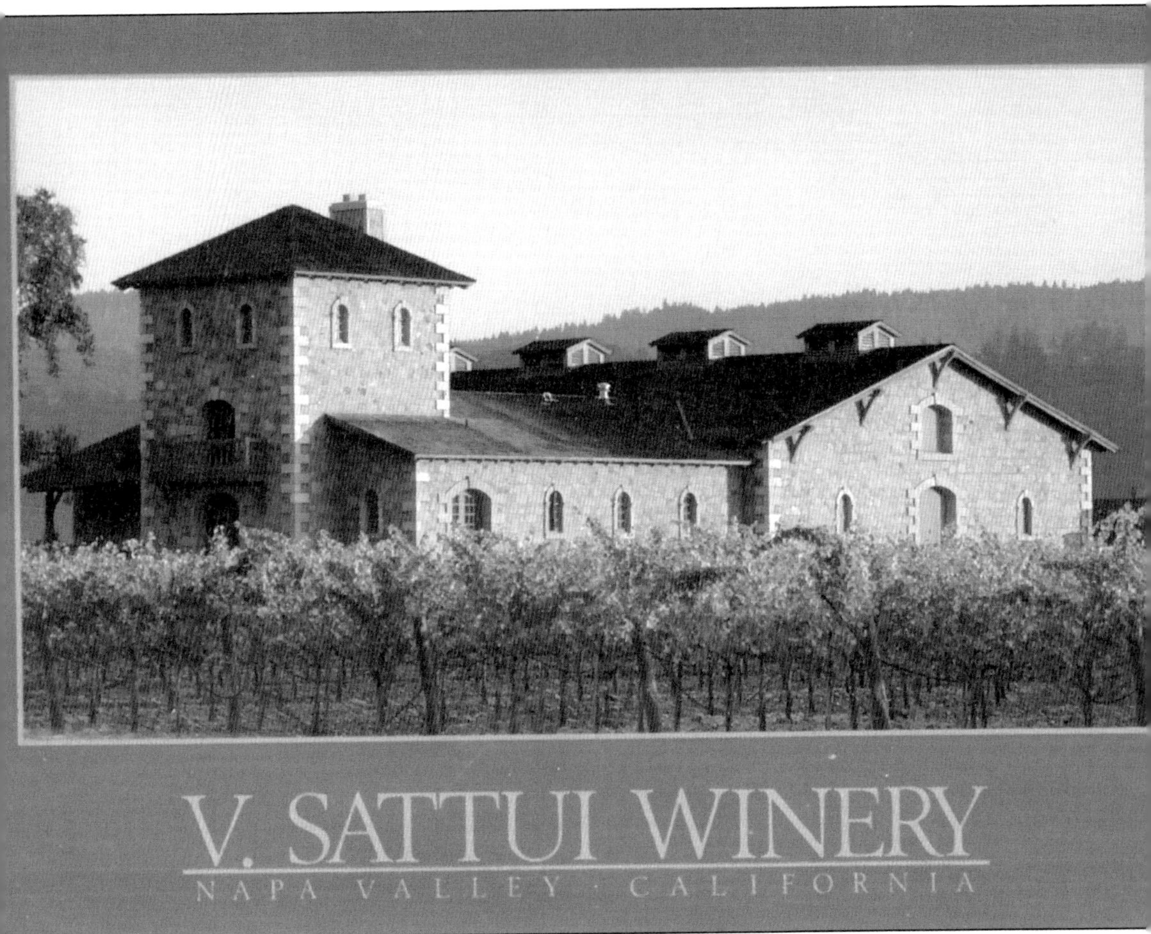

The V. Sattui Winery's history dates to 1885, when Vittorio Sattui opened a winery named the St. Helena Winery in San Francisco. Prohibition forced it to close. In 1976, Dario Sattui, the great-grandson of Vittorio, reopened the V. Sattui Winery. It has become a fixture along Highway 29 at the south end of St. Helena. It is a favorite stop for many visitors due to its inviting picnic grounds. (Author's collection.)

Four

Napa

The City of Napa as we know it today was born from the mind of Nathan Coombs. Coombs and John Grigsby received the land as payment for carpentry work done for landowner Nicholas Higuera. In 1847, Coombs laid out the initial streets of what was to become Napa; the area was initially named Coombsville. The city's first boundaries were from Brown Street on the west to the Napa River on the east, and from the Napa Creek on the north to the foot of Main Street on the south, the location of the steamboat landing.

Napa was positioned at the northerly terminus of the navigable portion of the Napa River. As such, it became an important freight and trading post.

Harrison Pierce built Napa's first permanent structure, the Empire Saloon at the southeast corner of Main and Third Streets. The town was nearly abandoned during the gold fever of 1848; it blossomed, however, after the disillusioned would-be miners returned and began building in earnest.

In 1849, Napa became the county seat of the newly formed Napa County. Napa continued to grow steadily over the years. An influx of workers moved in during the 1940s to help support the war efforts of the nearby naval bases and Kaiser Steel's shipyard.

Today Napa's downtown is undergoing a transformation. There has been extensive work along the riverfront as part of the corps of engineers' flood control work. New boutique hotels and mixed-use condominium and retail projects are being built. Napa's population stands at over 75,000 people, making it the largest city in the valley.

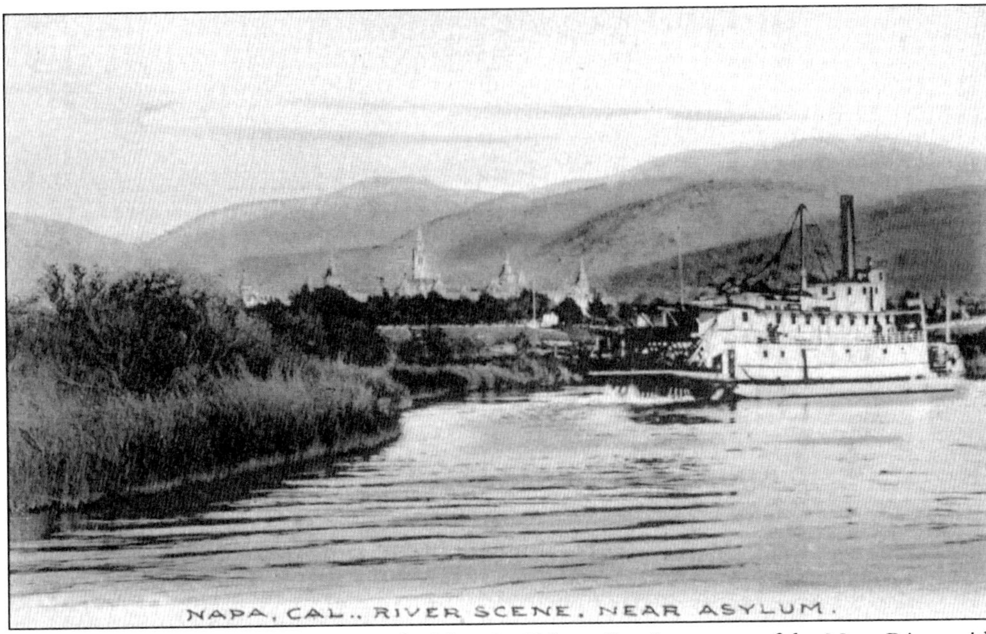

A steamship, most likely either the *Zinfandel* or *St. Helena*, plies the waters of the Napa River with the Napa State Hospital in the background. The ship is north of the Suscol docks, an area favored due to its deep channel, even at low tide. The Napa River was later dredged near Napa, allowing larger ships to dock just south of the Third Street Bridge. (Author's collection.)

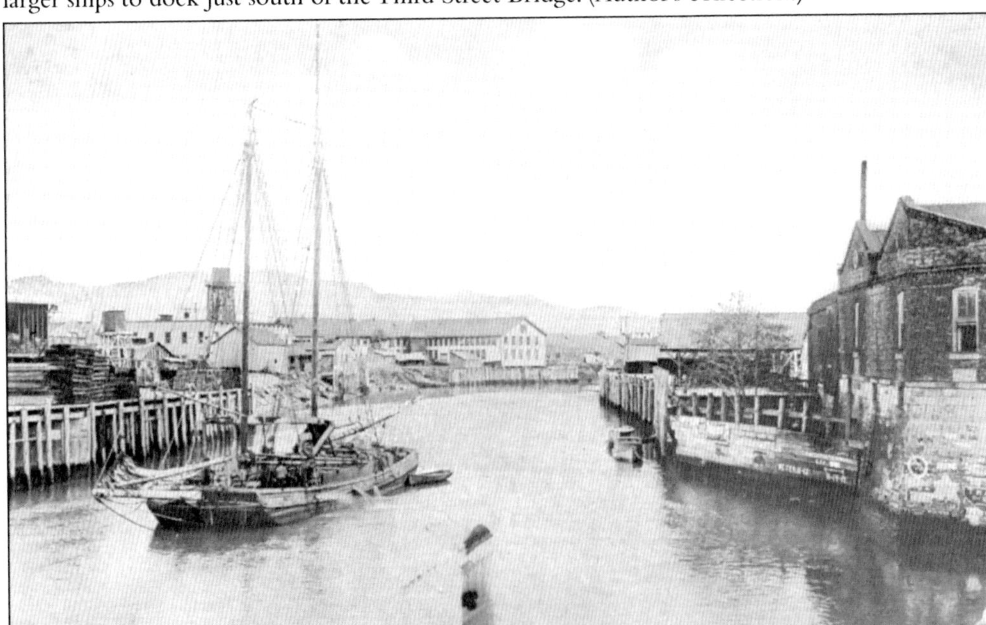

The scow schooner *Cinderella* is visible on the river just south of Third Street. Scow schooners were frequently used on the Napa River because their shallow drafts allowed them to navigate more easily in the sometimes shallow river. Larger vessels would have to offload their cargo at the Suscol landing south of Napa, where it would be transferred to smaller ships for transport to Napa. (Author's collection.)

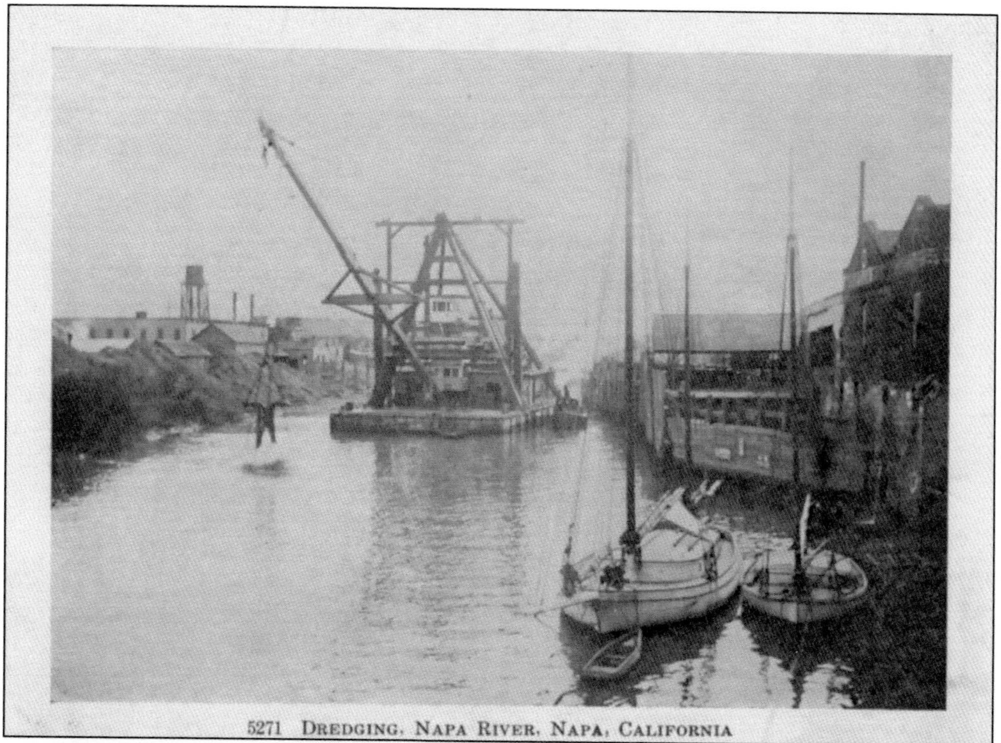

This postcard shows river dredging on the Napa River just south of Third Street *c.* 1908. The dredging of the river allowed larger vessels to travel north to Napa, bypassing the docks of Suscol. The dredging and advent of the railroad and electric railway were the death knell for the tiny hamlet of Suscol. (Courtesy of Mike Vanwormer.)

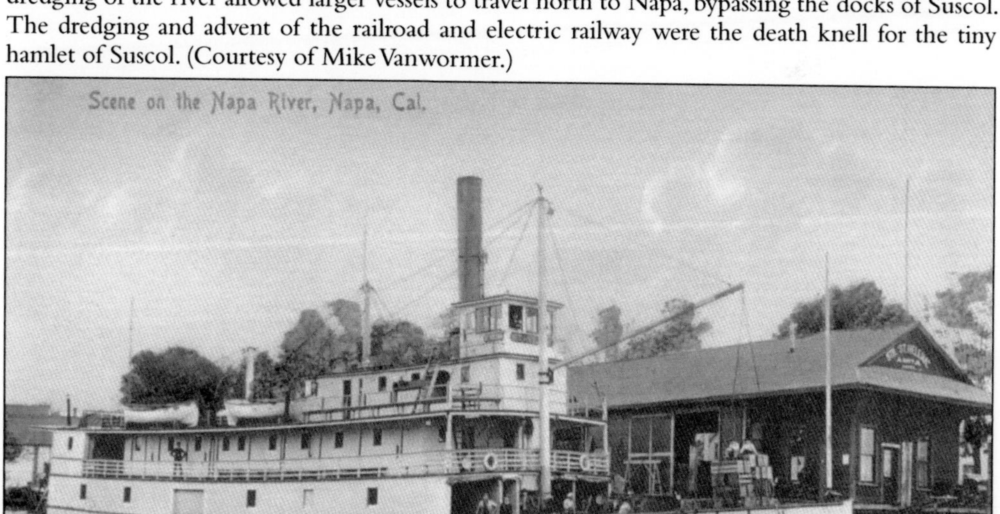

The sternwheel steamer *St. Helena* docked in Napa. It was one of the many ships that made the regular trek back and forth between San Francisco and Napa, transporting goods and passengers. The *St. Helena* began service in 1902 and featured 25 staterooms. (Author's collection.)

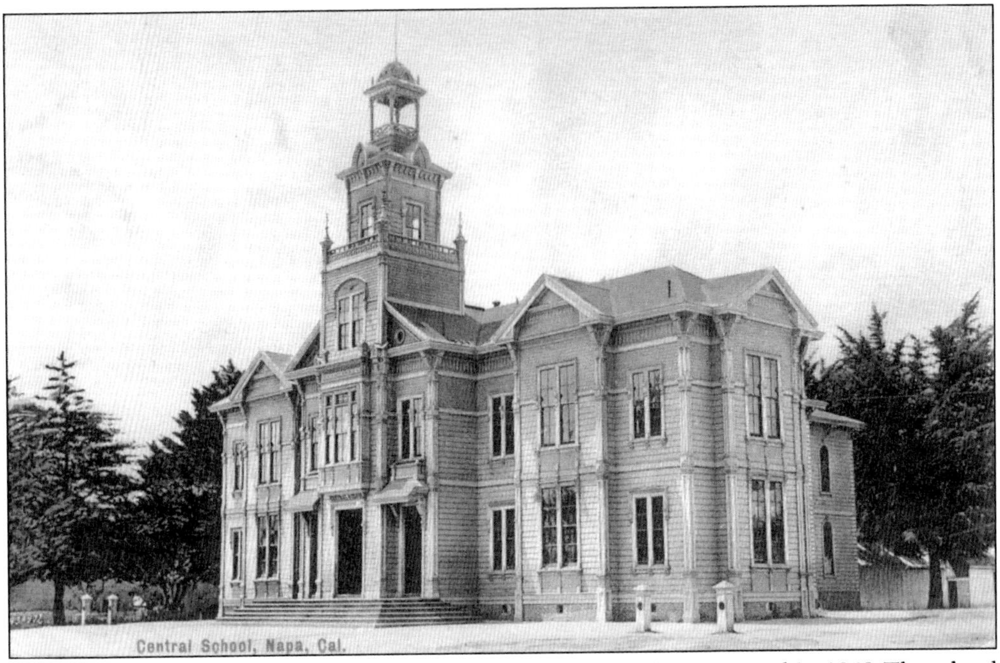

The Central School was Napa's first eight-year grammar school, constructed in 1868. The school featured two stories of classrooms, a cupola with a bell, and a widow's walk. It was built for $17,000 with funding from a special tax placed on residents. The school's most famous principal was John L. Shearer, who served in that capacity until its closing in 1921. The site of the school is the present location of Napa City Hall on School Street. (Author's collection.)

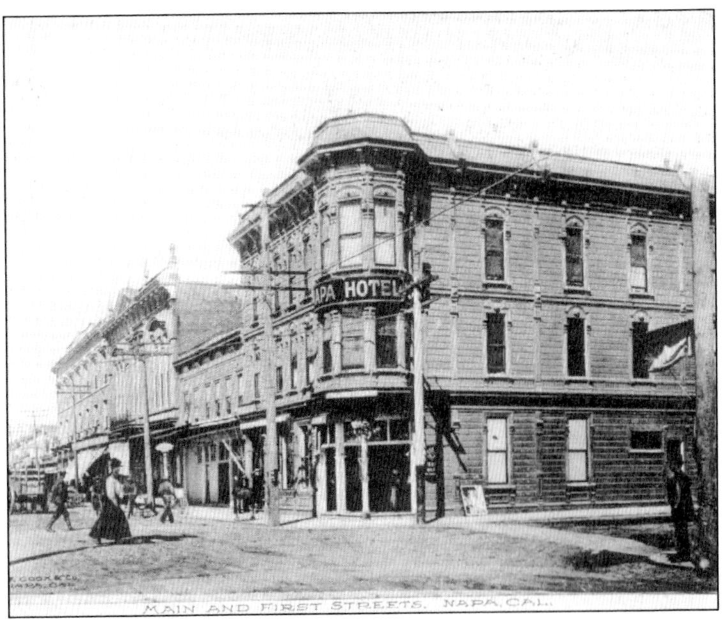

This postcard shows the Napa Hotel and First Street, looking north. The Napa Hotel was built in 1885 at the northeast corner of First and Main Streets to replace its predecessor, which burned a year prior. The hotel featured a covered walkway that connected the back of it to the nearby Napa Opera House. One of the hotel's early managers was David Dunlap, who went on to become the Napa County sheriff. (Author's collection.)

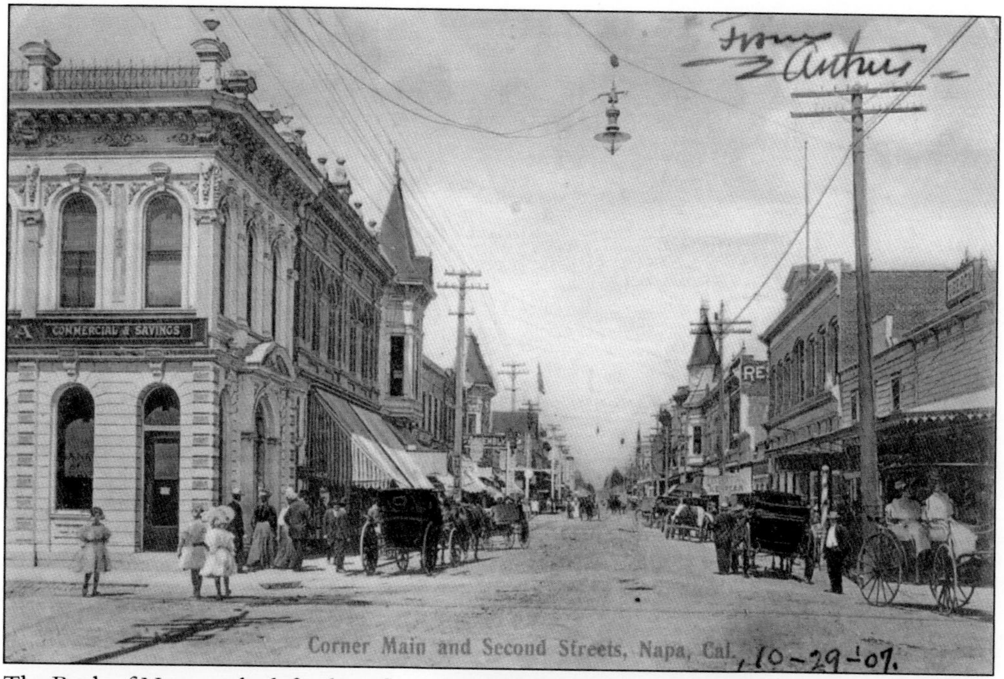

The Bank of Napa, at the left edge of this postcard, was built in 1923 and is located at 903 Main Street. It is now a Wells Fargo Bank. Next door is the Haas Stationary Store, with the striped awning. Many of the early Napa postcards were produced by the Haas brothers and hand-colored in Germany. On the far right is the Oberon Bar, which burned down in 1934. The site now houses Downtown Joe's Restaurant and Microbrewery. (Author's collection.)

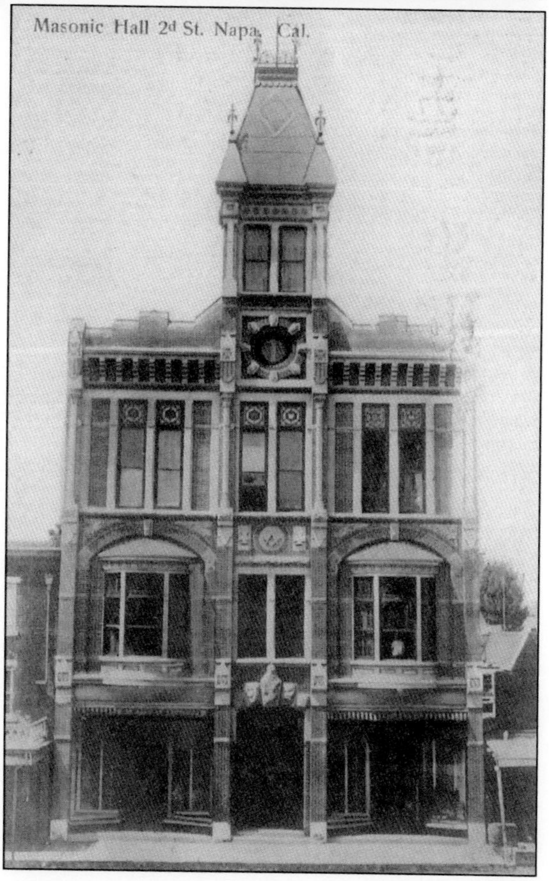

This imposing structure is the Masonic temple as it appeared *c.* 1907. The temple was built in 1889 for a cost of $50,000. It was located on Second Street between Coombs and Brown Streets. The temple was demolished in 1974 to make way for a public parking garage. (Author's collection.)

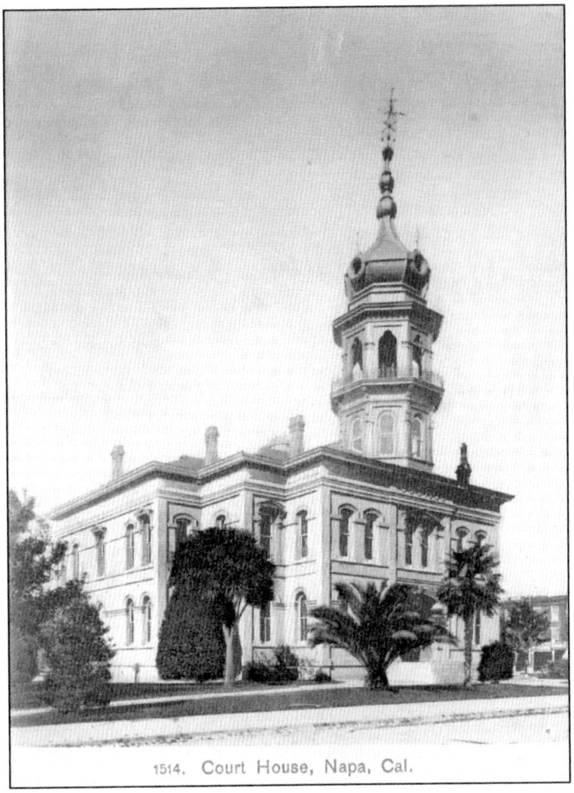

The Napa County Courthouse is pictured here as it appeared *c.* 1907. This was the third courthouse built on the site, completed in 1879. In addition to the courtrooms, the building also housed the county offices of the treasurer, assessor, recorder, clerk, surveyor, superintendant of schools, and sheriff. In 1897, the last public execution in California was on the courthouse grounds. (Author's collection.)

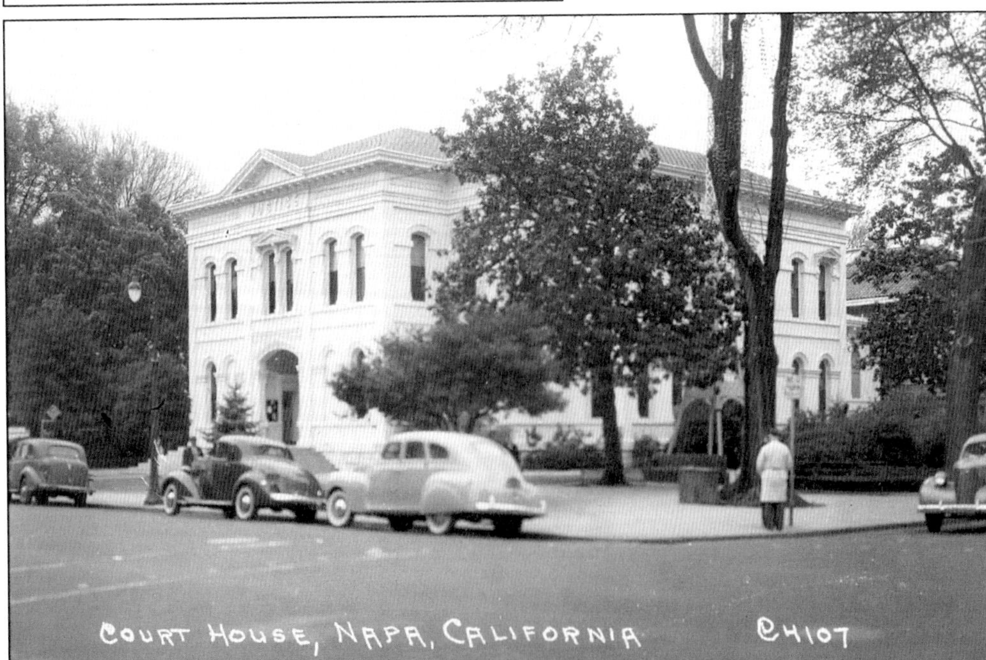

This later postcard shows the courthouse minus its distinctive cupola, which was removed in the 1930s. The building is still used today, although a modern courthouse was constructed across the street in 1999. (Author's collection.)

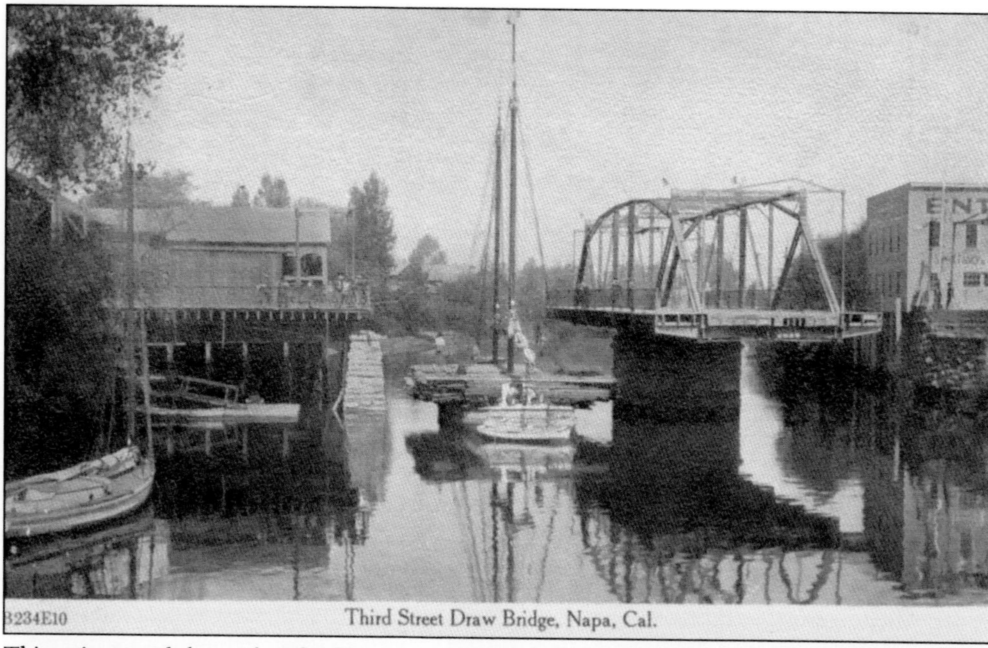

This unique card shows the Third Street steel drawbridge in its open position. The bridge was built in 1892 and served as the primary means of east-west travel in the city. Prior to that time, a ferry operated at the foot of Third Street. The bridge also contained railroad tracks that served the electric railway as it traversed the city and continued north up the valley. (Courtesy of Mike Vanwormer.)

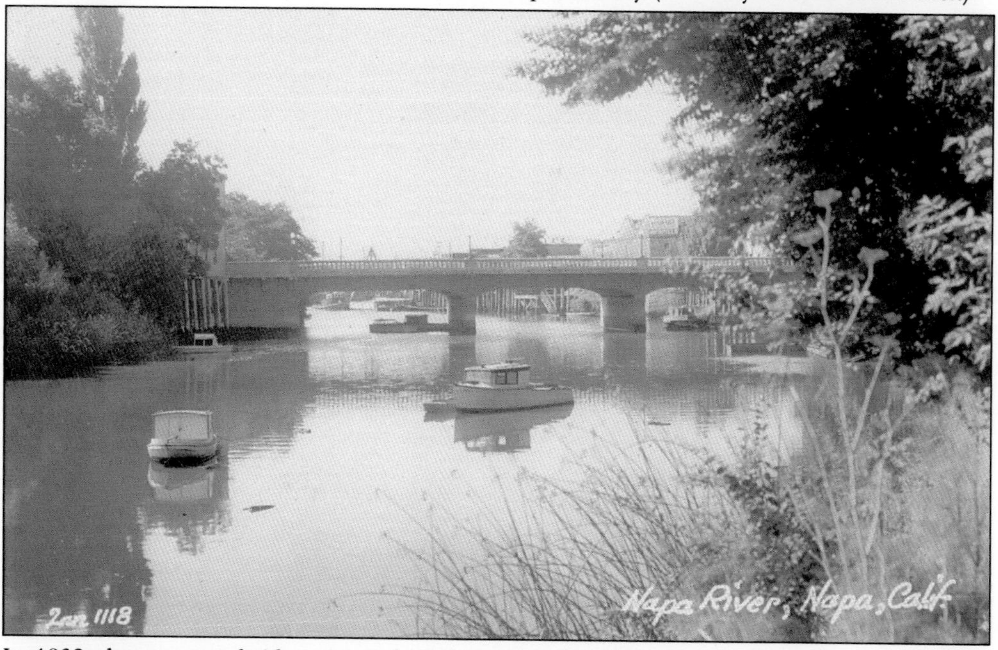

In 1932, the concrete bridge pictured in this postcard replaced the long-standing Third Street drawbridge. This bridge would serve Napans for 70 years. In 2002, it was replaced as part of the Napa River flood control project. The current bridge is wider and higher, allowing for a pedestrian promenade to follow the west bank of the river. The promenade runs from the Hatt Building north, past Veteran's Park, ending at First Street. (Author's collection.)

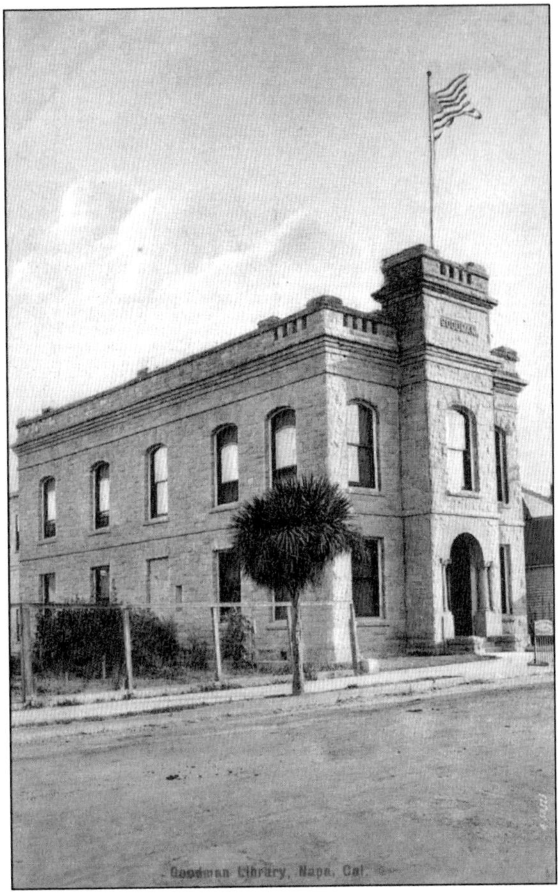

This postcard shows the Goodman Library as it appeared in 1907. The building, located on First Street west of Coombs Street, was erected and donated to the city by banker George Goodman in 1901. It served as the city's library until 1963, when a new facility was built farther south on Coombs Street. Today the Goodman Library is the home of the Napa County Historical Society. (Author's collection.)

The Palace Hotel was built in 1875, the same year Napa incorporated as a city. The Palace, which was located on the southwest corner of Third Street and Soscol Avenue, was one of the "big three" hotels that operated in early Napa, along with the Napa and Revere House Hotels. The Palace was torn down in the 1930s; a gas station and Noyes Lumber Company later used the site. (Author's collection.)

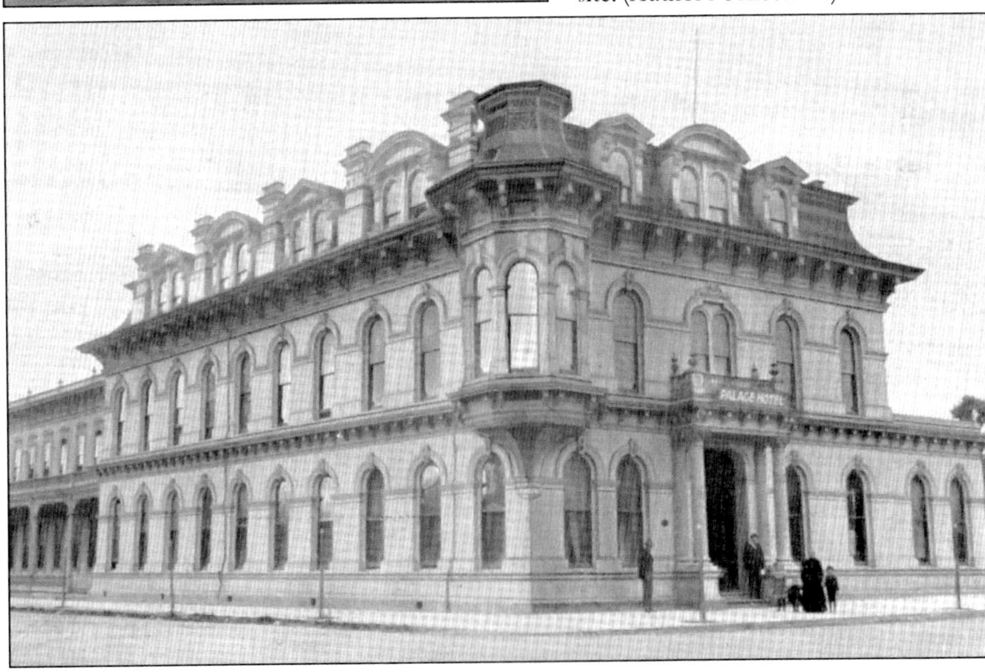

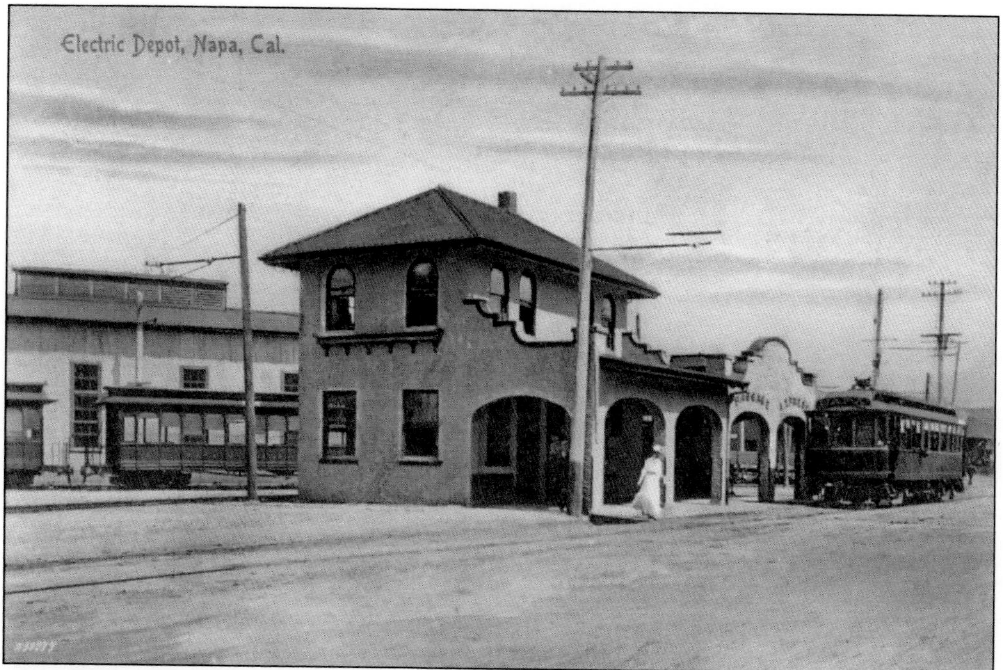

The electric railroad was a fixture in Napa from 1905 to 1938. The Napa Depot was constructed at the southeast corner of what are now Soscol Avenue and Third Street, directly across the street from the Palace Hotel. The depot featured covered and enclosed waiting areas on the first floor and a railroad office on the second floor. The train cars visible in the background were built in 1902 and purchased used from Los Angeles for use in Napa. (Author's collection.)

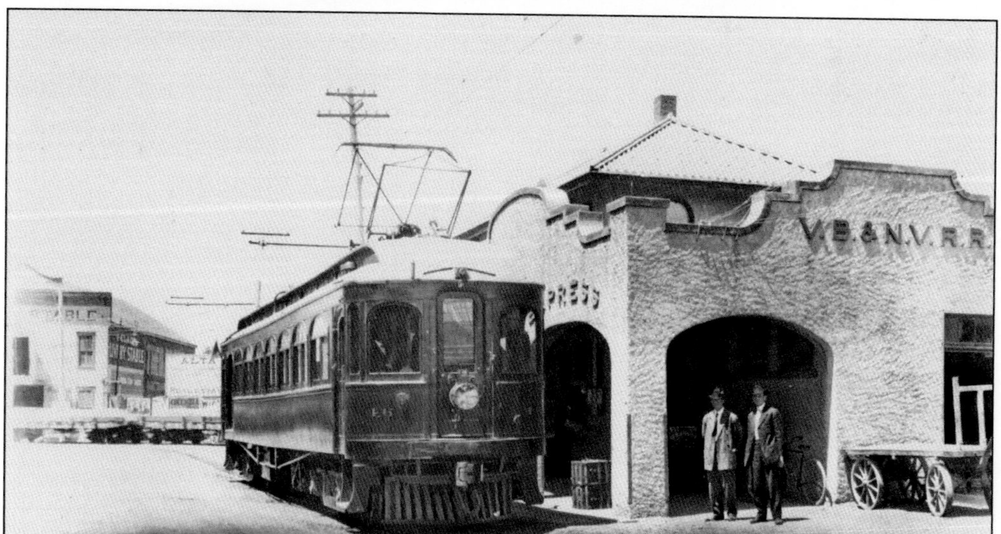

After stopping at the depot, the electric railroad crossed the Third Street Bridge and continued west until reaching Jefferson Street, where it veered north, finally traveling northbound along Calistoga Avenue (now renamed as an extension of Jefferson Street) out of town. In 1930, the tracks through downtown Napa were abandoned, and the electric railroad began using Southern Pacific tracks at the east edge of the city. (Courtesy of the Napa County Historical Society.)

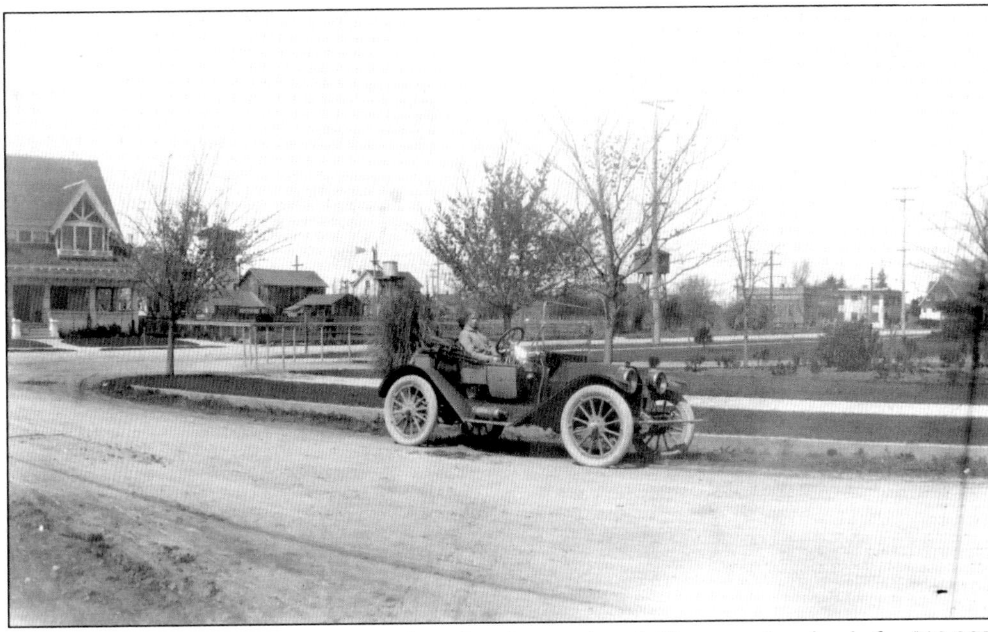

Napa's first city park began in 1905 when the city purchased 10 acres of orchards for $10,000. Originally named Oak Street Park, it was renamed Fuller Park in 1910 in honor of Mayor Jack Fuller. This postcard dates to the 1910s and shows Eula Salomonson posing in the automobile belonging to local legend Boon Fly. The auto is parked on the south side of the park, on Laurel Street, just east of Jefferson Street. (Courtesy of the Napa County Historical Society.)

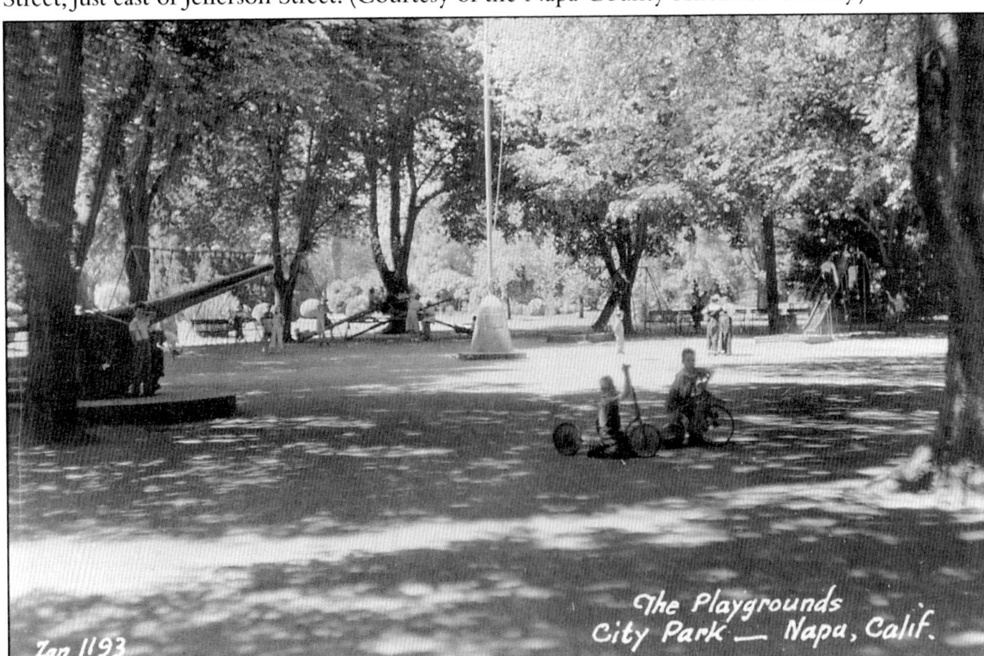

Fuller Park's playground is visible in this 1930s postcard. The cannon at the left edge of the card had been mounted on a warship in Manila Bay during the Spanish-American War. In 1942, the city returned the cannon to the federal government to be melted down and used for scrap metal during World War II. (Author's collection.)

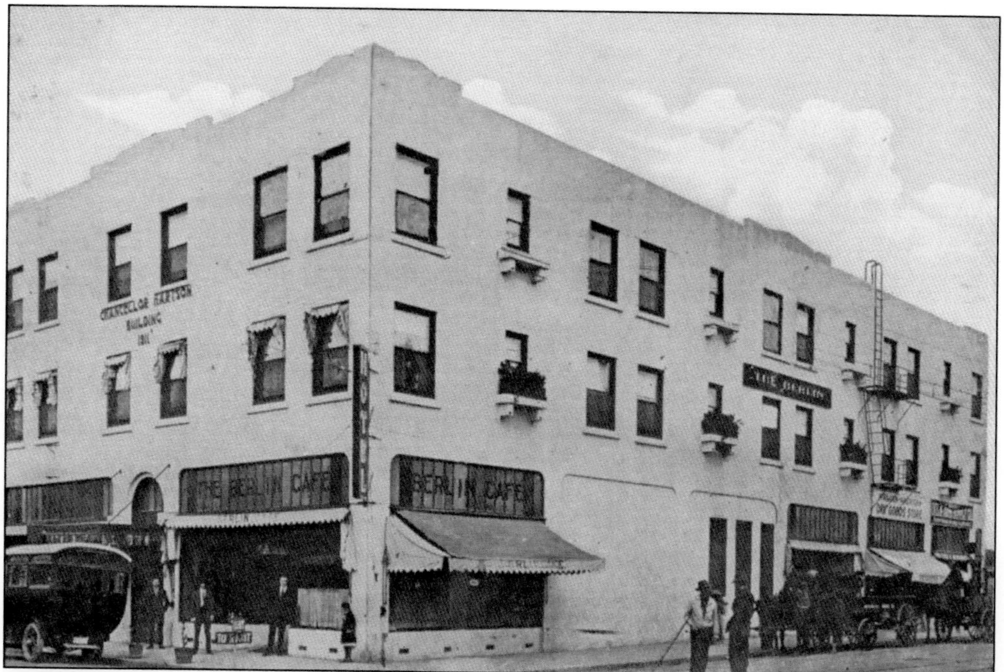

The Chancellor Hartson Building was constructed in 1911 at the northeast corner of Main and Third Streets and named for him by his daughter Anne Cope. Hartson was the district attorney of Napa County in the 1850s and later a judge; he also founded the Bank of Napa and the Aetna Springs Resort. In its early years, the building housed the Berlin Hotel, as is pictured in this postcard. (Courtesy of Mike Vanwormer.)

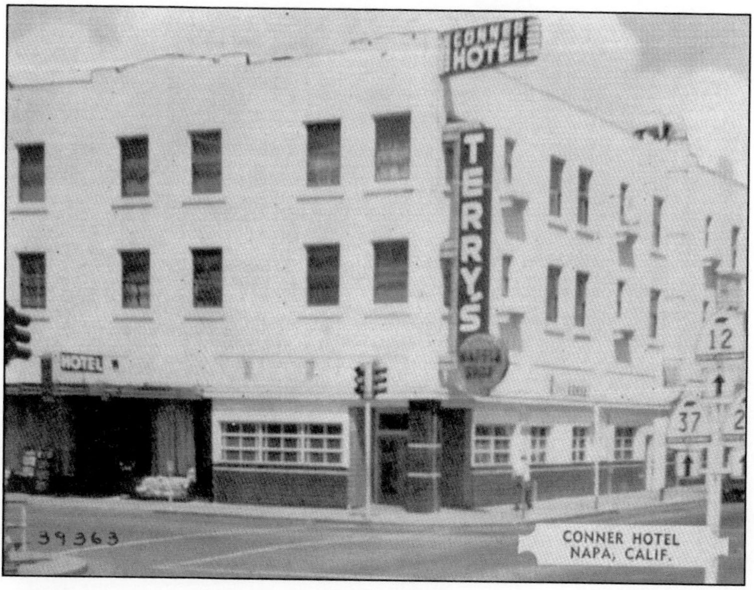

In its later years, the Hartson Building was remodeled and became the Conner Hotel. The hotel was a hideout for a short time for gangsters Joe "Fatso" Negri and "Baby Face" Nelson in the 1920s. The site of the hotel is now Veteran's Park, which was recently remodeled as part of the ongoing flood control project along the Napa River. (Author's collection.)

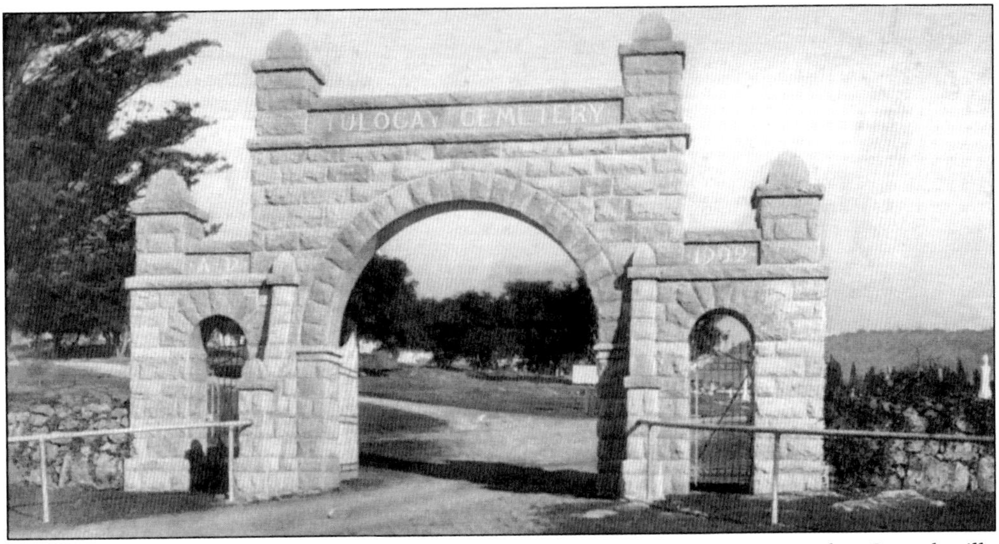

Tulocay Cemetery was first established in 1858 when 50 acres along present-day Coombsville Road were deeded by Don Cayetano Juarez. The name "Tulocay" was adapted from the name of Juarez's original Mexican land grant, Rancho Tulocay. The cemetery is the resting place of many prominent early Napa pioneers. The stone archway visible in this postcard was constructed in 1902 and still covers the main entrance to the cemetery. (Author's collection.)

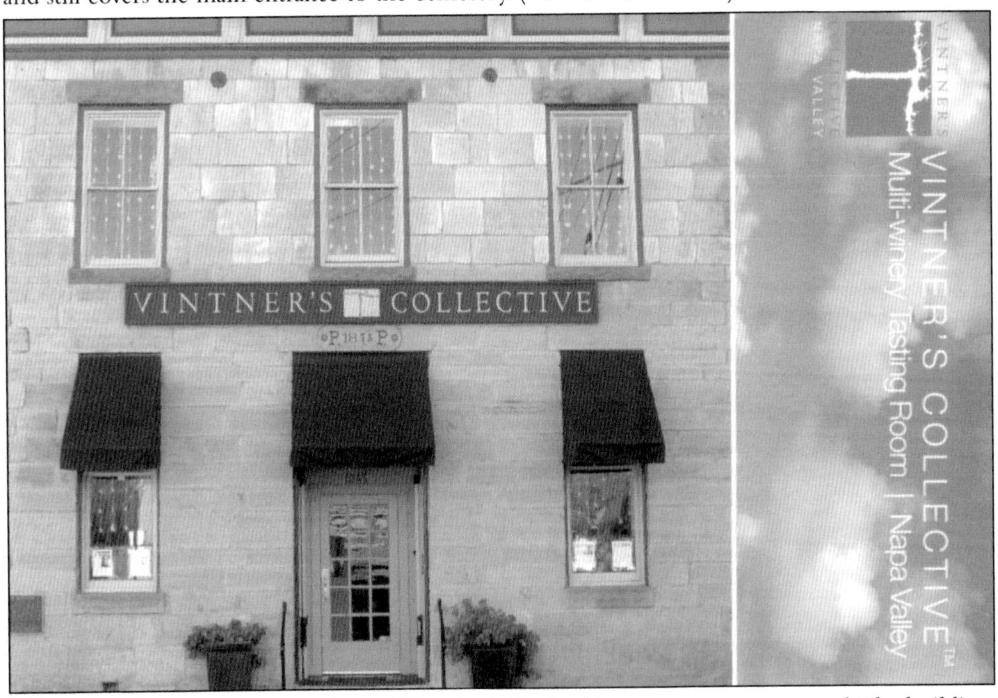

The front of the Sam Kee Laundry Building is visible in this contemporary postcard. The building, located at 1245 Main Street, is Napa's oldest surviving commercial building. Bavarian immigrant Philip Pfeiffer built it in 1875 to house a brewery. Rumor has it the upper floor was used as a brothel at the start of the 20th century. For many years, it housed the Sam Kee Laundry, one of the last vestiges of a once-thriving Chinatown area. Today the building is home to the Vintner's Collective, a wine tasting room. (Author's collection.)

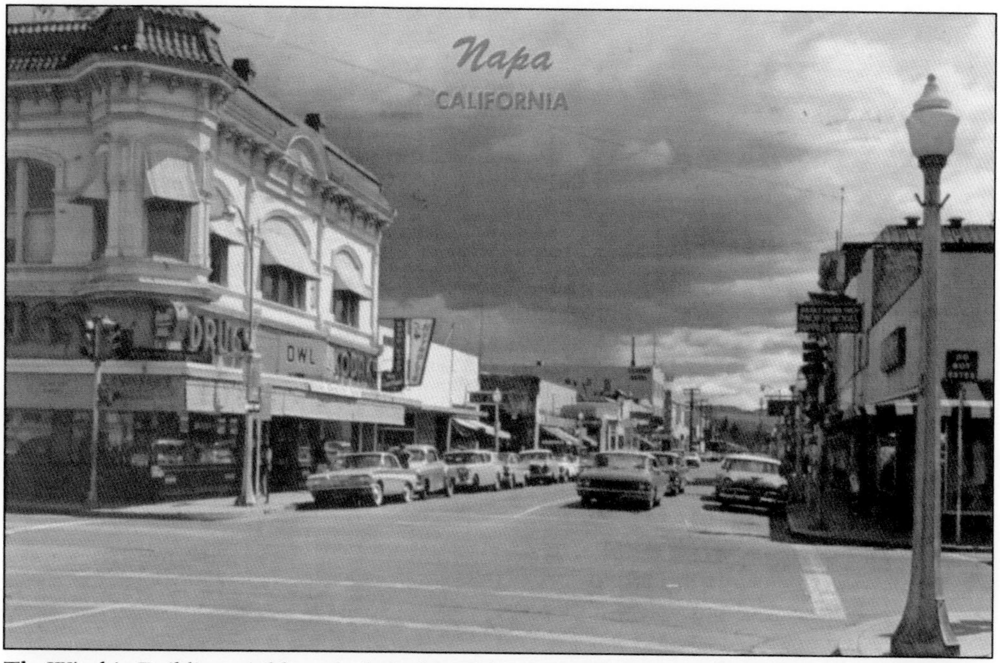

The Winship Building, visible at the left edge of this postcard, was a creation of noted Napa architect Luther Turton. Built in 1888, it still stands at the southeast corner of Main and First Streets. It is one of many Napa buildings on the National Register of Historic Places. The building's tower and spire were damaged and removed after the 1906 earthquake; they were reconstructed 100 years later during the building's recent restoration. (Author's collection.)

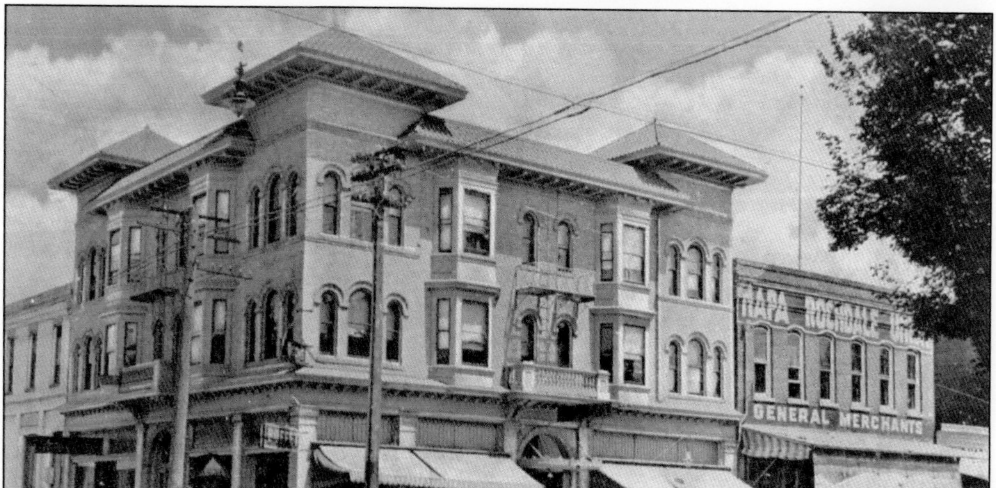

This postcard shows Alexandria Hotel as it appeared *c.* 1910. The hotel, built in 1910, is located on the southeast corner of Second and Brown Streets. The last surviving historic downtown hotel, it was later converted into office and retail space. (Courtesy of the Napa County Historical Society.)

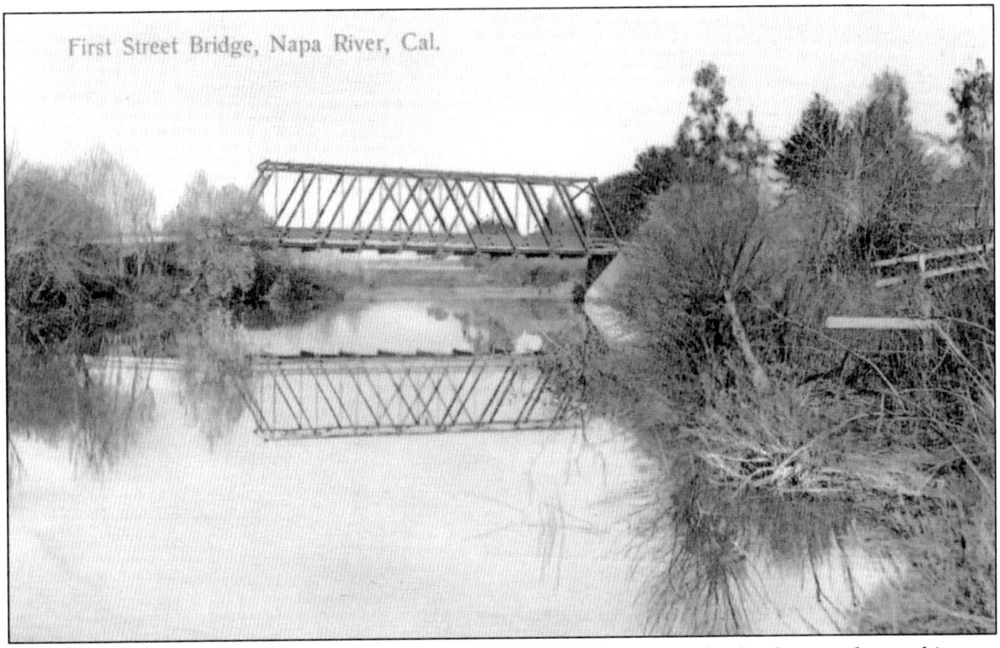

The First Street Bridge as it looked *c.* 1900 appears in this postcard. This bridge was located in east Napa just west of Juarez Street. The area is known as the Oxbow due to the curvature of the Napa River. It had recently seen a reissuance with the construction of the Oxbow Public Market and the planned Ritz-Carlton Hotel. (Author's collection.)

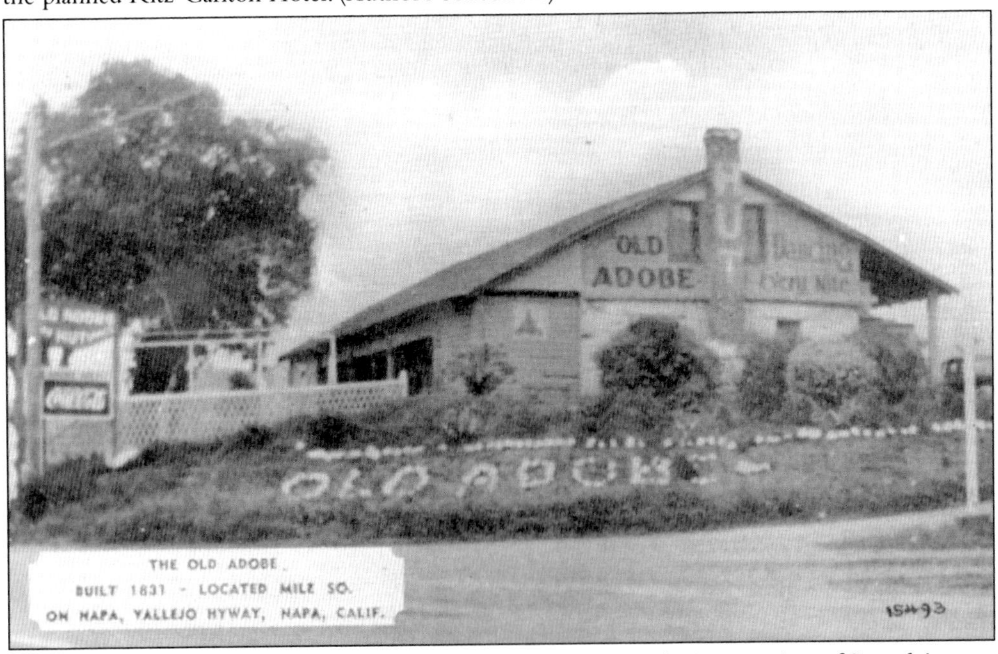

This postcard shows the Old Adobe Hut Restaurant located at the intersection of Soscol Avenue and Silverado Trail. The building is the oldest standing adobe structure in Napa County. Don Cayetano Juarez built it in 1845. It has housed various restaurants and bars over the years. A community group is attempting to raise funds to purchase the adobe and preserve it as a historic structure. (Author's collection.)

The "Steel Stand Pipe" pictured in this postcard was actually a water storage tower located at the intersection of Pine and Seminary Streets. The tower was built in 1904, a project of the then-private Napa City Water Company. It had a 25-foot diameter and stood 100 feet tall. The tower's 367-gallon capacity was a major source of water for the city. The city took over operation of the Napa City Water Company in 1922. (Author's collection.)

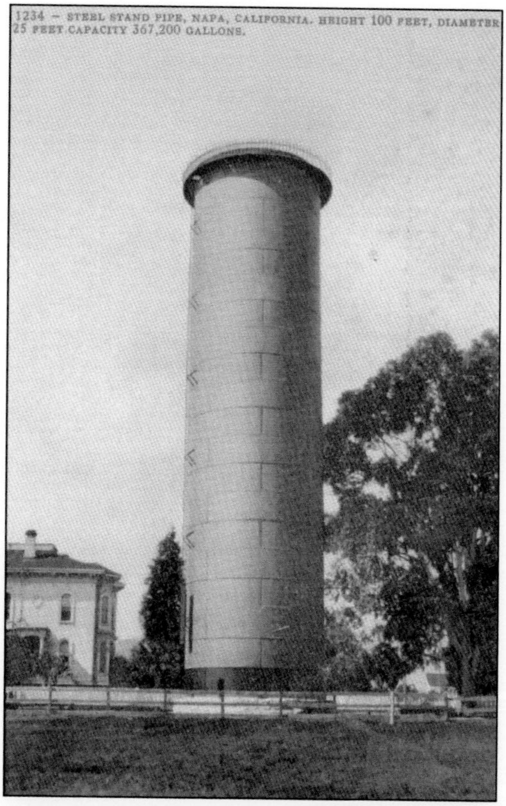

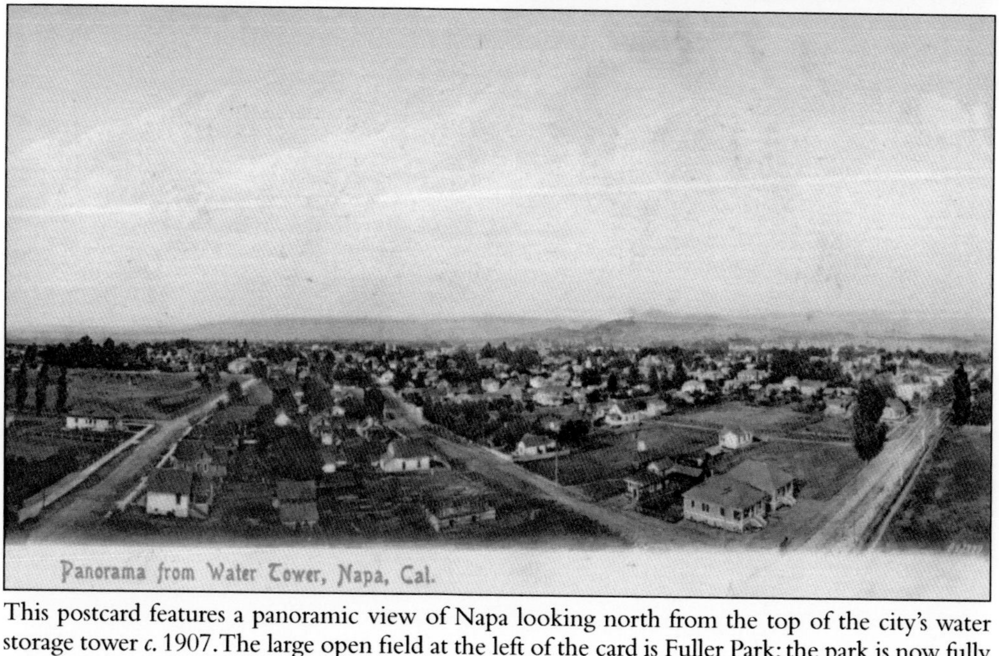

This postcard features a panoramic view of Napa looking north from the top of the city's water storage tower *c.* 1907. The large open field at the left of the card is Fuller Park; the park is now fully covered with a canopy of mature trees. The site of the water tower is now the home to Shearer Elementary School. (Author's collection.)

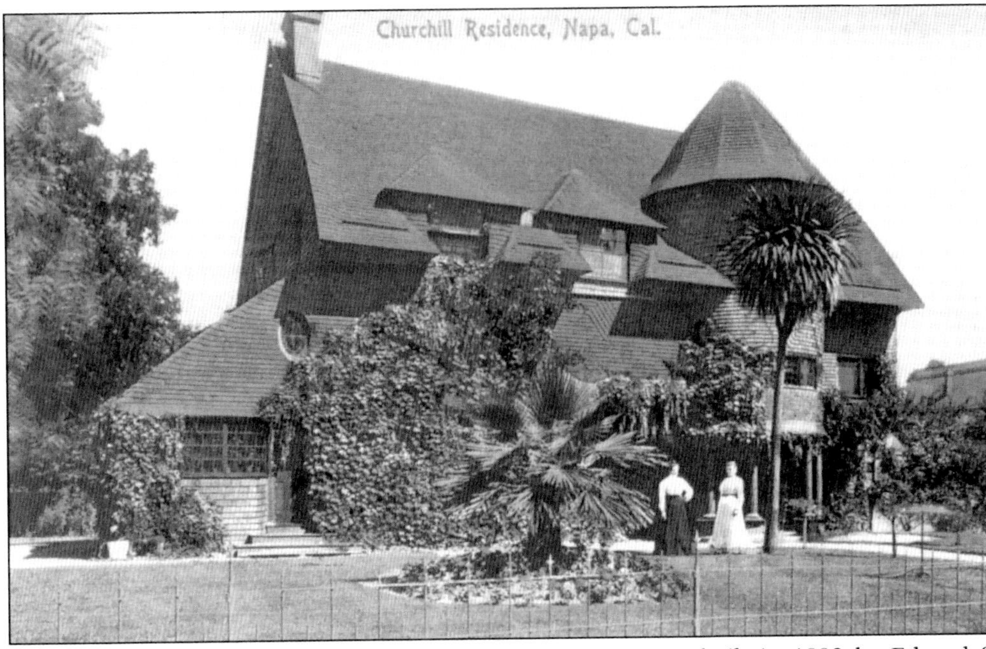

The Churchill House, located at Oak and Coombs Streets, was built in 1892 by Edward S. Churchill as a wedding present for his son, E. Wilder Churchill. During subsequent years, it became a boardinghouse, quarters for military nurses during World War II, and a day spa. The residence currently houses the Cedar Gables Inn, a bed and breakfast. (Courtesy of the Napa County Historical Society.)

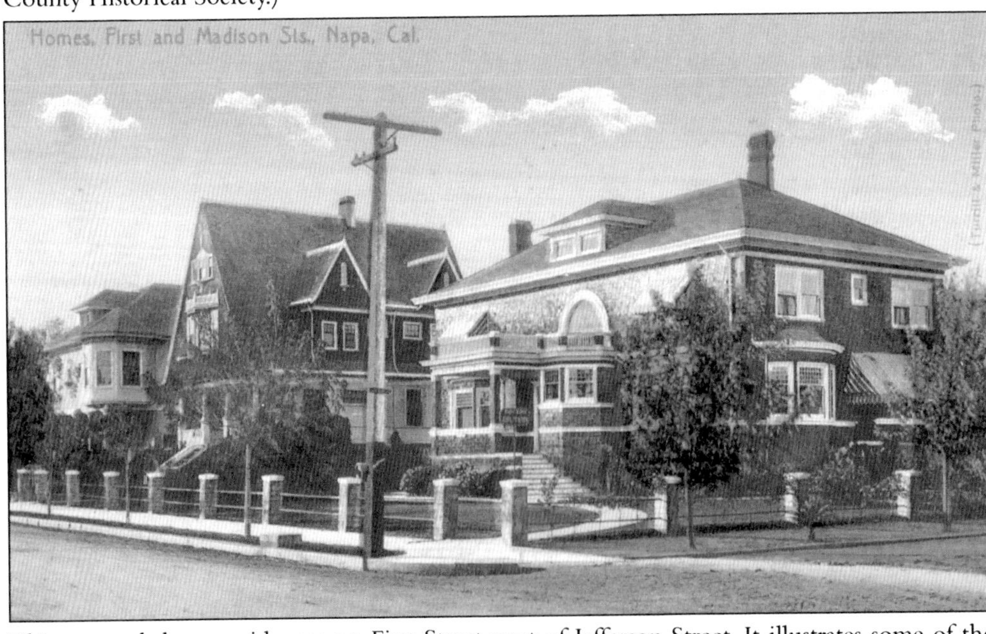

This postcard shows residences on First Street west of Jefferson Street. It illustrates some of the many architecturally significant residences in Napa. Visible at the right edge is the Kahl-Voorhees house, built in 1905. The house now serves as the Beazley House Bed and Breakfast Inn. Many restored Victorian-era homes in and around Napa have been converted to serve weary travelers. (Author's collection.)

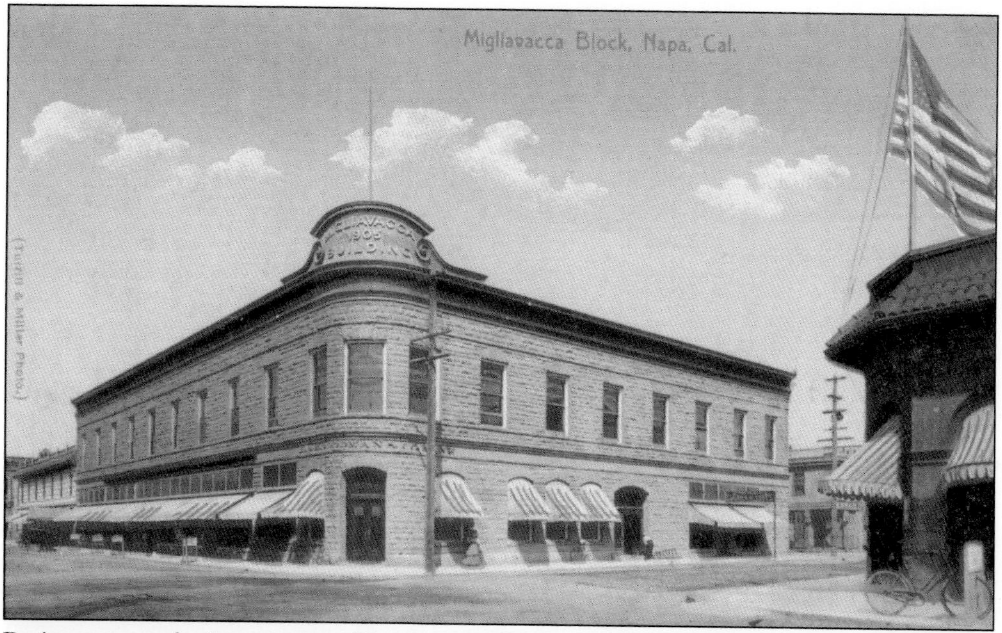

Businessman and winery owner Giacomo Migliavacca built a self-titled building on First and Brown Streets in 1904. Merchants and a bank occupied the first floor, and offices rented by attorneys and doctors were on the second story. It was a fixture on First Street until 1973, when it was torn down for redevelopment. More recently, the site held the Gore Clock Tower and now an outdoor seating area. (Author's collection.)

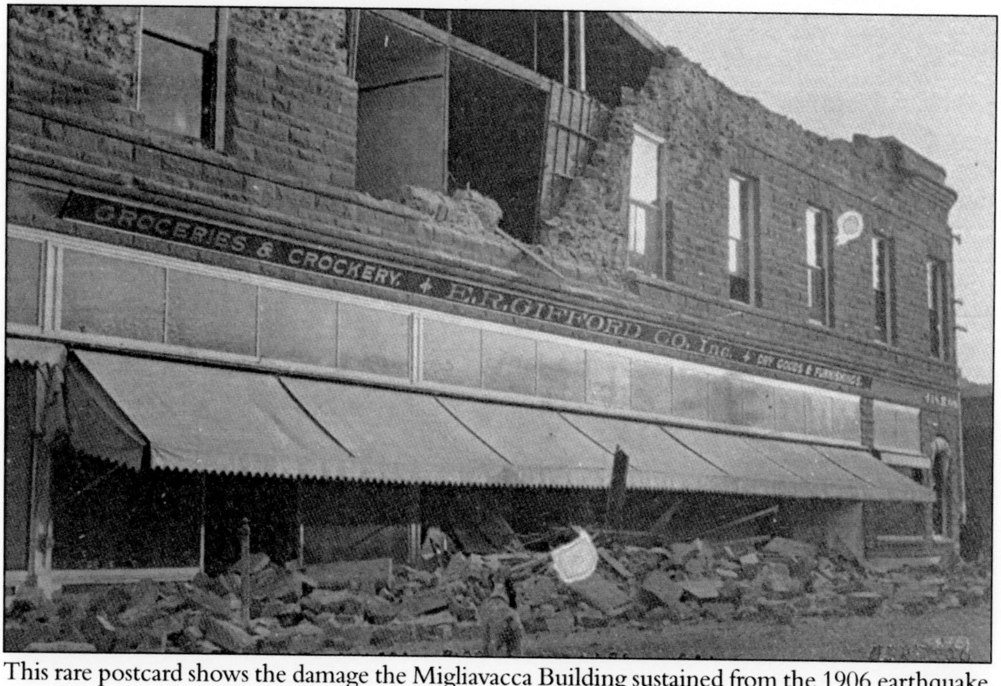

This rare postcard shows the damage the Migliavacca Building sustained from the 1906 earthquake, the same quake that destroyed San Francisco. The building's distinctive curved sign was not added until after the earthquake. The building's repairs and upgrades were completed within four months of the great quake. (Author's collection.)

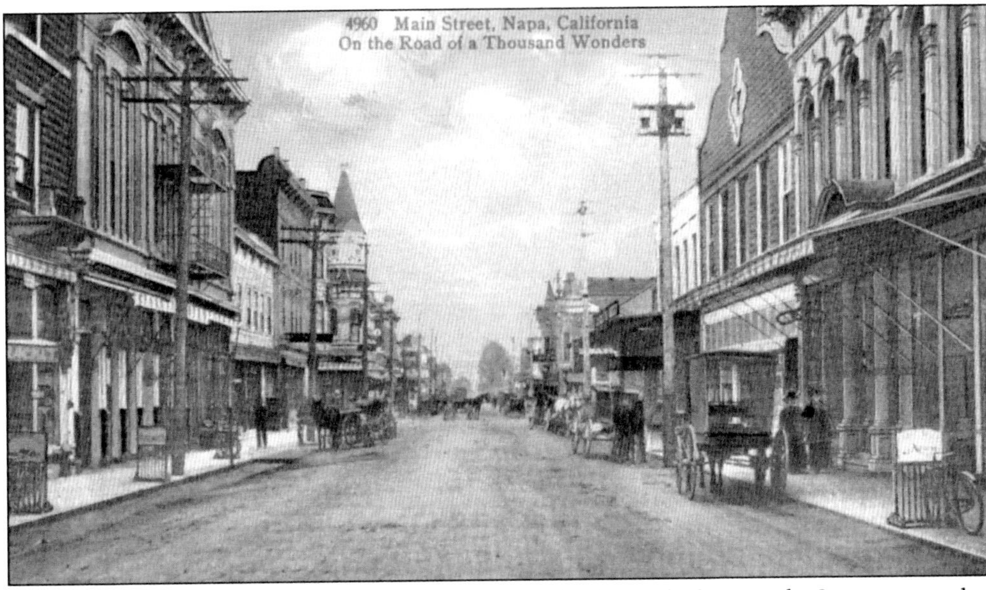

The Napa Opera House is visible on the left near the first telephone pole. It was opened as Crowey's Opera House in 1879 and was the center of entertainment in the young city, hosting light operas, band concerts, political rallies, and later vaudevillian acts. The Opera House stage was on the second floor; the first floor hosted three shops. The Opera House went dark in 1914 and was saved from the wrecking ball in the 1970s. It was restored and reopened as an entertainment venue in 2003. (Author's collection.)

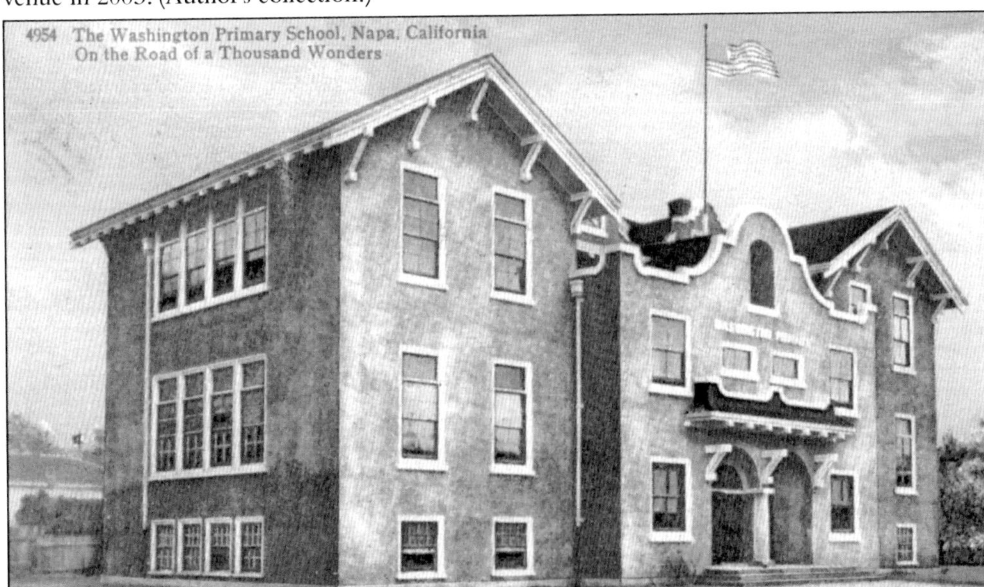

Pictured is the Washington School as it appeared around the beginning of the 20th century. It was located at the corner of Polk and Seminary Streets. Constructed in 1909 as an elementary school, the building was converted to county offices in the 1950s and ultimately abandoned in the early 1990s. Blue Oak School purchased the property in 2000 and renovated it, reopening it as a private school in 2002. (Author's collection.)

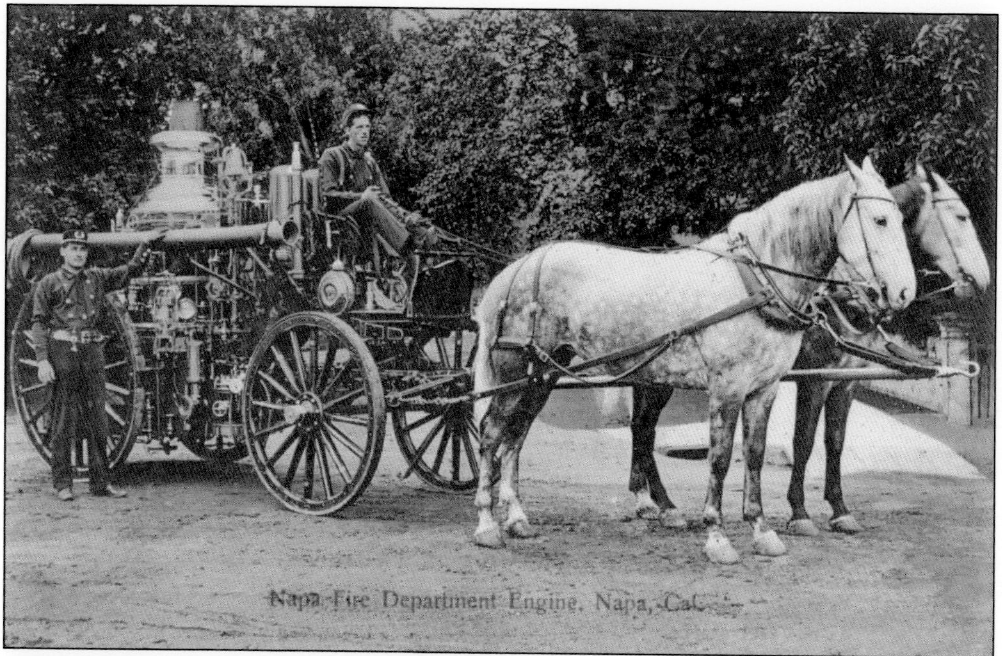

This postcard shows the Napa Fire Department's 1904 Nott Steamer, with driver Harry Bruton and engineer Jeff Smelser. The horses pictured were named Rock and Fly. This steamer is currently being restored by the Napa Firefighter's Museum. (Author's collection.)

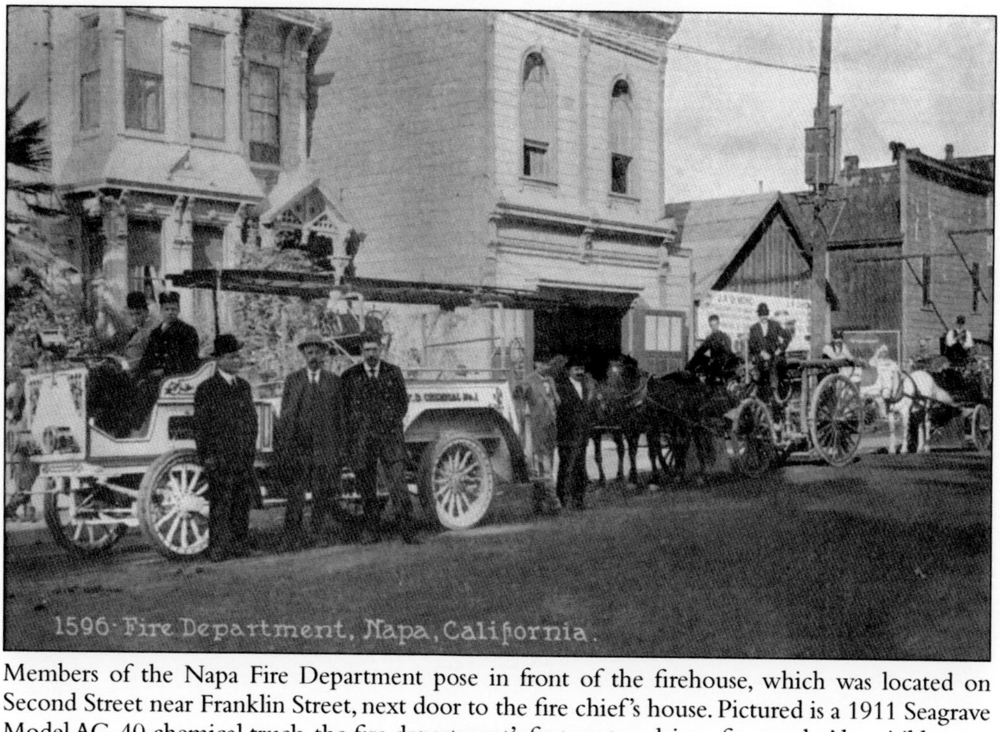

Members of the Napa Fire Department pose in front of the firehouse, which was located on Second Street near Franklin Street, next door to the fire chief's house. Pictured is a 1911 Seagrave Model AC-40 chemical truck, the fire department's first motor-driven fire truck. Also visible are a 1904 Nott Steamer and a hose wagon. (Author's collection.)

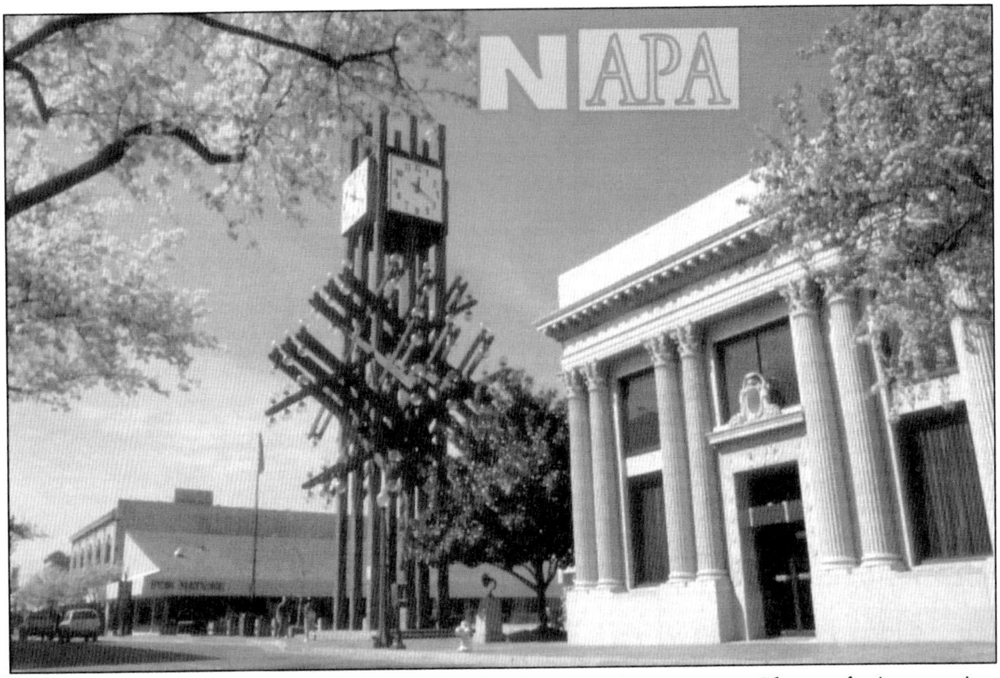

This postcard from the 1980s shows a view of several landmarks on Murray Plaza at the intersection of First and Brown Streets. The Gore Clock Tower was installed in the plaza in the 1970s; it was removed during a remodeling of the area in 2002. Visible under the tree next to the clock tower is a monument dedicated to Edwin Pridham and Peter Jensen, founders of Magnavox, who invented the loudspeaker in their F Street laboratory in 1915. (Courtesy of Mike Vanwormer.)

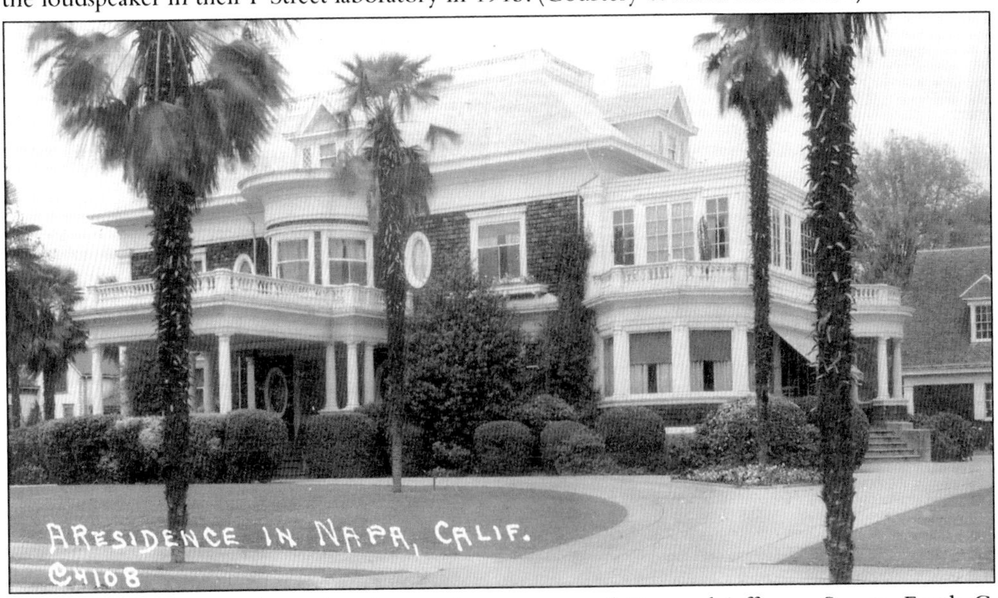

The Noyes Mansion is located at the northeast corner of First and Jefferson Streets. Frank G. Noyes, a lumberyard owner, built the residence and adjacent carriage house in 1903. Over the years, the residence was subdivided into offices and shops. The carriage house served as a restaurant and later a nightclub. In 2004, *Wine Spectator* magazine purchased the mansion and embarked on an extensive renovation and restoration of it. (Author's collection.)

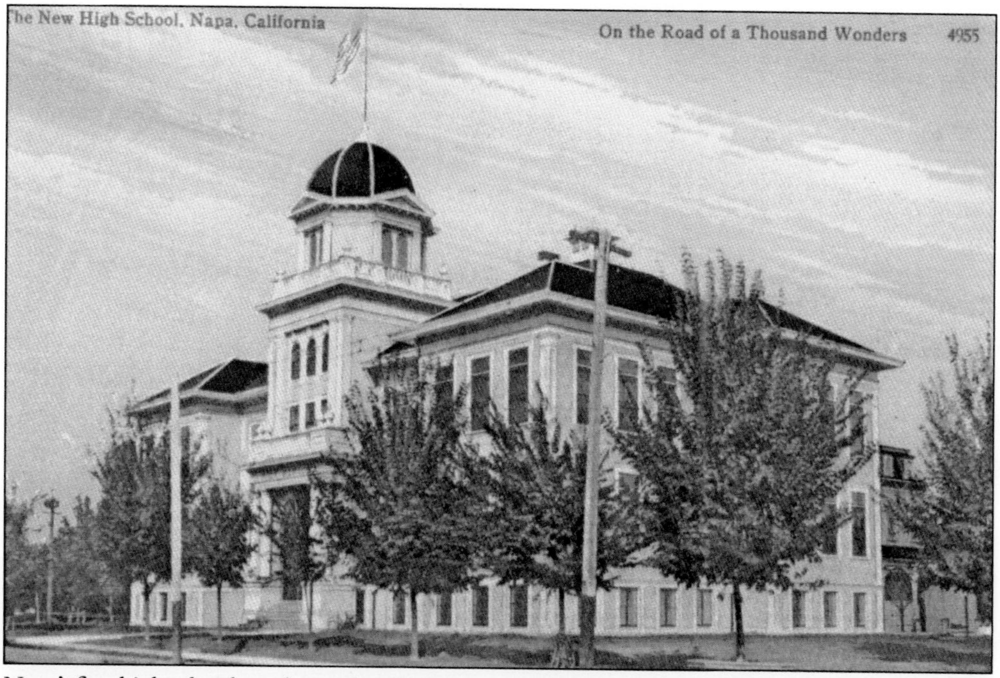

Napa's first high school was located on Polk Street and was founded in 1897. The building pictured here was constructed in 1909 on Jefferson Street, between Clay and Polk Streets. It served as the city's only high school until 1920, when a new building was constructed at Jefferson Street and Lincoln Avenue. The original building then became an intermediate school until the early 1950s, when it was torn down to make way for a shopping center. (Author's collection.)

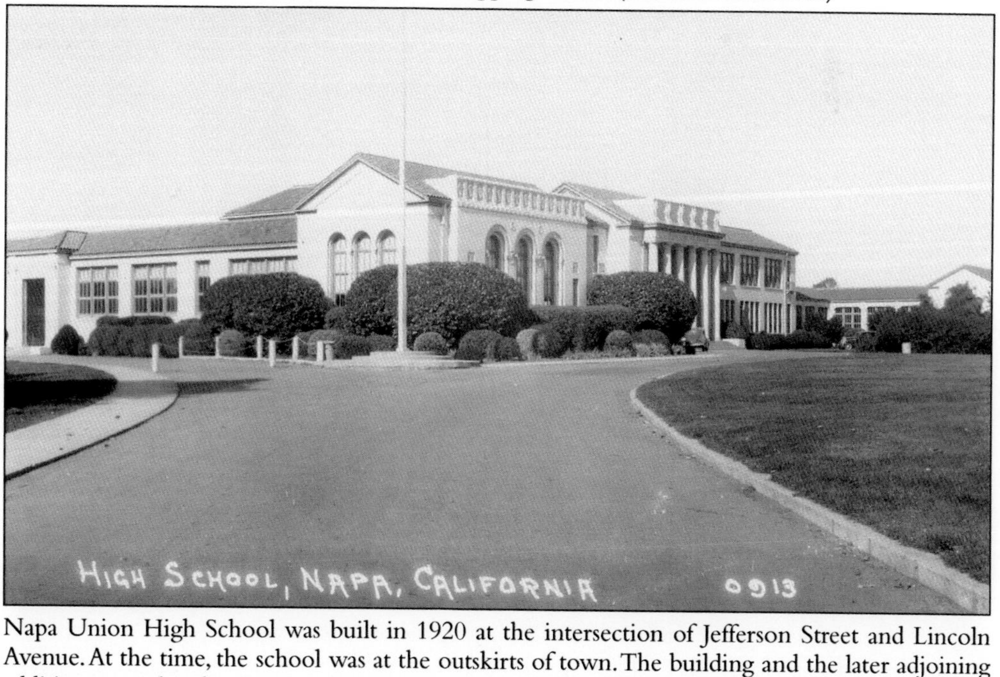

Napa Union High School was built in 1920 at the intersection of Jefferson Street and Lincoln Avenue. At the time, the school was at the outskirts of town. The building and the later adjoining additions served as the town's only high school until 1972, when Vintage High School was opened. Today the building houses the Napa Valley Unified School District offices. (Author's collection.)

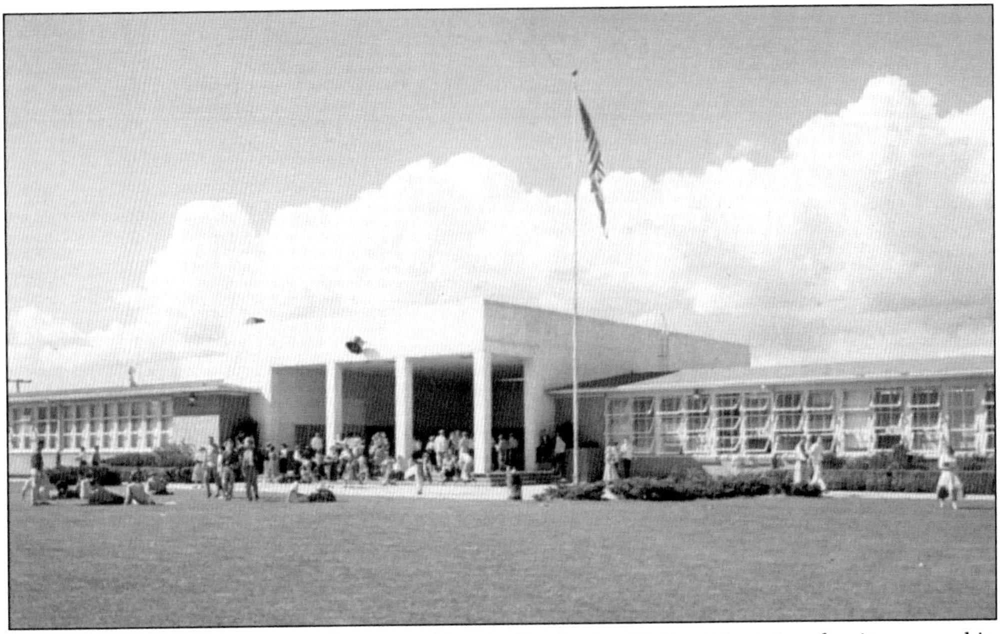

The Napa Junior College (now known as Napa Valley Junior College) is pictured as it appeared in the 1950s. At the time, it was located on Jefferson Street at the present site of Napa High School; the college was located there from 1944 to 1965. It is now located on Highway 221 just south of Imola Avenue. The college is known for its viticulture program and criminal justice training center. It also operated a satellite campus in St. Helena. (Author's collection.)

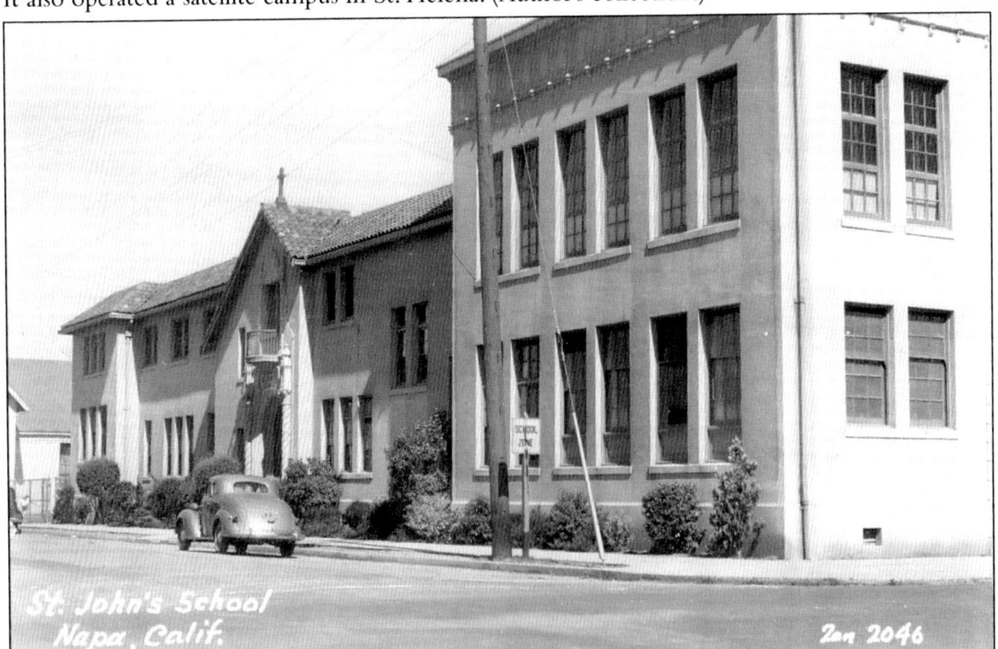

St. John's, the first catholic school in Napa County, opened in 1912. It was located in a building that was formerly the Napa Baths indoor pool complex. The Dominican Sisters of San Rafael ran the school. In 1926, the school moved to the location pictured, at the corner of Main and Napa Streets adjacent to St. John's Catholic Church. (Author's collection.)

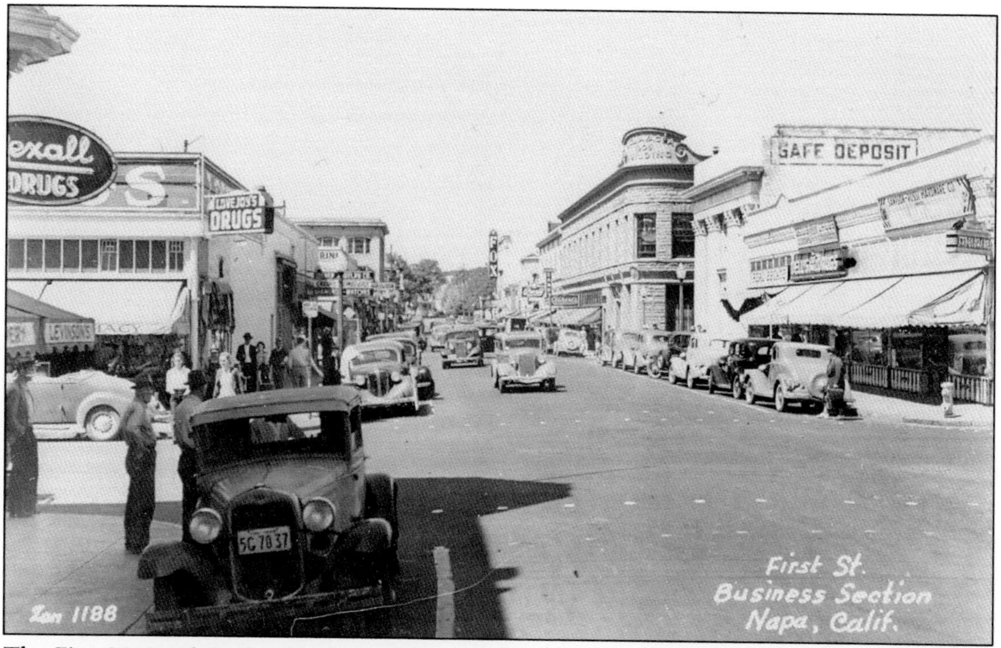

The First National Bank of Napa building is located on the right side of the street, marked on its side "Safe Deposit." It was constructed in 1917, and it later housed Bank of America and then the Napa Federal Savings and Loan. In 1993, the building became the home of Napa County Landmarks, a historic preservation group. The structure currently houses the Ristorante Allegria, at which patrons can dine inside the old bank vault. (Author's collection.)

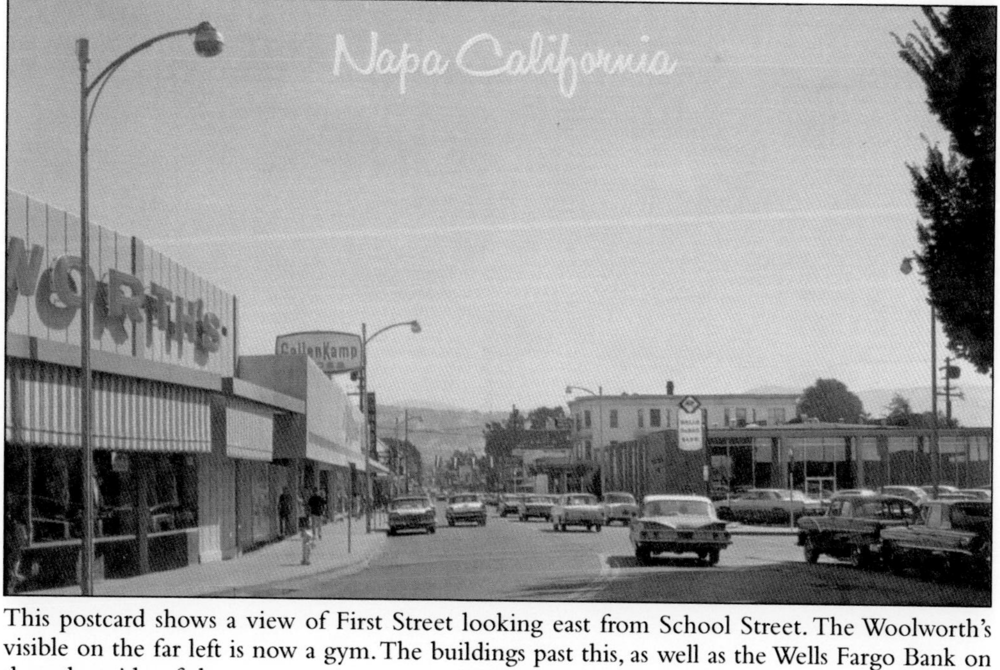

This postcard shows a view of First Street looking east from School Street. The Woolworth's visible on the far left is now a gym. The buildings past this, as well as the Wells Fargo Bank on the other side of the street, are now gone. Wells Fargo is being replaced by the Napa Square office building, and the other side of the street will be the home for the new boutique hotel, the Avia. (Author's collection.)

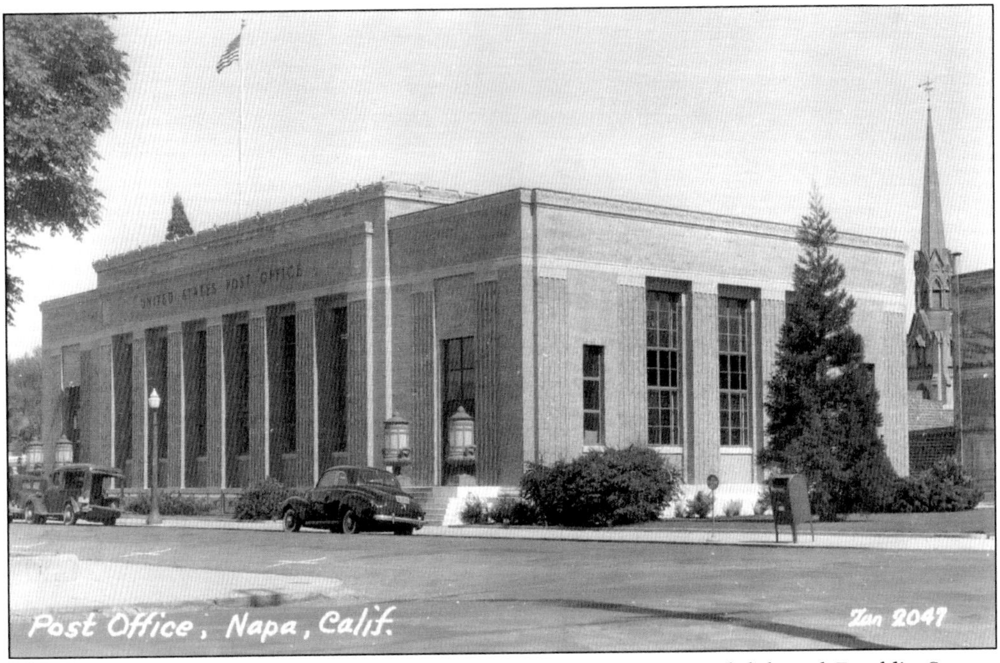

The downtown post office is located on Second Street between Randolph and Franklin Streets. The building was constructed in 1933, one of the projects undertaken during President Roosevelt's Depression-era New Deal building campaign. Although remodeled in 1965 to make it wheelchair accessible, it remains relatively unchanged since it was built. Visible in the background at the right is the steeple of the historic Presbyterian church building. (Author's collection.)

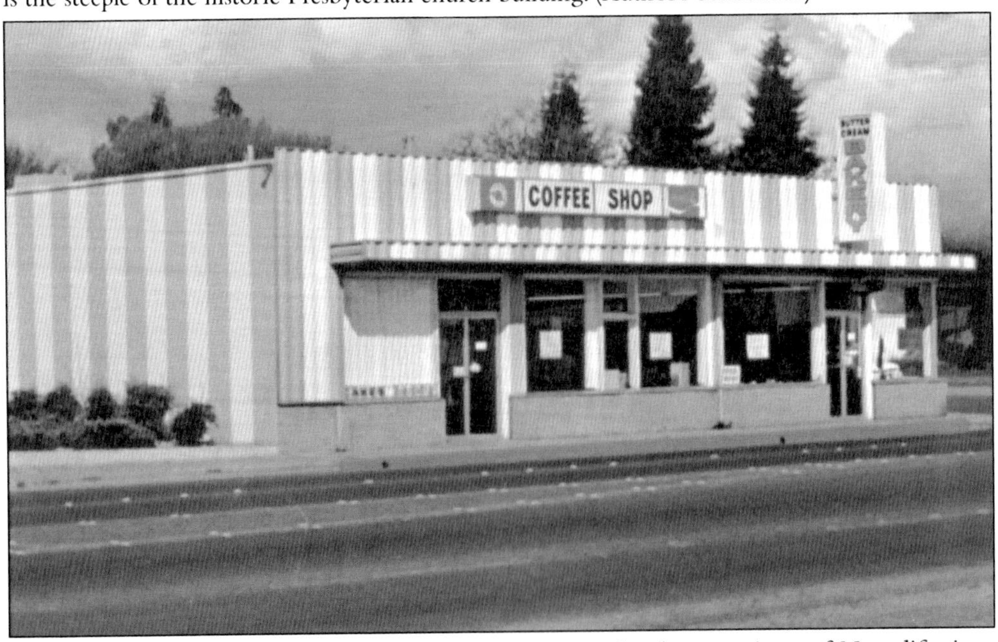

The Buttercream Bakery, located at 2297 Jefferson Street, has been an icon of Napa life since David and Bobbi Closs opened it in 1948. The bakery features a bevy of baked goods as well as a full-service diner. Buttercream was restored in 2001 and is now run by the Closs's son, Gerry. (Author's collection.)

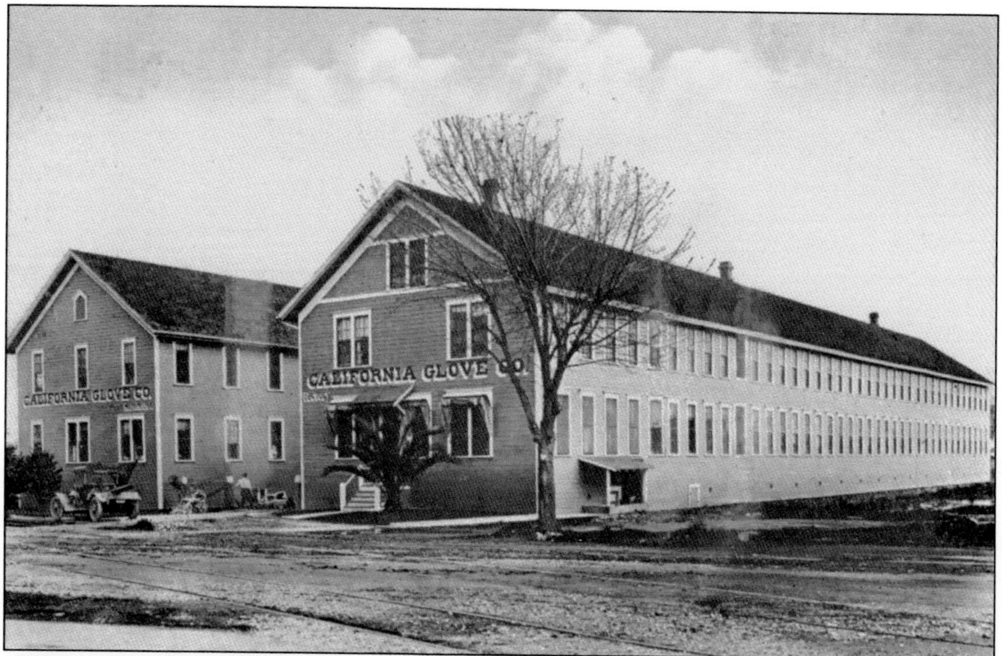

Shown here is the Napa Glove Company *c.* 1920. The company was founded in 1903 by R. Raymond and former workers of the California Glove Company. It was located on Soscol Avenue south of town. This was one of the many factories that lined the Napa River; in the days before environmental protection laws, these factories dumped the byproducts of their production directly into the river. (Author's collection.)

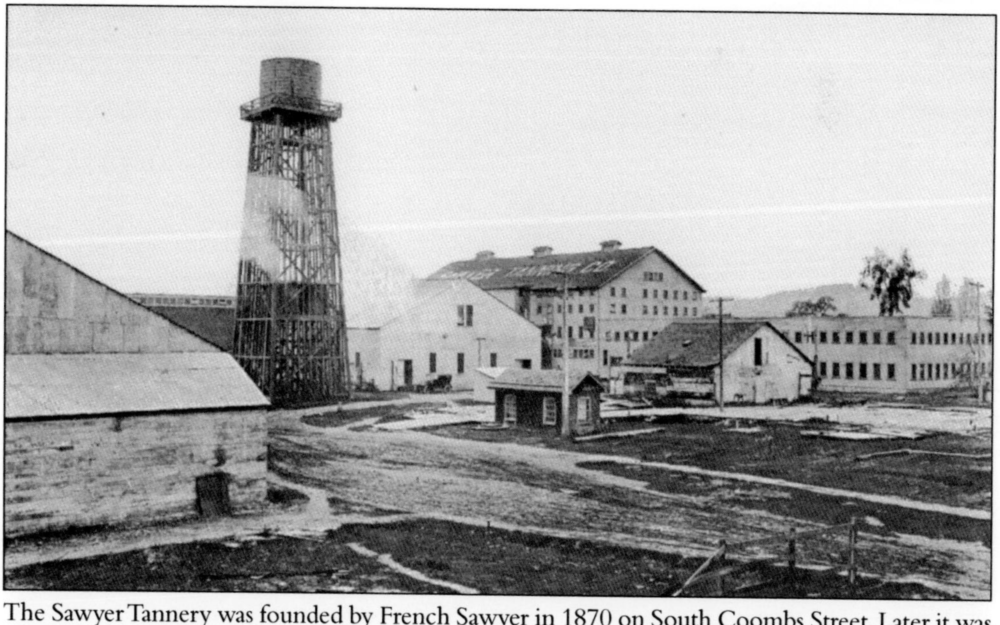

The Sawyer Tannery was founded by French Sawyer in 1870 on South Coombs Street. Later it was run and co-owned by Emmanuel Manasse. The tannery produced patent leather garments, wool-lined coats, and gloves. Development of Napa leather by the tannery resulted in an alternative definition for Napa being created in the dictionary. The tannery survived economic upturns and downturns and the Depression; it finally closed in 1990. (Courtesy of Stan France.)

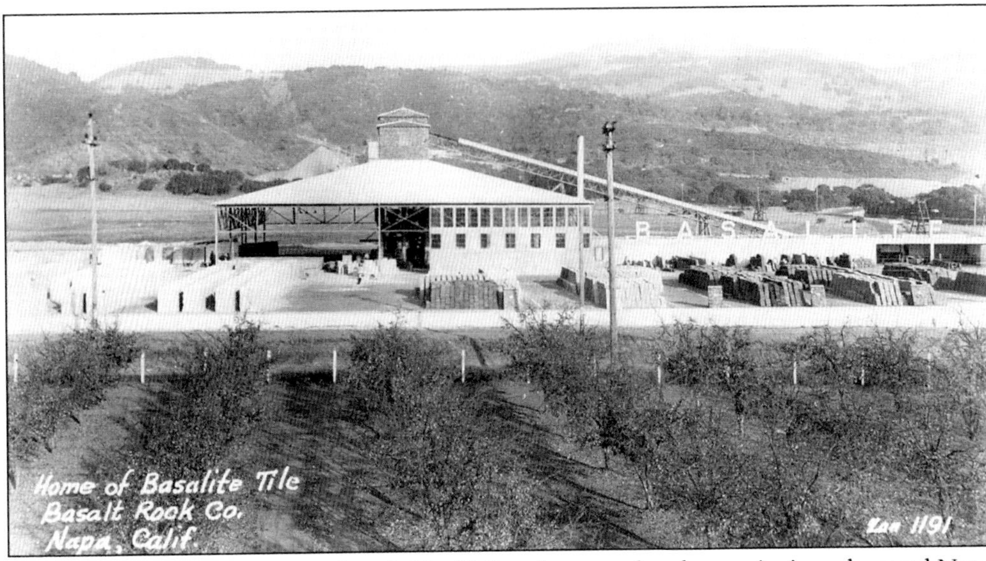

The Basalt Rock Company was founded in 1920 and operated rock quarries in and around Napa. In 1938, the company branched out by building its own barges to transport rock down the Napa River. Basalt joined the war effort during World War II, constructing a full shipbuilding works, including a dry dock. They produced barges, tankers, and salvage-rescue tugs. The shipyard later became the Napa Pipe Company. Basalt's other major facilities on Highway 221 are now home to Syar Industries. (Author's collection.)

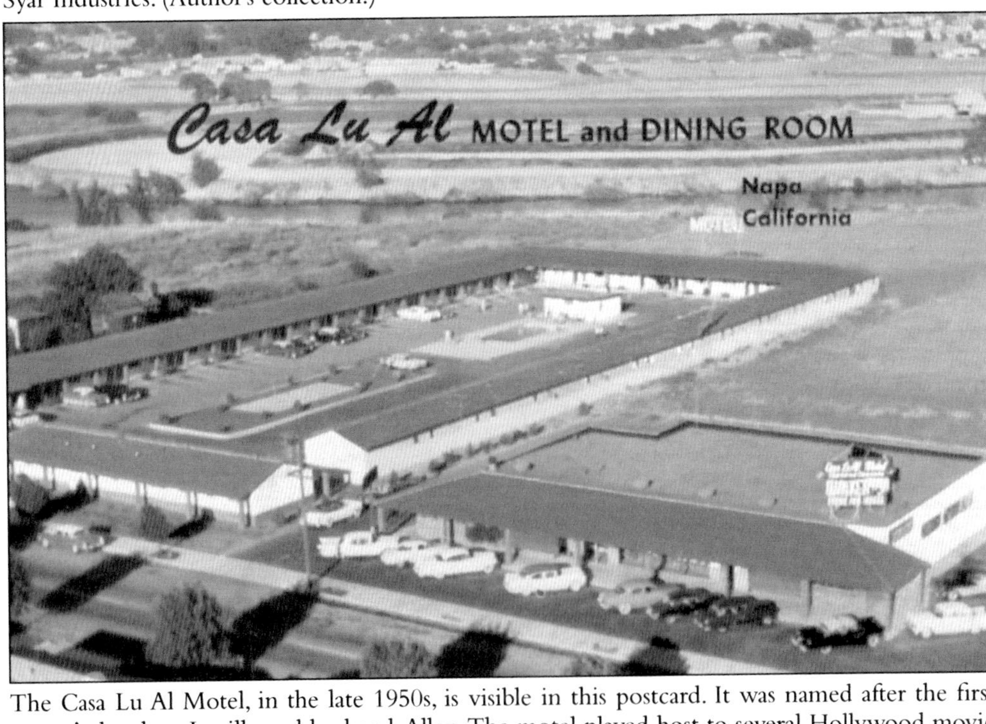

The Casa Lu Al Motel, in the late 1950s, is visible in this postcard. It was named after the first owner's daughter Lucille and husband, Allen. The motel played host to several Hollywood movie crews. In 1959, *This Earth is Mine* was filmed, starring Rock Hudson. Two years later, Elvis Presley arrived in Napa to film *Wild in the Country*. The motel has been extensively renovated and is now known as the Wine Valley Lodge. (Author's collection.)

The First Presbyterian Church began in 1853, first meeting in the courthouse and then in a building located on property donated by Nathan Coombs. The cornerstone of the original structure was relayed as the cornerstone of this building on August 20, 1874. Architects R. H. Daley and Theodore Eisen created the Victorian Gothic–style building. The church was designated a historical landmark by the State of California in 1975. (Author's collection.)

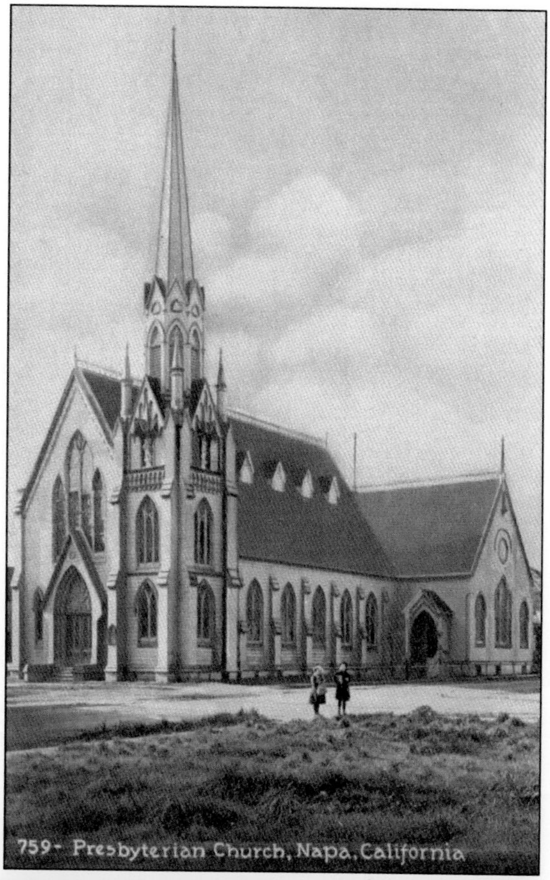

The interior of the First Presbyterian Church clearly shows the pipe organ that has been a fixture of the sanctuary since 1875. The organ was brought from San Francisco on a ferry up the Napa River. (Author's collection.)

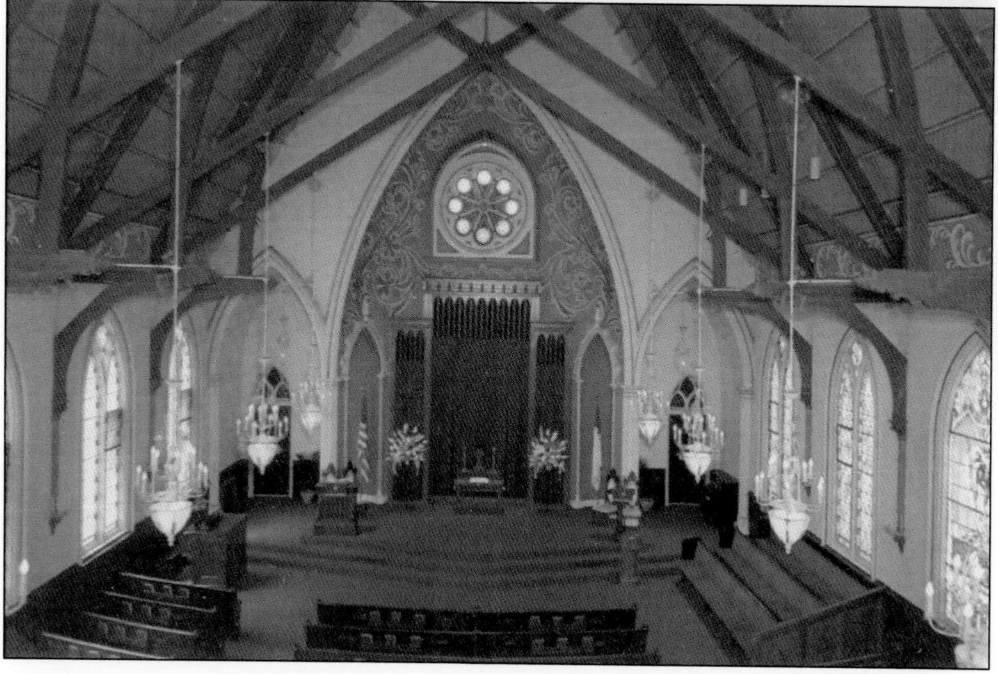

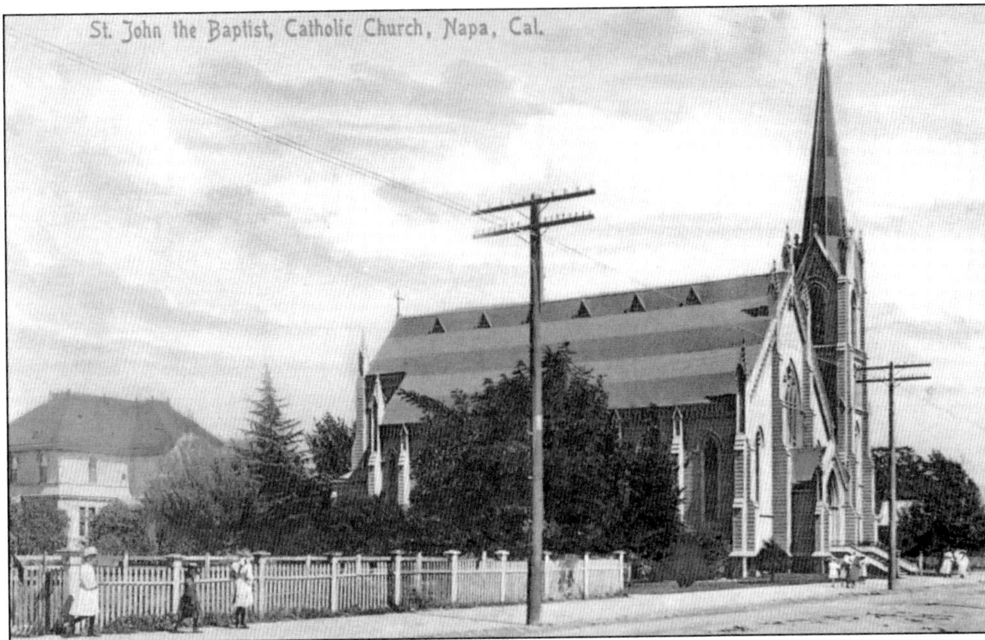

St. John the Baptist Catholic Church was first built in 1858. Prior to that time, services were held in various members' homes. Until 1865, one priest was assigned to cover Lake, Napa, Sonoma, and Solano Counties; mass was performed on alternating Sundays. The church building pictured in this postcard was constructed in 1881. It was demolished in 1965 to make way for the current building. (Author's collection.)

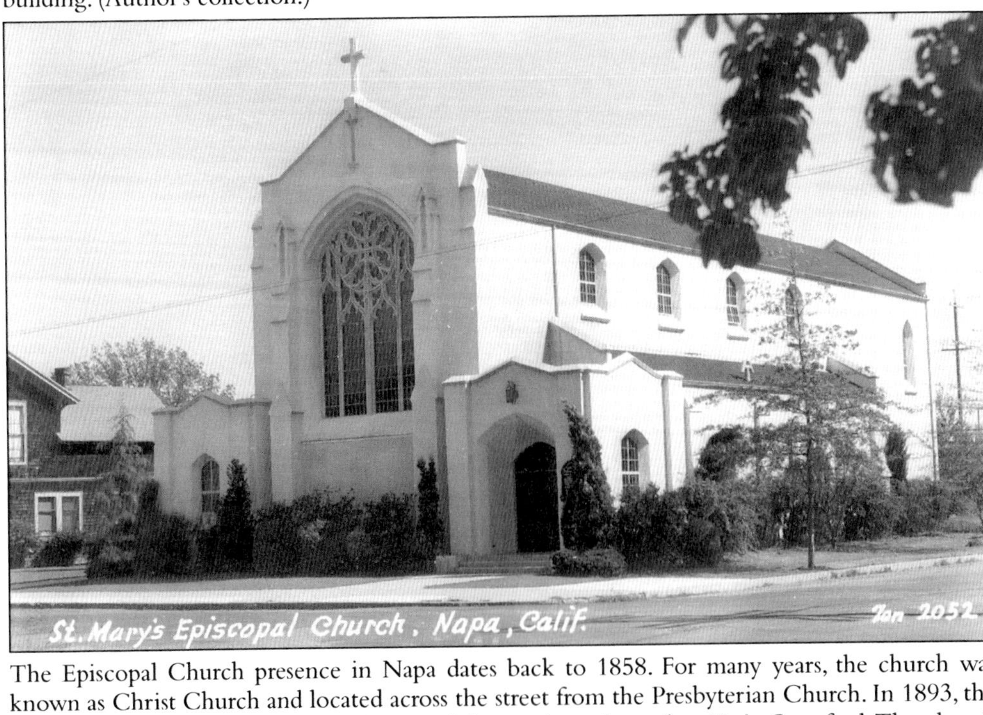

The Episcopal Church presence in Napa dates back to 1858. For many years, the church was known as Christ Church and located across the street from the Presbyterian Church. In 1893, the church was renamed St. Mary's in honor of the mother of member H. A. Crawford. The church building pictured above was constructed in 1932 at 1917 Third Street. (Author's collection.)

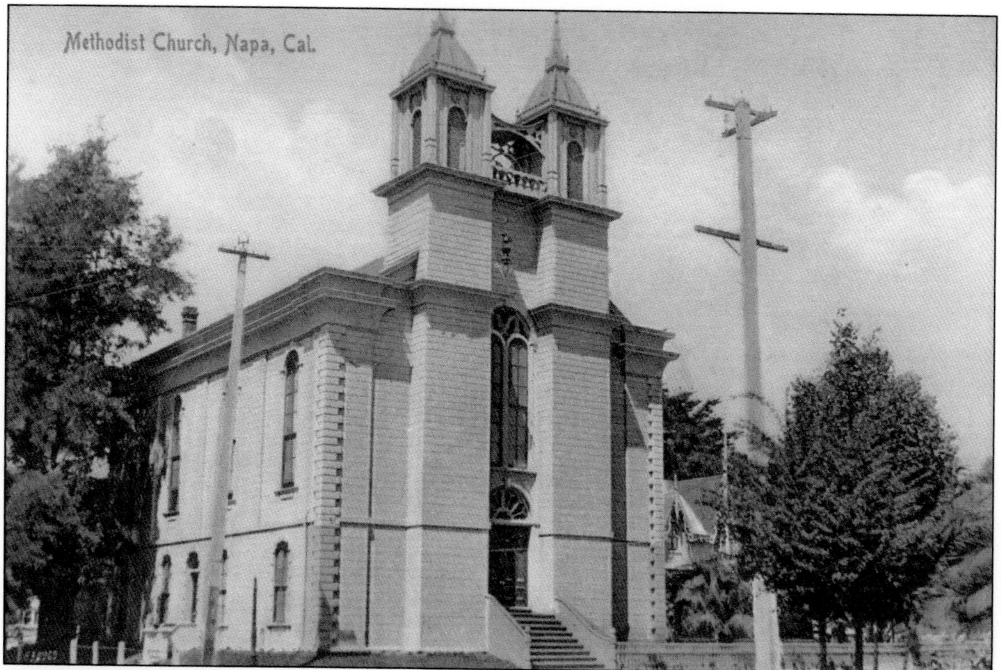

The first building for the Methodist Church was a wooden church constructed in 1856 at the corner of Fifth and Randolph Streets. The building pictured here replaced the original church in 1876, when fire destroyed its predecessor. The new church building would serve the congregation until it was demolished in 1916 to make way for the current structure. (Author's collection.)

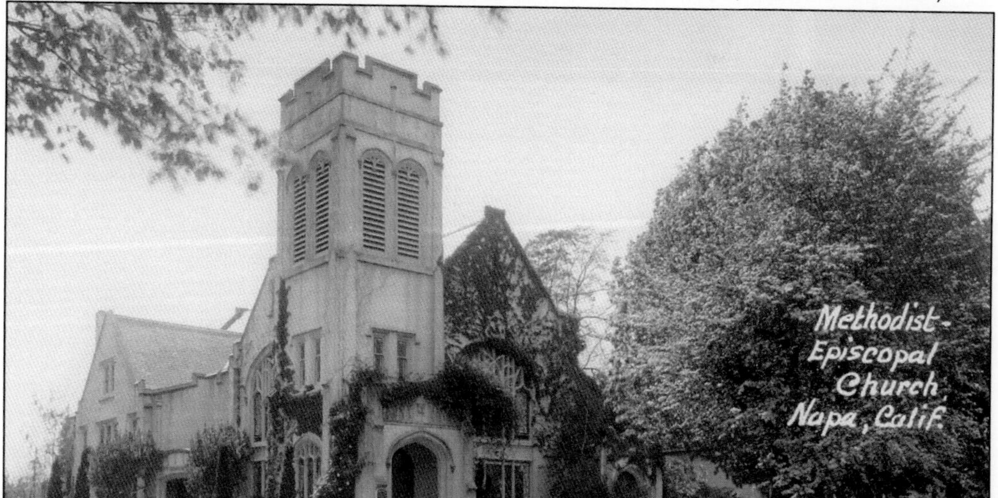

The Methodist Church is located at 625 Randolph Street. Built in 1917, the church is noted on this postcard as the Methodist Episcopal Church; the name was later changed to simply Methodist Church. A social hall was added in 1952, which now serves as the Hope Center, a daytime drop-in center for the homeless of Napa. (Author's collection.)

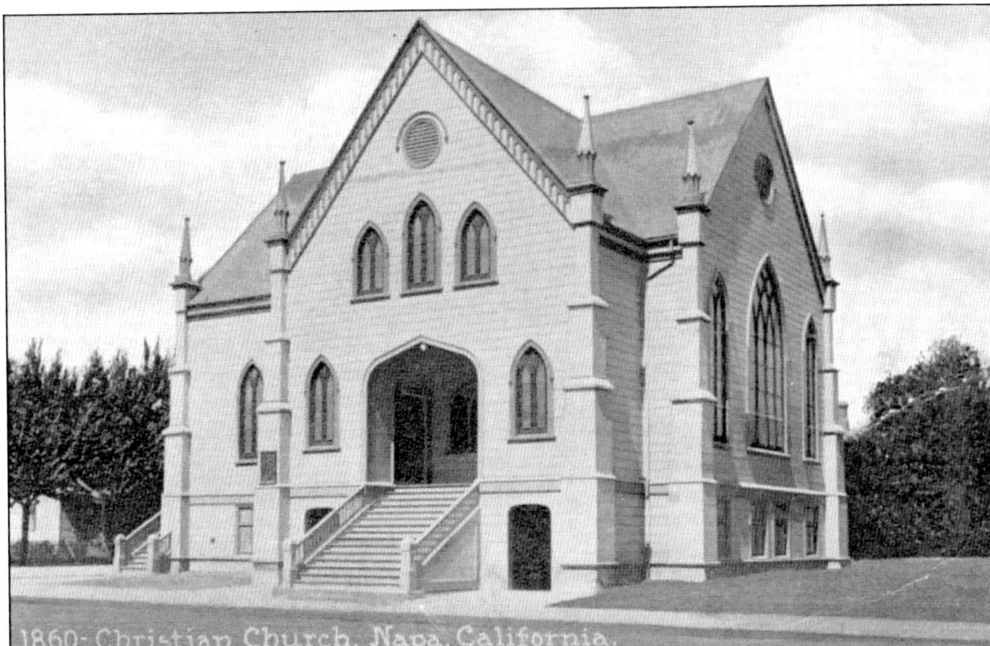

The Christian Church was located at the corner of Pearl and Randolph Streets. The church roots in Napa County date back to the early 1850s, with congregations in the towns of Yountville, St. Helena, and the Berryessa and Monticello area. The Napa congregation was originally located in the Browns Valley area, but it moved into town in 1870. The site is now the home of the local American Legion Post building. (Courtesy of Stan France.)

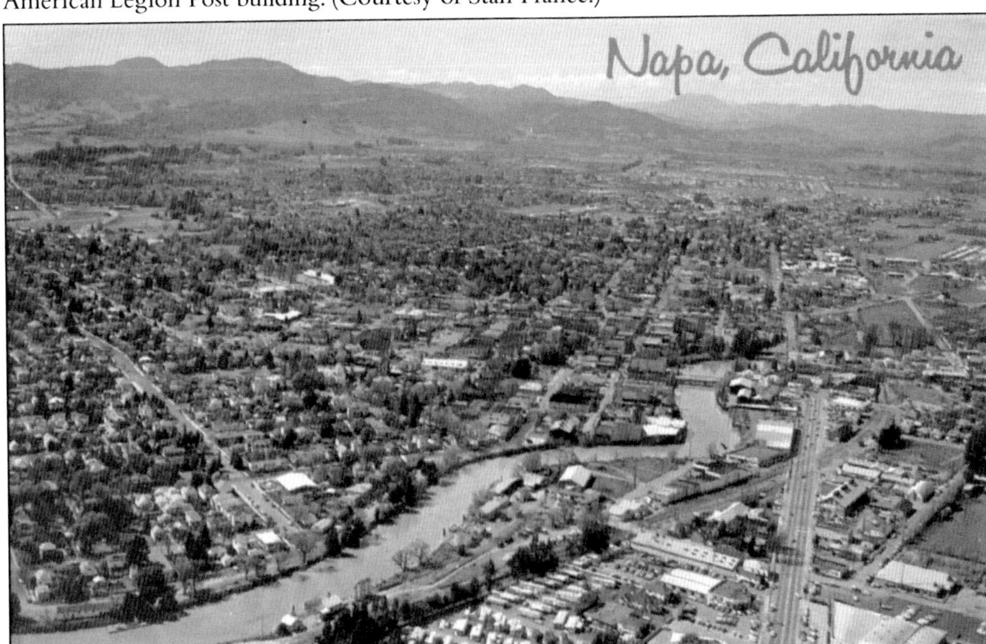

This aerial view of downtown Napa shows the route of Soscol Avenue running diagonally at the lower right in the foreground. At the time, Soscol Avenue stopped at Third Street, as pictured above. Today it continues north, ending at the intersection with Trancas Street. (Author's collection.)

Five

Yountville

The town of Yountville began its life when, in 1836, Napa County pioneer George C. Yount received a land grant of 12,000 acres from Mariano Vallejo in exchange for producing wood shingles for Vallejo's Sonoma home. The Caymus land grant encompassed the area of present day Yountville, Oakville, and Rutherford.

George Yount, who was known as "Captain Buckskin" due to the rugged clothing he preferred, originally named the settlement he founded in 1855 Sebastopol; however it was renamed in his honor after his death in 1865.

Yountville consisted of a train station, a small business district, and a population of about 150 in 1884, the year the Veteran's Home of California was constructed. It grew rapidly as support workers for the veteran's home moved into the area.

Yountville has become more than a company town for the veteran's home. It now boasts a vibrant downtown, which includes the shopping destination of the V1870 complex. It also has several resort hotels and noted restaurants, including Thomas Kellar's French Laundry, widely regarded as one of the best restaurants in the world. Today Yountville boasts a population of nearly 3,000 people.

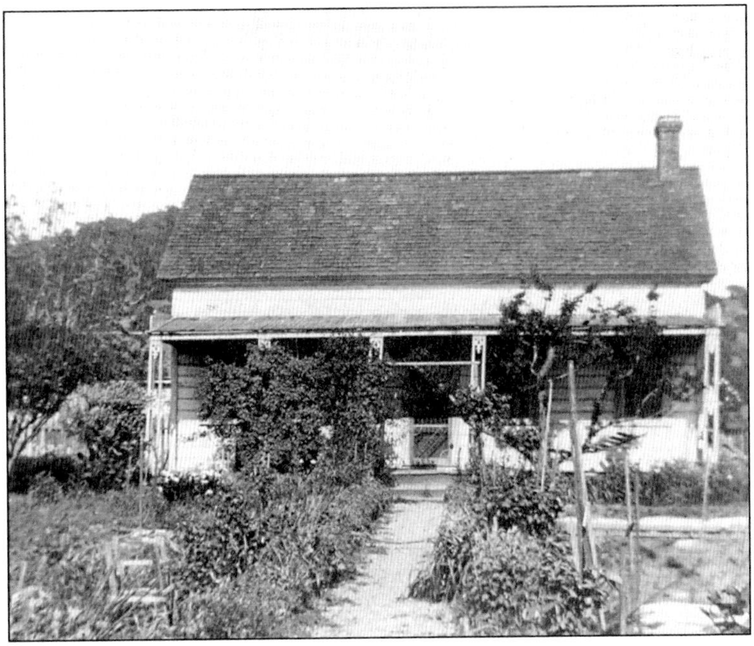

A typical farmhouse of the early 20th century is pictured here in this 1909 postcard from Lila Kohler. At the time, Lila and her husband, Fredrick, farmed a plot of land in rural Yountville. (Author's collection.)

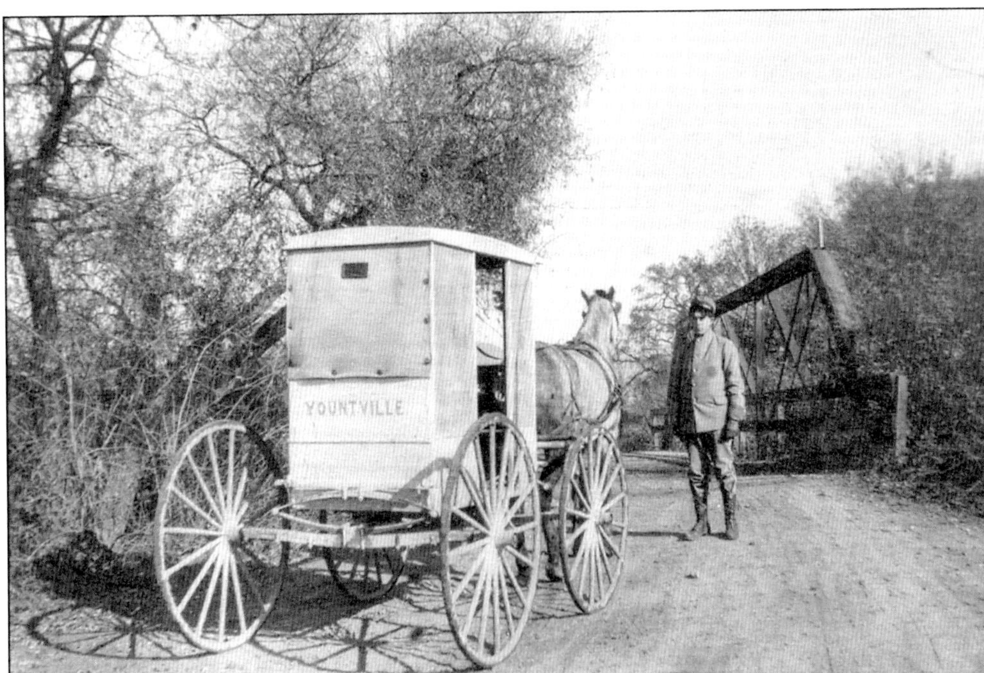

Postman chancellor W. Johnson poses by his mail wagon *c.* 1906. Johnson was part of the postal service's rural free delivery, which began during the early 1900s. Johnson would serve the citizens in and around Yountville for almost 40 years. He started with the horse-drawn wagon shown, and he then transitioned to a motorcycle and finally an automobile. (Courtesy of Stan France.)

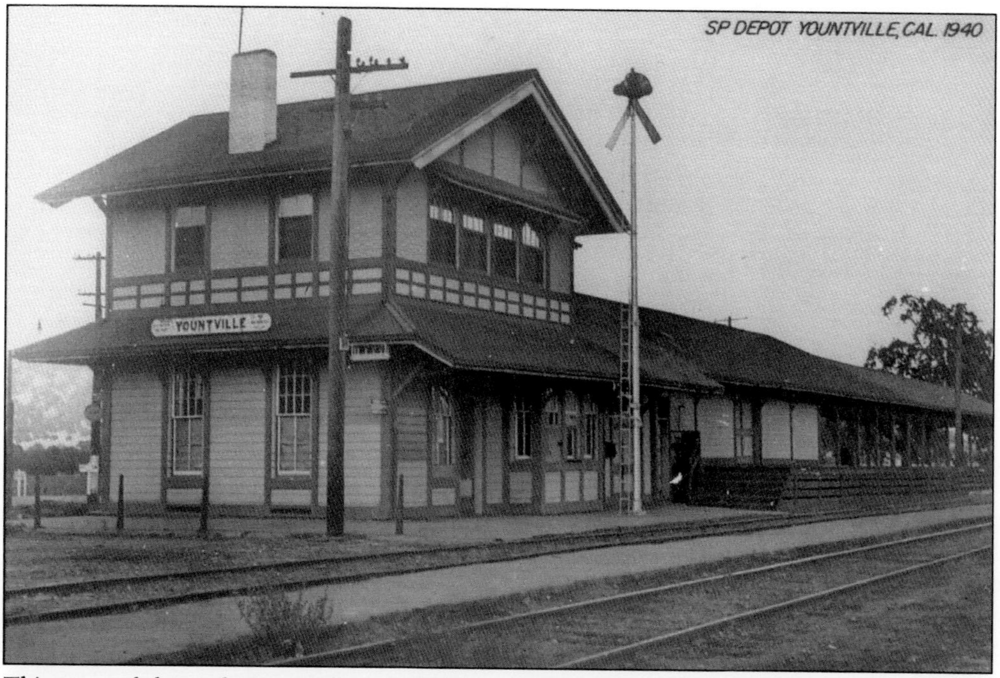

This postcard shows the Yountville train station as it appeared in 1940. By this time, the Southern Pacific had already abandoned its passenger service to Napa County. The station was constructed in 1868 as part of the building boom, which resulted in the extension of rail service to Sam Brannan's Hot Springs Resort in present-day Calistoga. (Courtesy of Mike Vanwormer.)

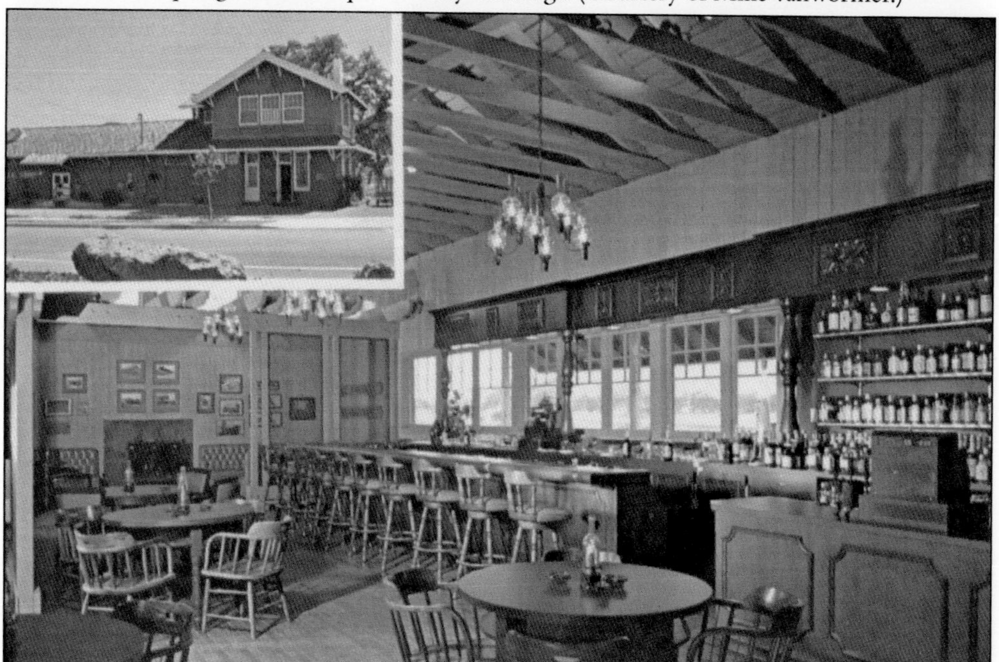

The Whistle Stop Tavern advertised in this 1970s-era postcard was in Yountville's former train station. The building, located at 6505 Washington Street, now houses the Overland Sheepskin Factory. (Author's collection.)

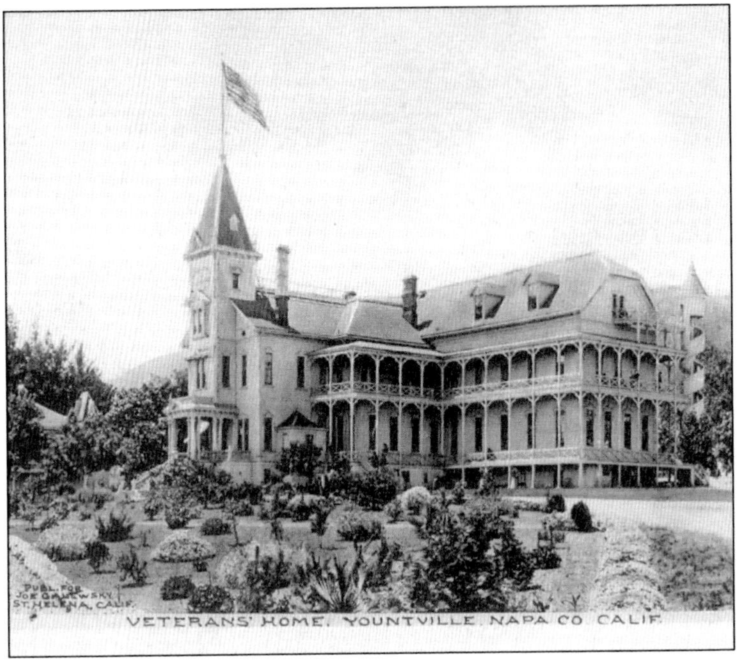

The Veterans Home of California at Yountville was founded in 1884. It was originally run by the Grand Army of the Republic, which bought 910 acres of land in Yountville for $17,500. Initial structures included a central building and five-room wooden cottages surrounding it. There were 42 veteran residents when it first opened. The state took over operation of the home in 1897. (Courtesy of Mike Vanwormer.)

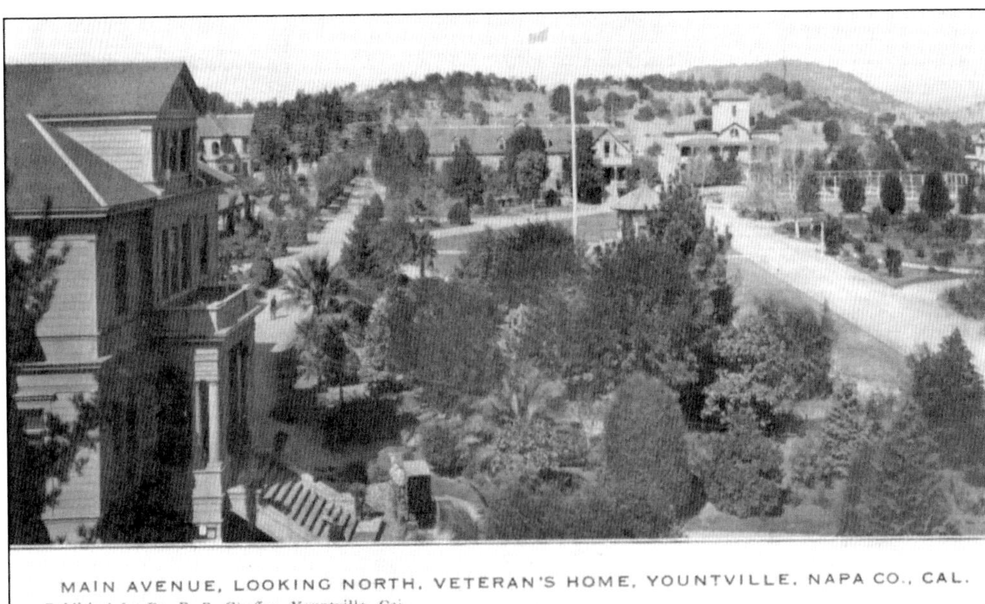

This postcard shows what was called the Main Avenue of the veteran's home in 1914. Visible at the center is a parade ground and outdoor pavilion. The bucolic setting of the veteran's home has attracted veterans since it first opened its doors. Today there are three veteran's homes in California, with five more planned. (Author's collection.)

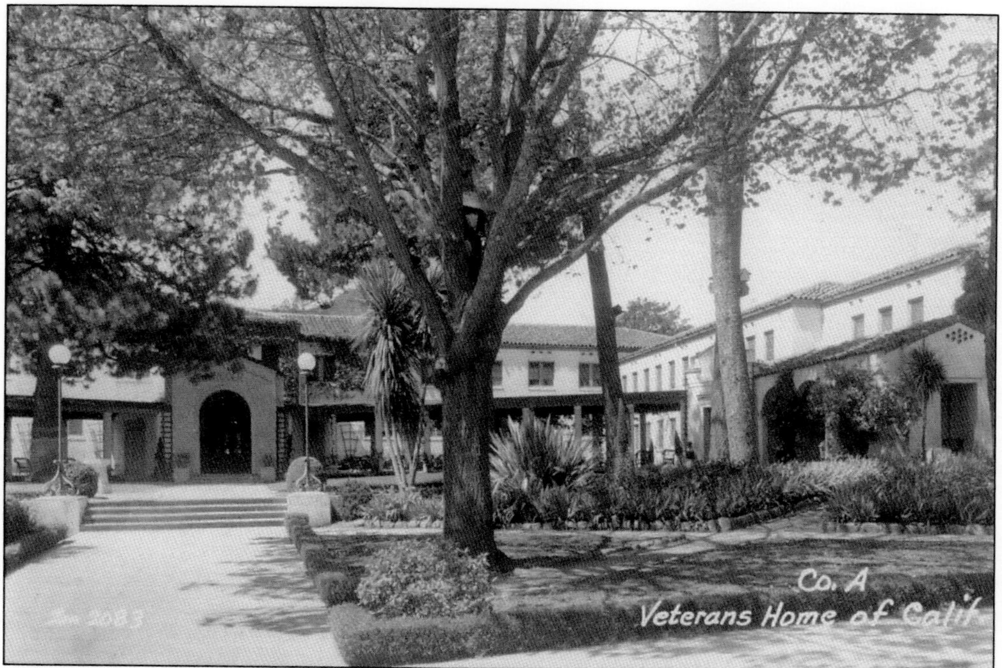

This 1950s-era postcard features one of the residence buildings on the grounds of the veteran's home. Each building was given a designated letter similar to a military unit, as in Company A. Today the buildings are known as sections. (Author's collection.)

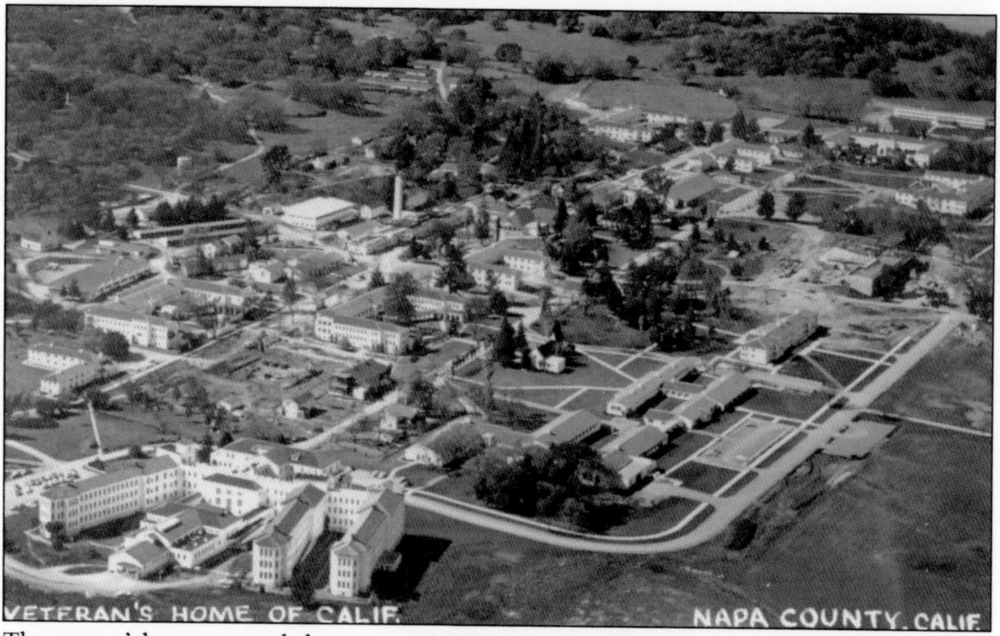

The veteran's home currently houses over 1,100 veterans and has many features, including a 1,200-seat theater, a 9-hole golf course, 35,000-volume library, a creative arts center, swimming pool and fitness center, resident-operated television station, baseball stadium, RV park, bowling lanes, auto hobby shop, a base exchange store, chapel, and coffee shop. It is currently the largest veteran's home in the United States. (Courtesy of the Napa County Historical Society.)

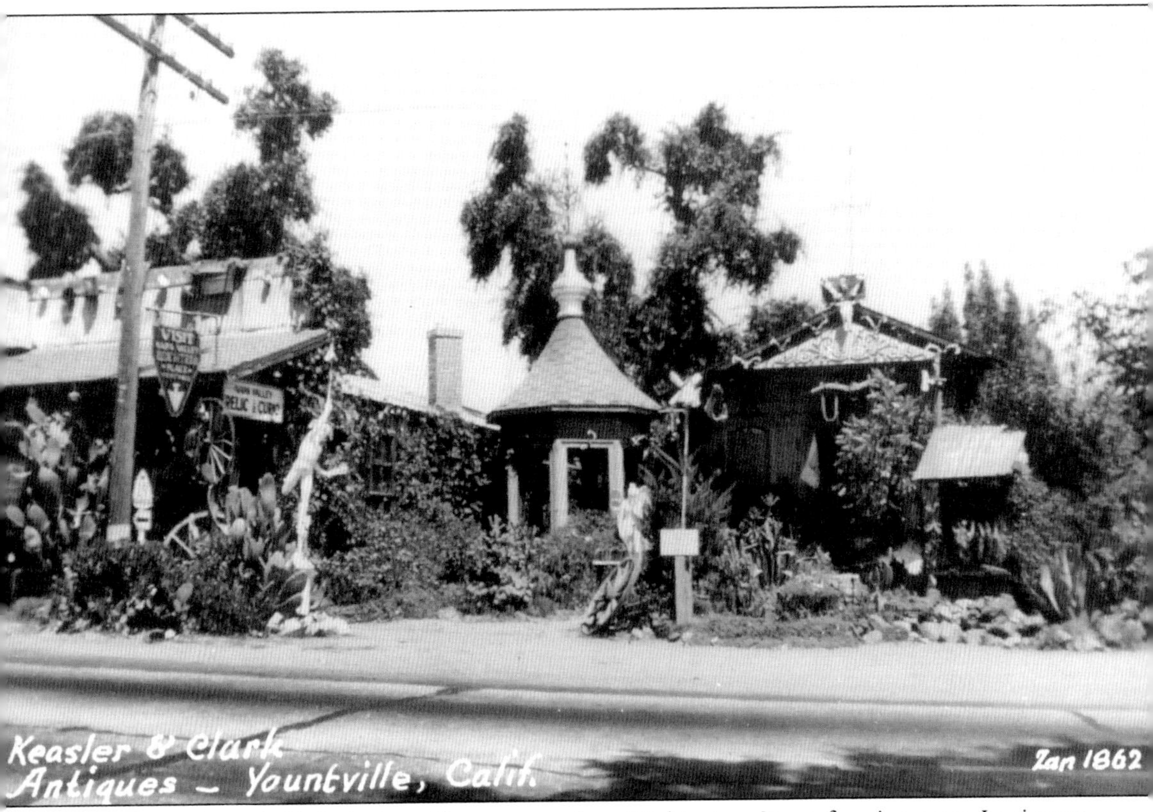

The Keasler and Clark Antique Shop operated on Washington Street for nine years. Its signage indicates that it was home to Napa Valley "relics and curios." The gazebo visible in this postcard was later moved to its present location in front of the V1870 Marketplace. (Courtesy of the Napa County Historical Society.)

Six

St. Helena

The town of St. Helena is located within the Carne Humana Rancho, the land grant given to Dr. Edward Bale. In 1853, businessman J. Henry Still bought 126 acres from Bale for a little over $1,000. He immediately went to work by building a general store at the site of his planned town. In an effort to promote his dream of a new town, Still offered free lots to anyone who would open a business.

Still and fellow businessman William Taylor named the city, probably in honor of the nearby Mount St. Helena. The city incorporated in 1876 and reincorporated in 1889. Wine pioneers such as Dr. Crane, Charles Krug, and the Beringer brothers chose to plant their vineyards outside of St. Helena. Ever since that time, the wine industry has been an important part of St. Helena's economy and way of life. The city was also a stopover location for those seeking the benefits of resorts such as White's Sulphur Springs and the nearby St. Helena Sanitarium.

Today St. Helena's vibrant Main Street (the portion of Highway 29 that runs north-south through the town) is home to an eclectic mixture of restaurants, boutiques, and art galleries. At the north end of town sits the Culinary Institute of America's west coast campus, located within the historic Greystone Winery. St. Helena's population today stands at 6,000 people.

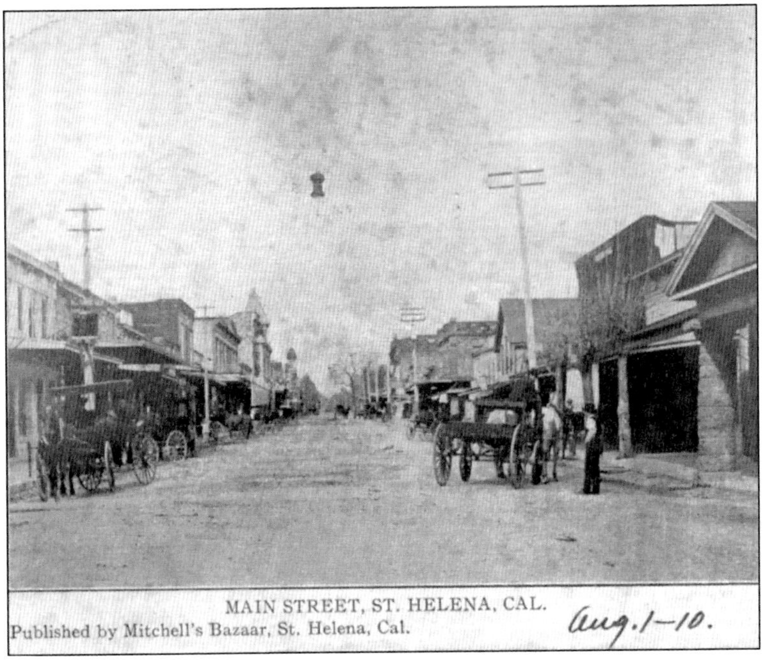

This 1910 postcard shows downtown St. Helena looking north from Spring Street. The Ritchie Block Building, with its distinctive curved roofline and cupola, is clearly visible midway on the left side of the street. One structure to the left of the Ritchie Building was the Windsor Hotel. (Courtesy of the Napa County Historical Society.)

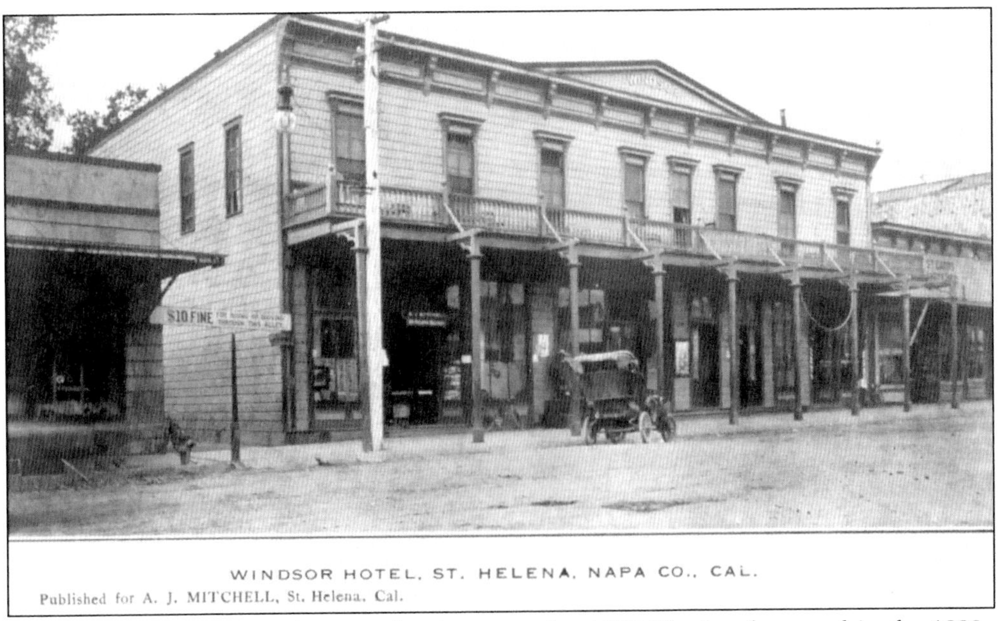

The image shows the Windsor Hotel as it appeared *c.* 1908. The hotel, opened in the 1880s, was the brainchild of Swen Alstrom, a former manager of the nearby White's Sulphur Springs Resort. Note the early automobile, most likely a Ford Model T, parked in front of the hotel. The hotel was located just south of the Ritchie Block Building. (Courtesy of the Napa County Historical Society.)

The Richie Block Building was constructed in 1892. Although it has had many stores fill its first floor since 1893, the majority of the second floor has been home to the local lodge of the Masons. This postcard of the building, located at 1331 Main Street, shows first floor tenant St. Helena Home Furnishings. (Author's collection.)

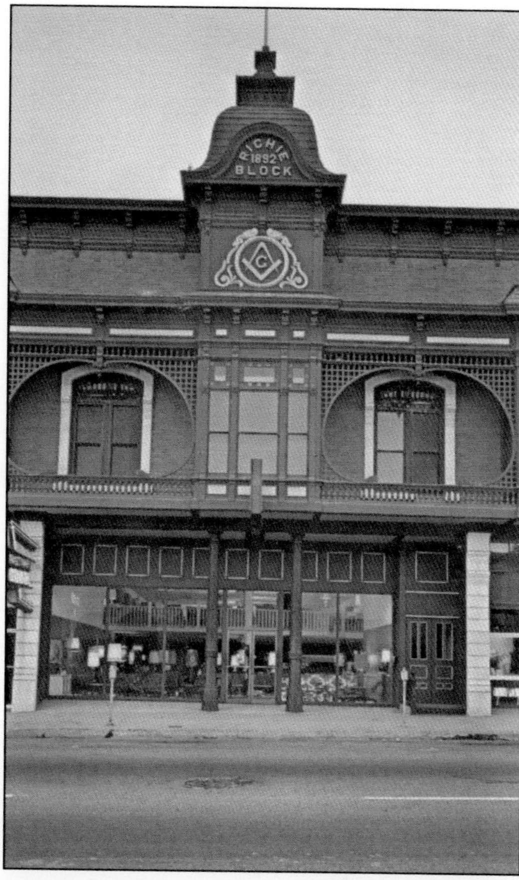

This postcard shows Main Street looking north from Spring Street. Visible down the center of the street are the electric railway tracks, although the lack of overhead lines shows that the postcard is from after the railway stopped operation, in 1938. The town's distinctive streetlights are also visible. The lights were purchased in 1915 from an auction of surplus items after the end of the Pan-American Exposition in San Francisco. (Courtesy of Stan France.)

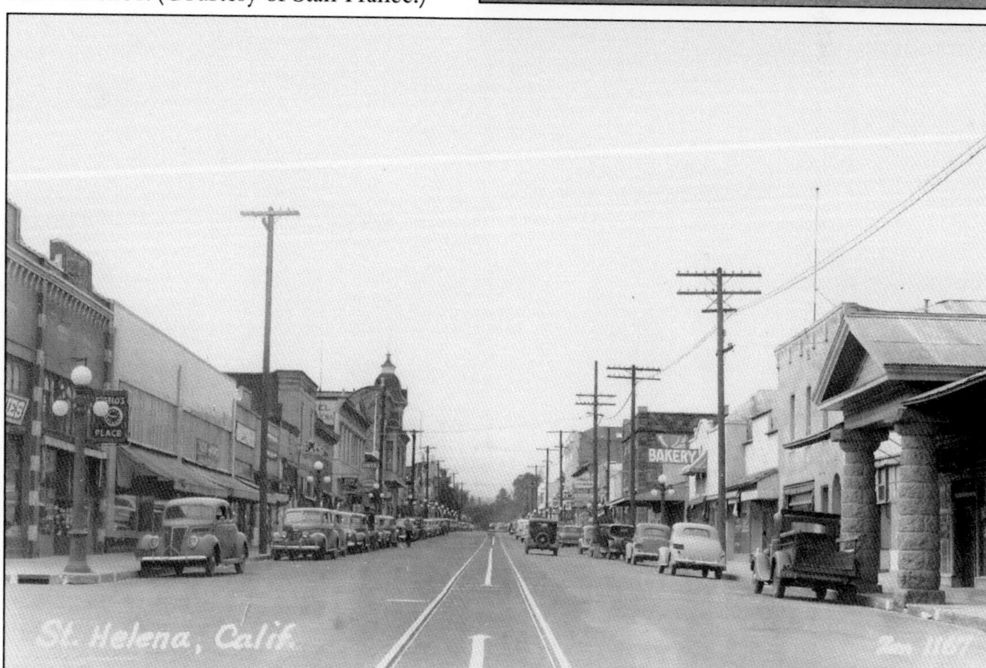

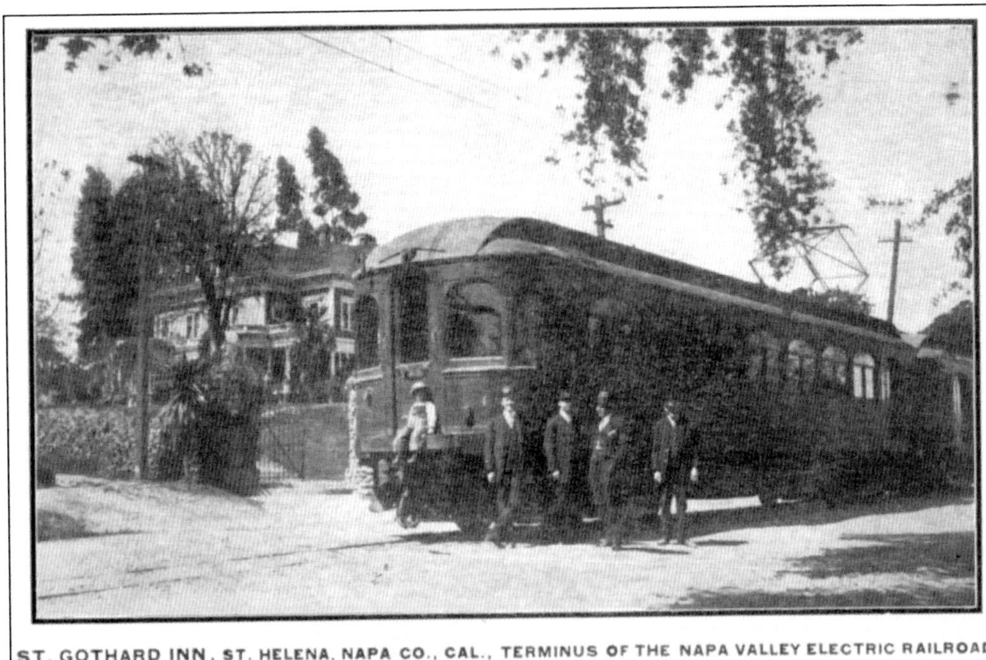

This postcard is of the St. Gothard Inn and Tavern, which was located at 1915 Main Street at the north end of town, just south of the Beringer Winery. The postcard dates to before 1912, when the electric railroad's most northerly stop was at St. Helena. After that time, the electric railroad extended to downtown Calistoga. (Courtesy of the Napa County Historical Society.)

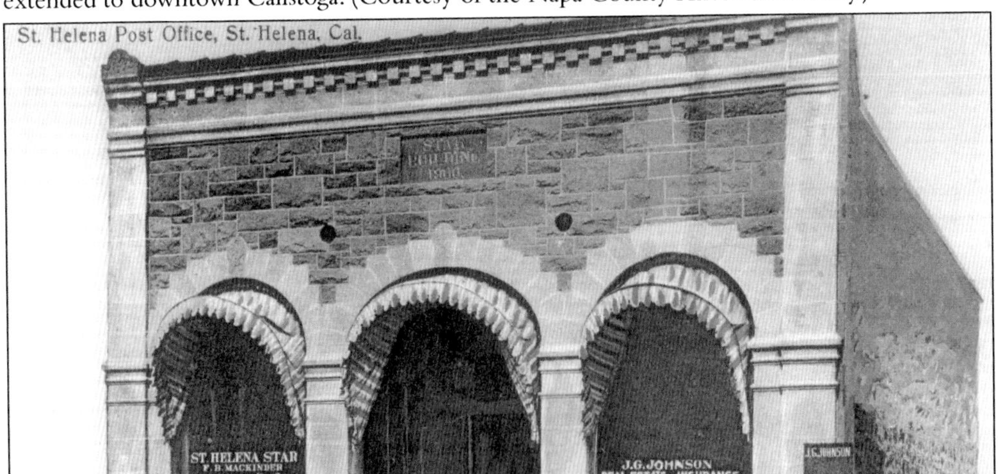

The Star Building is located at 1328 Main Street. It housed the *St. Helena Star* newspaper from 1900 to 2003. At the time of this postcard, around 1912, the publisher was Frank MacKinder. The building also housed MacKinder's brother's insurance business as well as the town's post office. Today it is home to the Caldwell-Snyder Art Gallery. (Author's collection.)

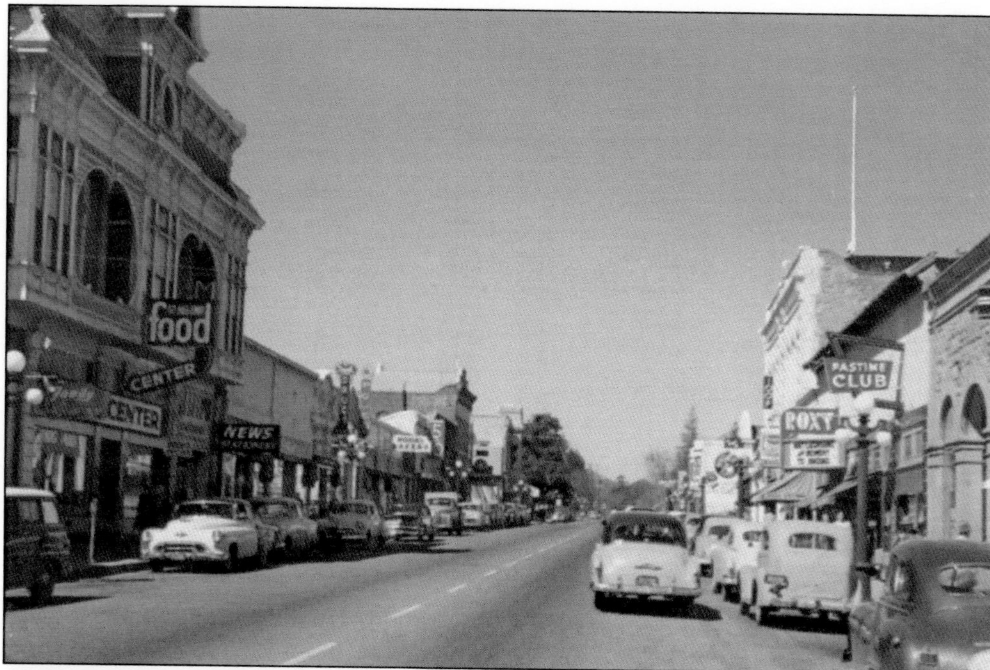

Several longtime St. Helena landmarks are visible in this 1950s postcard, including the Ritchie Block Building, the Model Bakery, and the Roxy Theater. The Roxy, located at 1340 Main Street, was originally built in 1915 and is now known as the Cameo Cinema. It is the longest continuously operated single-screen movie theater west of the Mississippi. (Author's collection.)

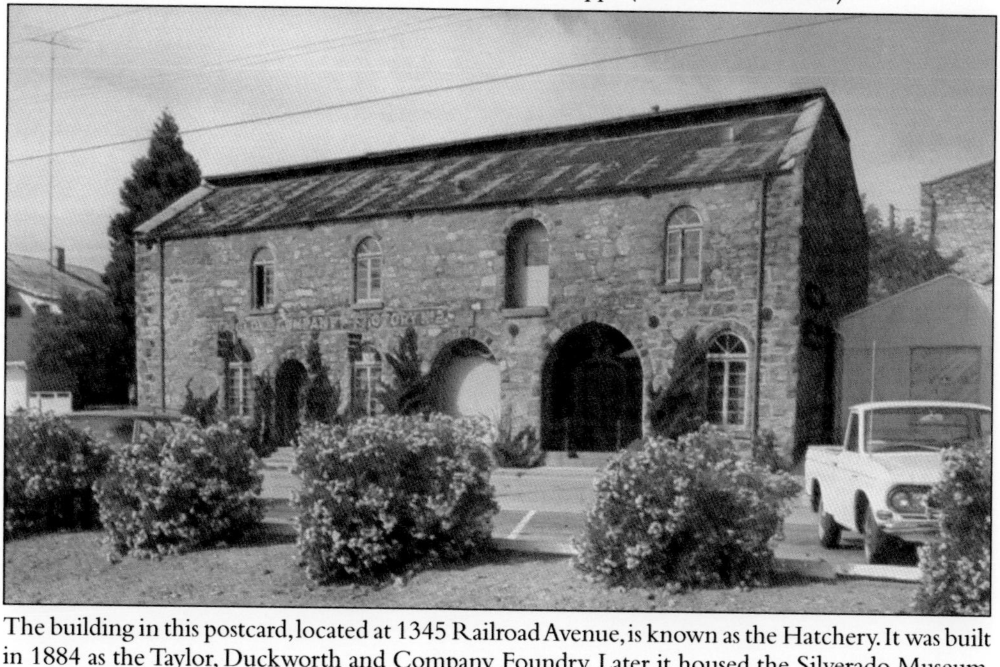

The building in this postcard, located at 1345 Railroad Avenue, is known as the Hatchery. It was built in 1884 as the Taylor, Duckworth and Company Foundry. Later it housed the Silverado Museum, until the museum moved to its current location adjacent to the library. The museum honors the life and accomplishments of Robert Louis Stevenson, and it was founded by bibliophile Norman H. Strouse. Today the Hatchery is home to a restaurant and offices. (Author's collection.)

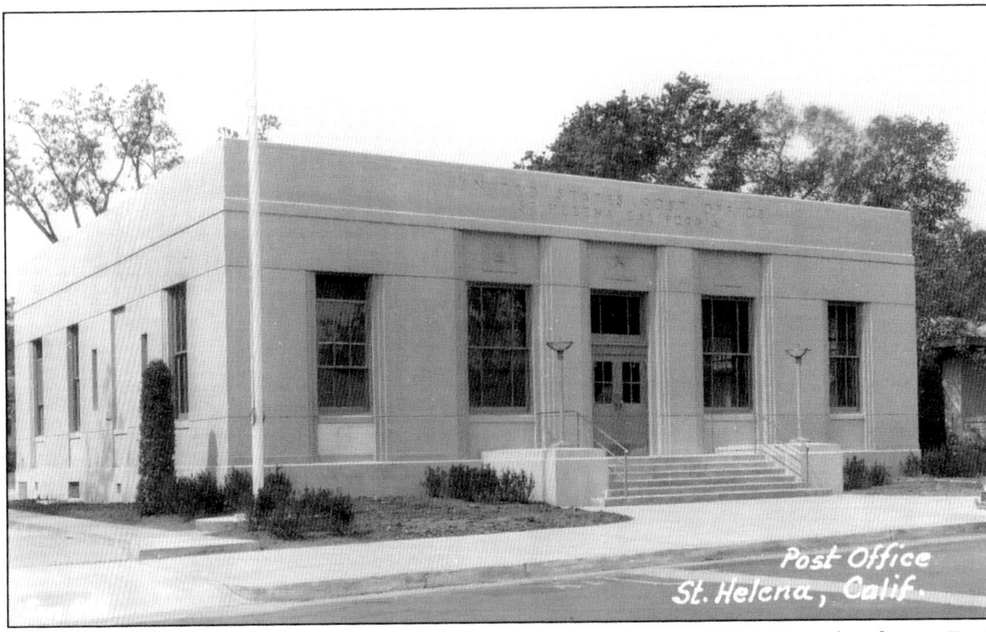

The post office in St. Helena is located at 1461 Main Street. It is another example of New Deal construction, as it was built in 1940. It is similar in design to the post office in downtown Napa. (Author's collection.)

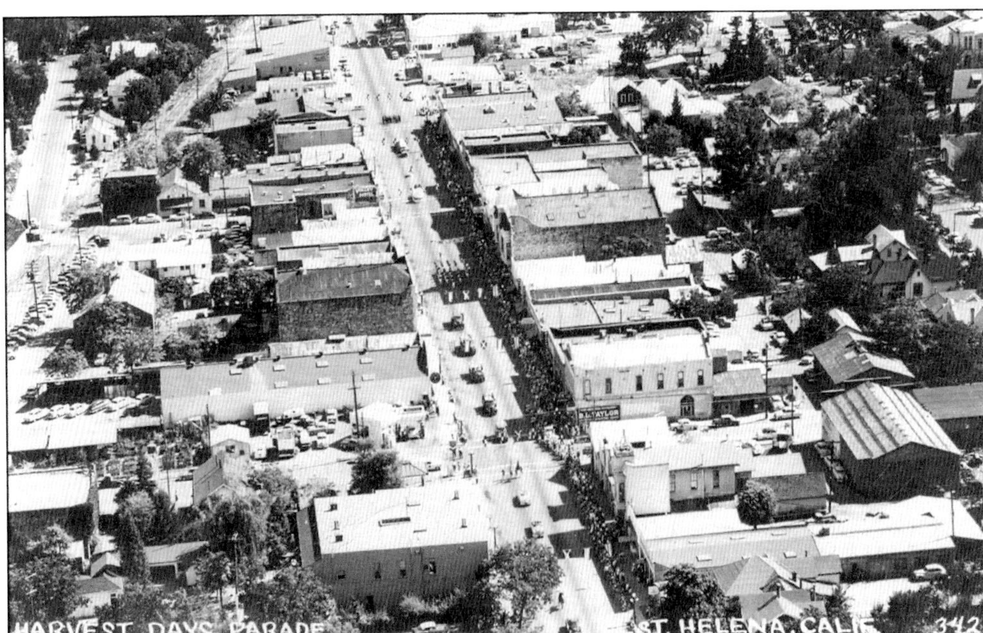

This postcard shows an aerial view of St. Helena during a parade for Harvest Days in the 1950s. The city still celebrates the annual end of the grape harvest season in October, although the celebration is now known as the Hometown Harvest Festival. (Author's collection.)

The Catholic presence in St. Helena dates to the 1860s, when a simple wooden church was built. The stone church pictured, located at 1340 Tainter Street, was constructed in 1892 under the direction of Father Becker. It was damaged by fire in 1945, but it was remodeled and continues to serve parishioners today. (Author's collection.)

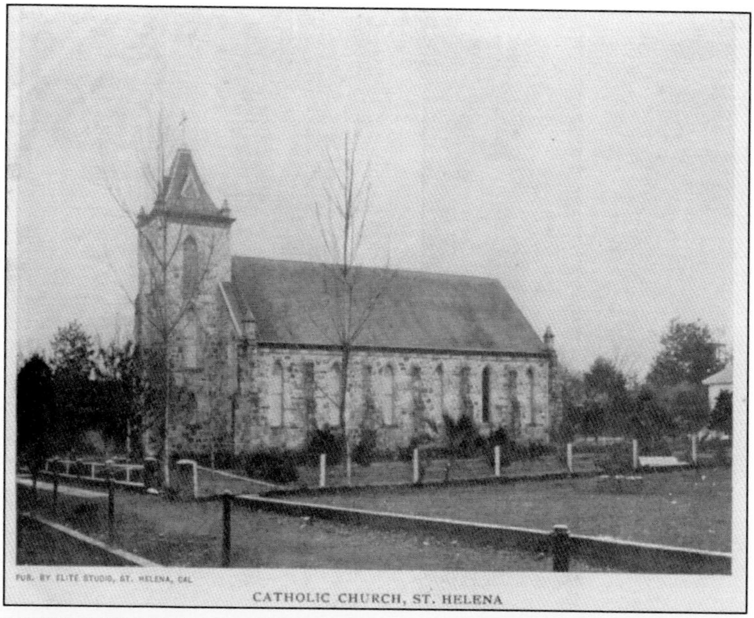

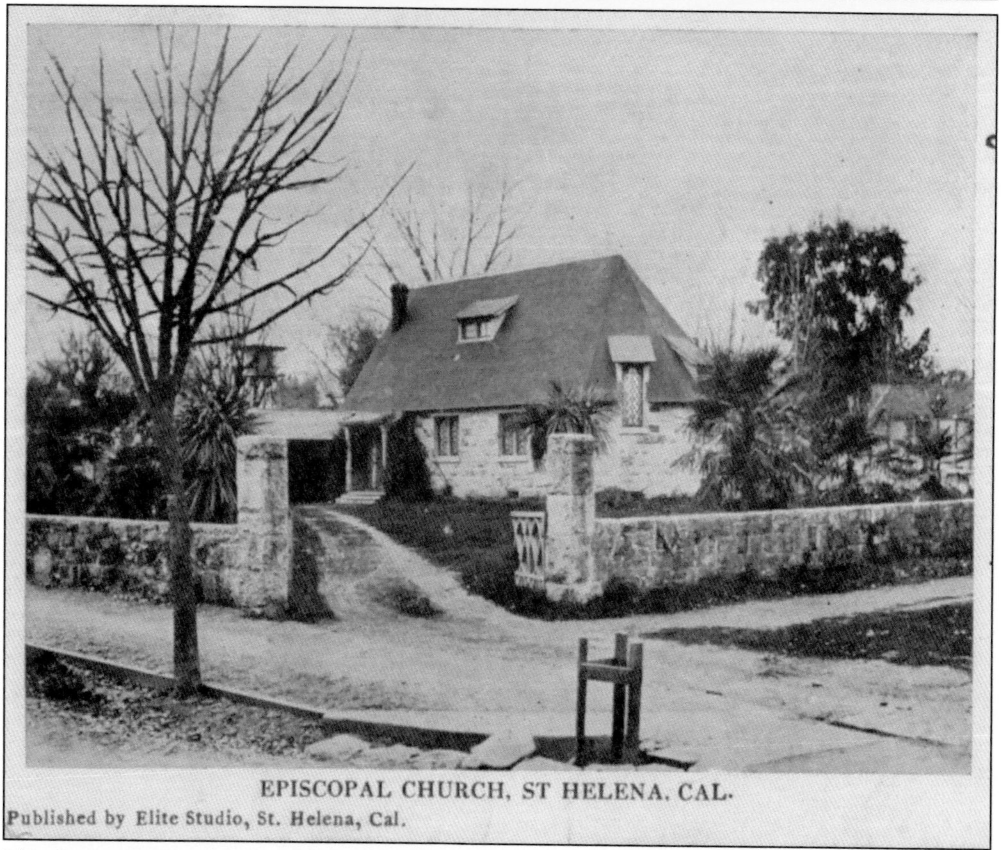

The Grace Episcopal Church is pictured in this postcard *c.* 1908. The building was constructed in 1895 and continues to serve the congregation, although it was expanded in 2007. (Courtesy of the Sharpsteen Museum of Calistoga History.)

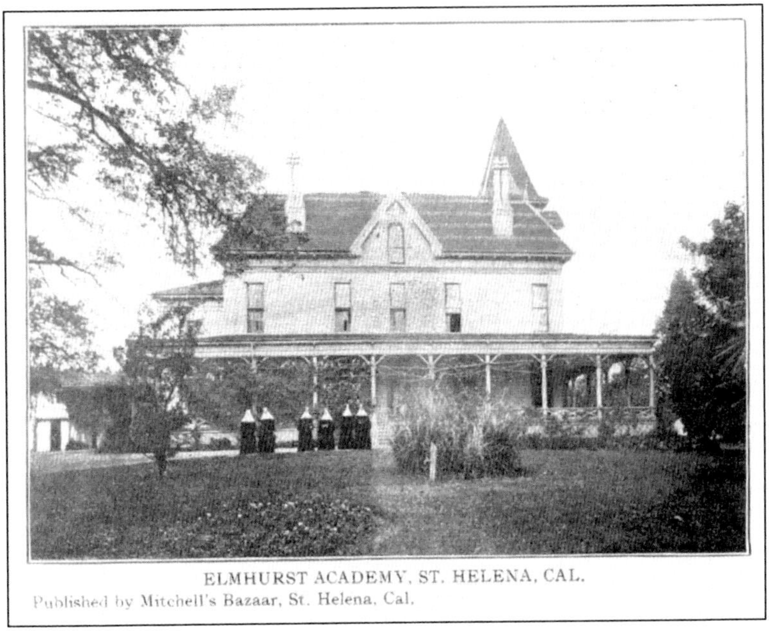

The Elmhurst Academy was a women's Catholic college established in St. Helena by the Ursuline Order in 1887. It accepted pupils of all denominations. The academy was shuttered in the 1910s. (Courtesy of the Napa County Historical Society.)

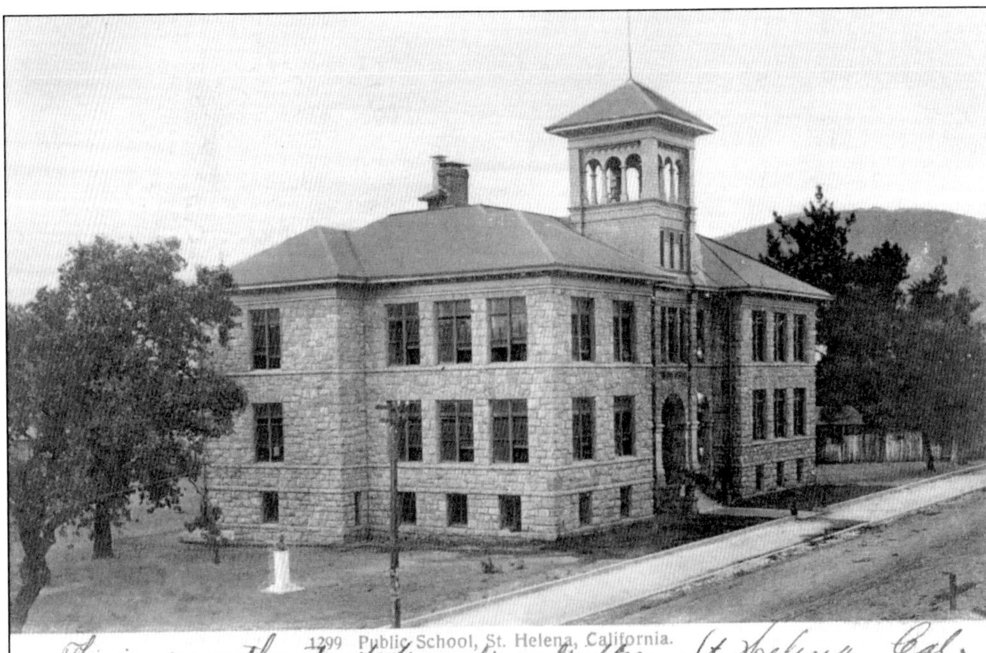

The St. Helena school pictured above was constructed in 1901; it was the first stone school building in the county. The building, which was located on Oak Street, was demolished in 1932 due to earthquake fears. (Courtesy of the Napa County Historical Society.)

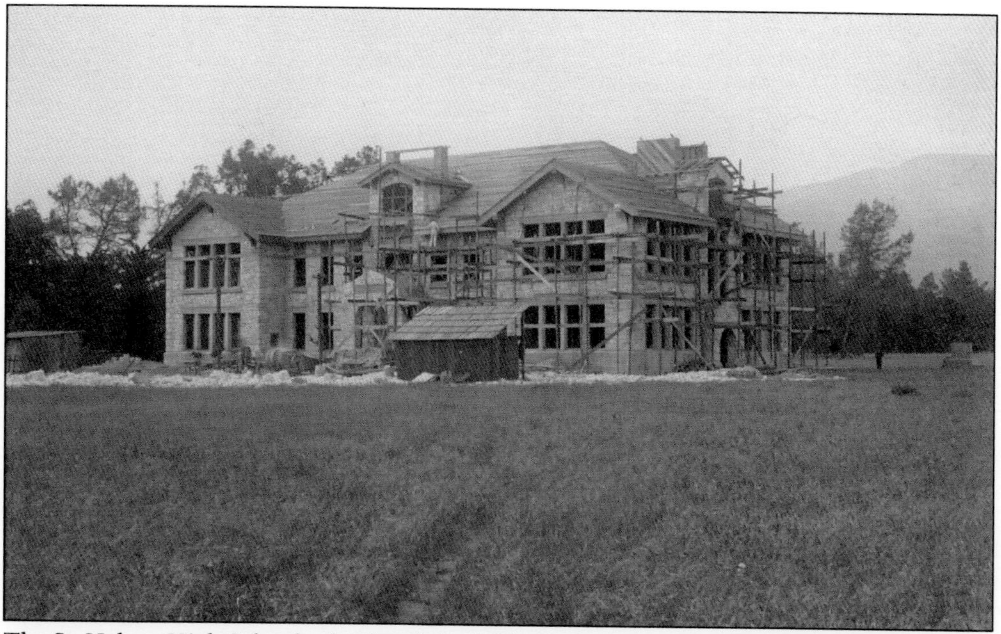

The St. Helena High School, a landmark, is visible in this postcard while under construction in 1912. The 16-acre school site was donated in 1908 to the city by the estate of Frances Grayson Crane for the purpose of building a high school. (Courtesy of the Sharpsteen Museum of Calistoga History.)

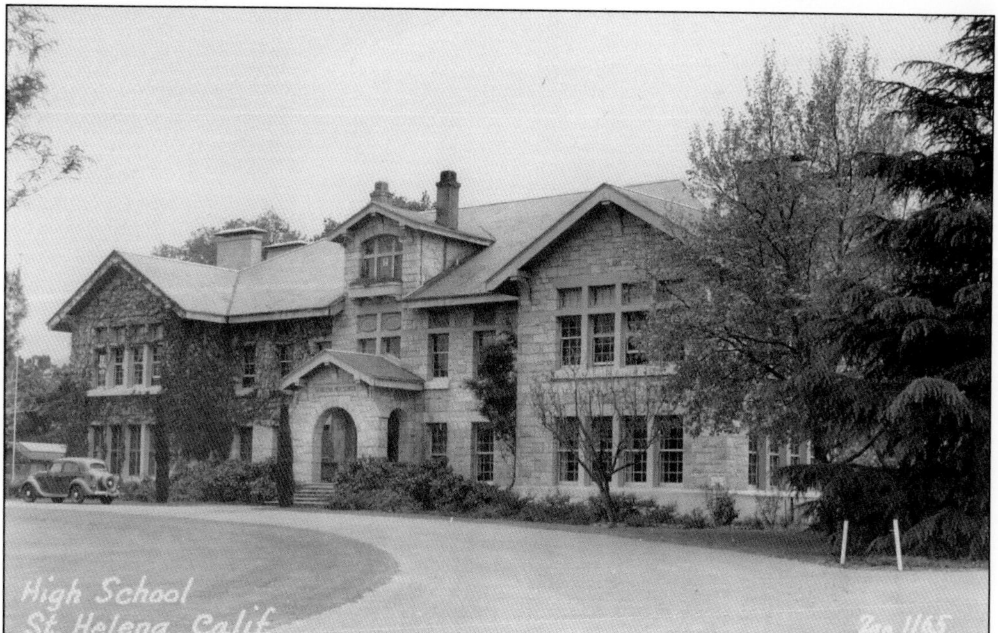

This 1930s postcard shows another view of St. Helena High School. The school building is a clearly visible landmark along Highway 29 for motorists as they enter St. Helena. Although additional school buildings have been constructed behind it, Vintage Hall, as it is known, still houses some classrooms, the cafeteria, and the St. Helena Unified School District offices. (Courtesy of Mike Vanwormer.)

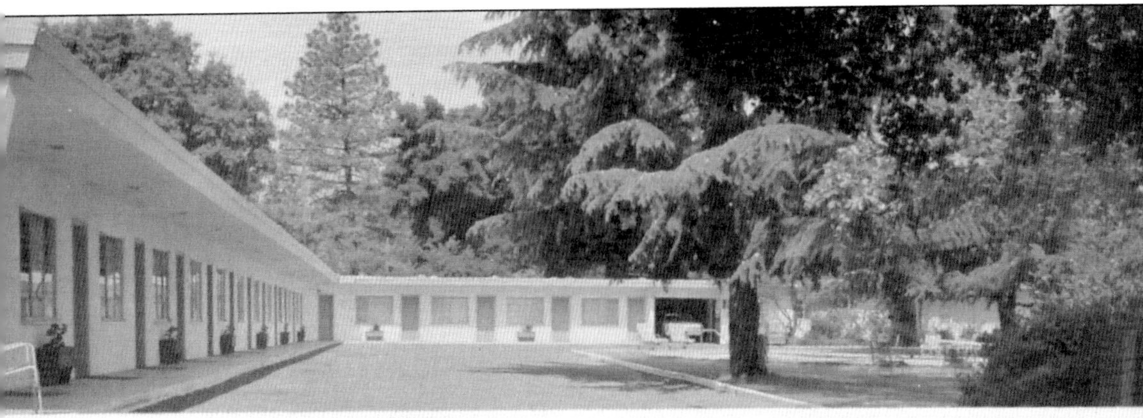

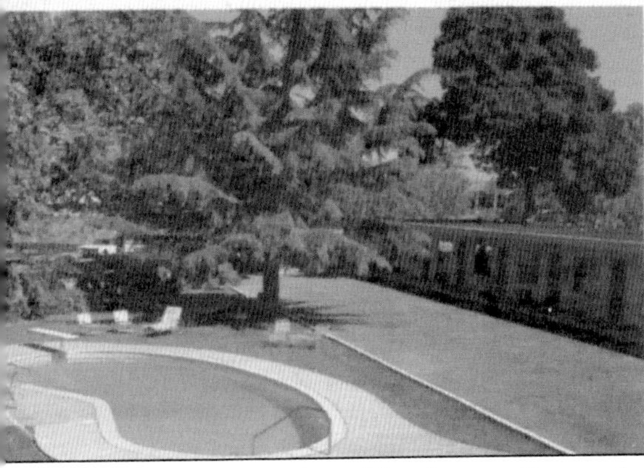

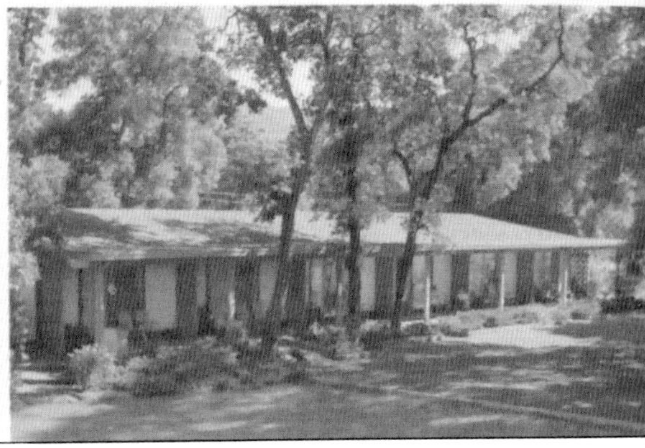

The El Bonita Motel has been a fixture along Highway 29 at the southern end of St. Helena since 1952. The area where the motel still stands started out as a religious retreat and campground in the 1940s. The original owners were named Elmer and Bonita, hence the name of the motel. (Author's collection.)

Seven

Calistoga

Calistoga was first surveyed as a town site in 1860. Settlement of the town began in earnest when Sam Brannan developed his hot springs resort there. In a now infamous speech while a little tipsy, Brannan misspoke while trying to equate his new resort to the Saratoga area in the state of New York, instead saying it would be the "Calistoga of Sarifornia." Brannan and the citizens of the new town apparently liked the name, and Calistoga was born.

Brannan further brought progress to the area when he spearheaded the effort to bring the railroad northward from Napa to the town in 1868; his motivation was to provide an easy way for guests to get to his resort, and the side effect was a reliable way to ship goods south to the Bay Area. Eventually the electric railway would also travel to the town, bringing even more tourists to the area.

Brannan ran into financial troubles, selling his beloved resort in 1869. By this time, a town had sprung up around the Hot Springs Resort. Calistoga would go on to become an important jumping-off point for miners seeking riches in the silver mines of nearby Mount St. Helena and for tourists seeking recreation in the resorts of Lake County.

Calistoga transformed itself into a destination in its own right. Many entrepreneurs followed Brannan's example, setting up resorts and spas in and around the city. Names such as Pacheteau, Dr. Aalders, and Nance would follow.

Today Calistoga has a population of about 5,300 people. Visitors still arrive in Calistoga from all over the world to enjoy the fine dining and local wineries, relax in the natural hot springs and volcanic mud baths, embark on bicycle tours of the nearby vineyards, and hike the Oat Hill Grade and Mayacamas Mountains.

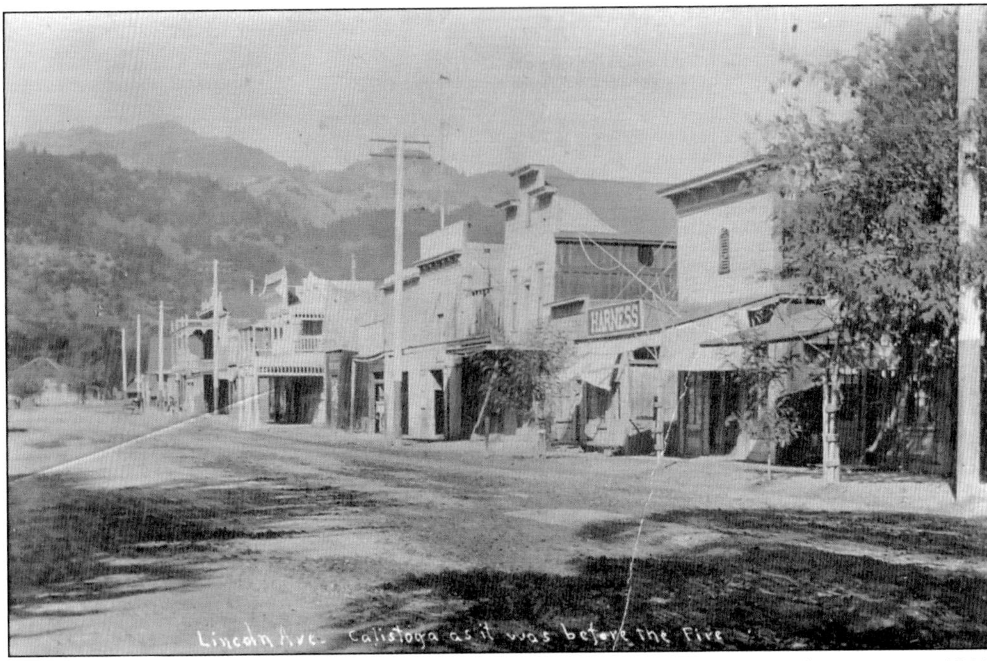

This early view of Calistoga shows Lincoln Avenue looking west and was taken prior to 1901, when a huge fire destroyed much of the downtown, including city hall. (Courtesy of the Sharpsteen Museum of Calistoga History.)

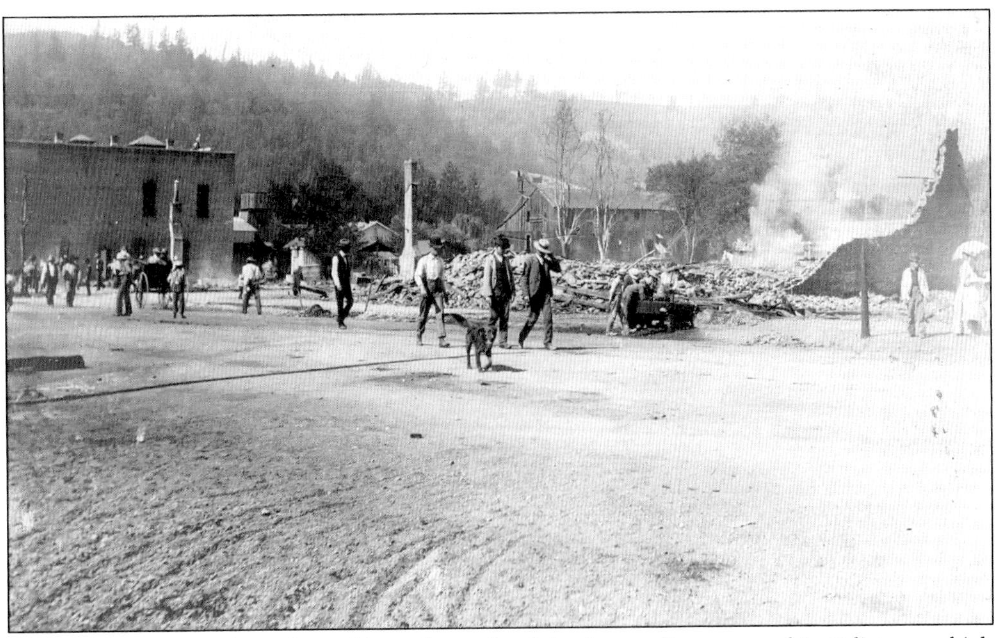

This postcard shows the still-smoking aftermath of the largest fire ever to hit Calistoga, which occurred on August 3, 1901. It started when gasoline drums in the back of a mercantile store on Lincoln Avenue exploded due to the scorching heat. The efforts of the firefighters were hampered when their hoses burned due to the fire's intense heat. (Courtesy of the Sharpsteen Museum of Calistoga History.)

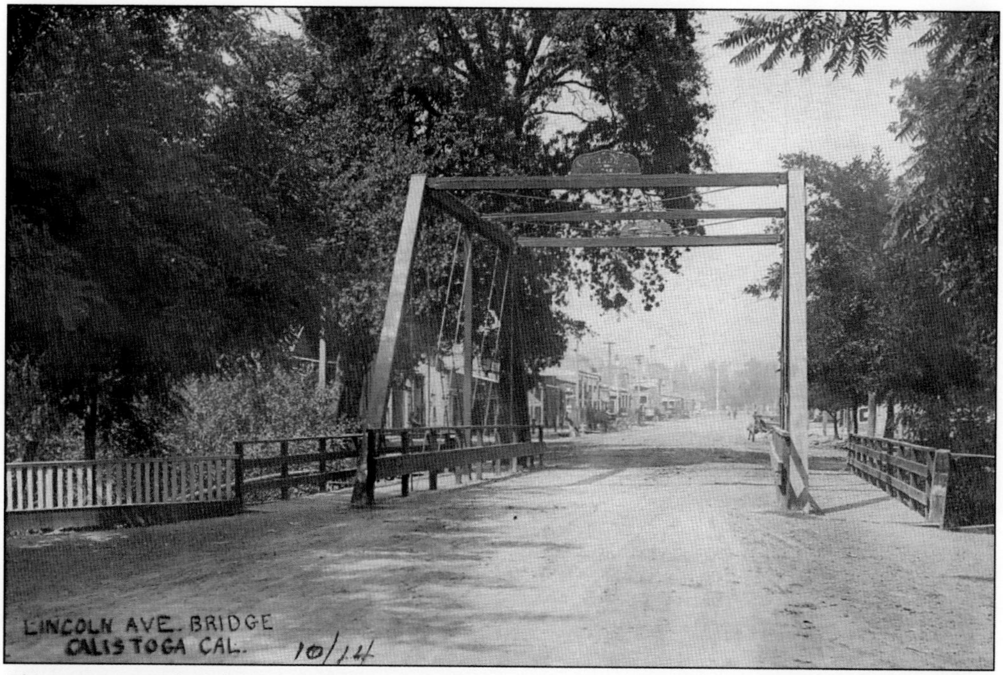

This image reveals Calistoga as viewed from the Lincoln Avenue Bridge, looking west *c.* 1914. This steel truss bridge was fabricated in San Francisco and transported to Calistoga. (Courtesy of the Sharpsteen Museum of Calistoga History.)

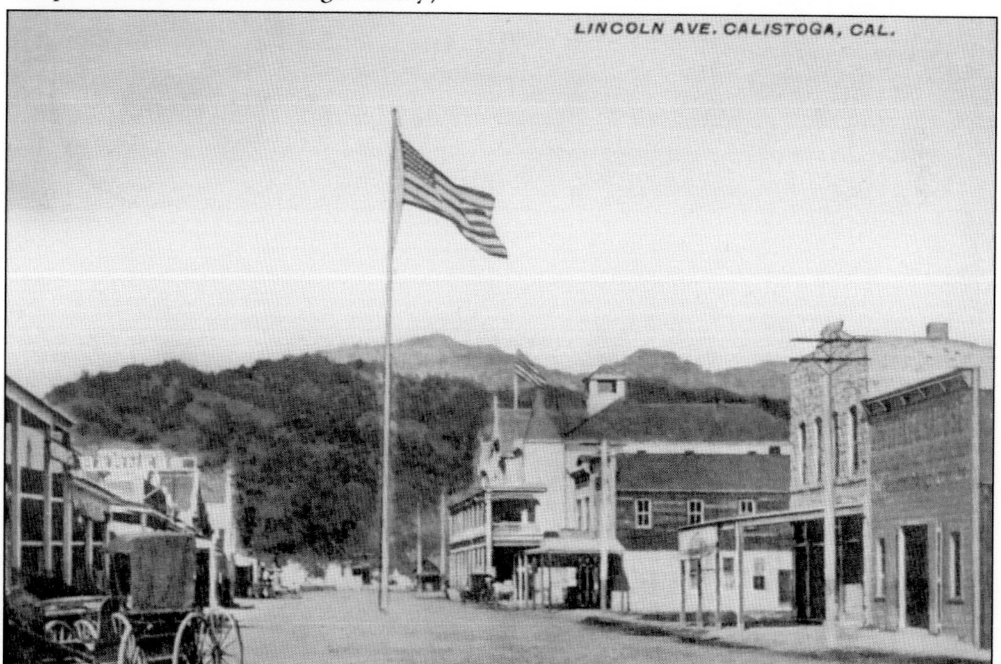

The flagpole visible in this 1911 postcard was a fixture of downtown Calistoga during the early part of the 20th century; it stood at the intersections of Lincoln Avenue and Washington Streets. The pole was removed in the 1920s as automobile traffic increased. The large building with its own flag, to the right of the pole, is the Hotel Calistoga. (Courtesy of Mike Vanwormer.)

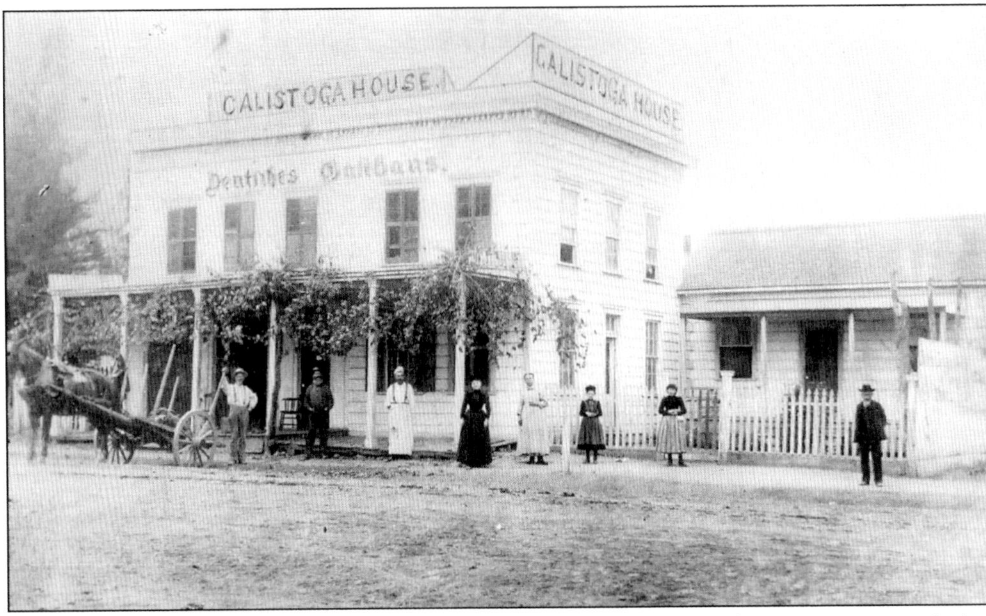

The Calistoga House Hotel was located on Lincoln Avenue, near Myrtle Street. It was typical of early hotels in the area. Note the German writing on the building, indicative of the many German immigrants who came and settled in Napa County. (Courtesy of the Sharpsteen Museum of Calistoga History.)

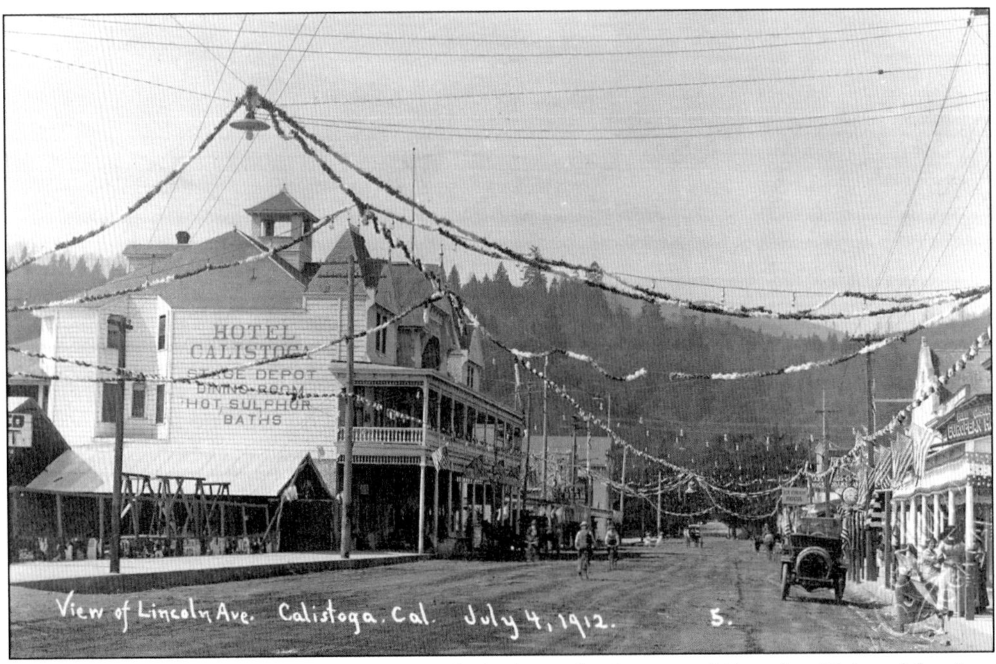

This 1912 postcard shows Lincoln Avenue decked out for the annual Fourth of July celebration. This year was particularly special because electric lines had just been run throughout the city. Visible at the far right, where the automobile is parked, is the European Hotel. The European was torn down in 1917 and is the site of the present-day Mount View Hotel. (Courtesy of the Sharpsteen Museum of Calistoga History.)

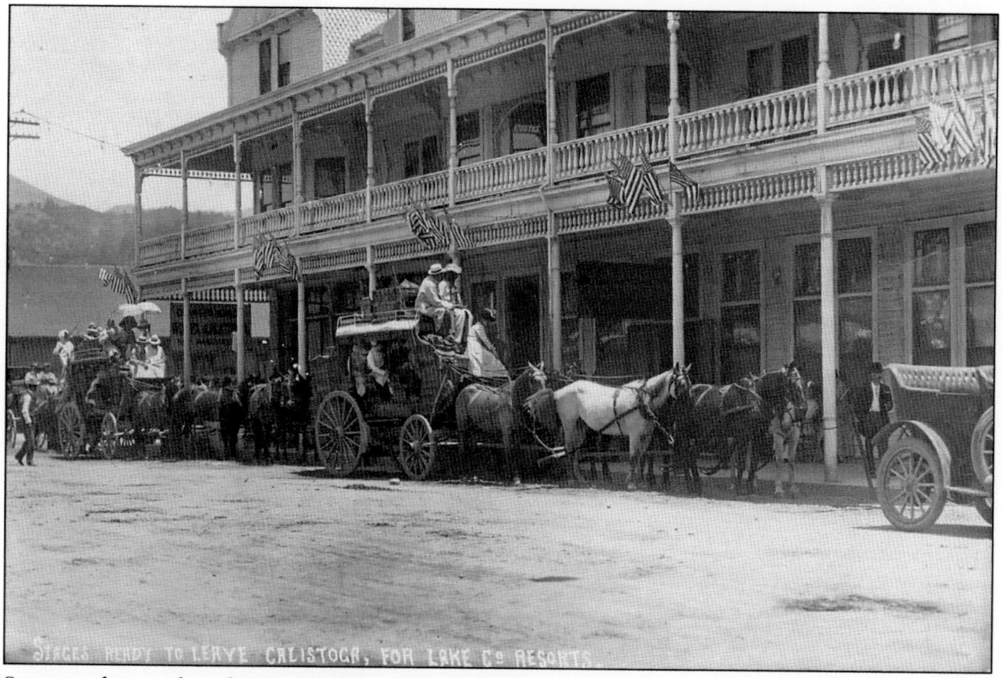

Stagecoaches and early automobiles are assembled in front of the Hotel Calistoga, awaiting departure up the Lawley Toll Road to Lake County resort areas and the quicksilver mines. The Calistoga train station is visible in the background at the left edge of the photograph. (Courtesy of the Sharpsteen Museum of Calistoga History.)

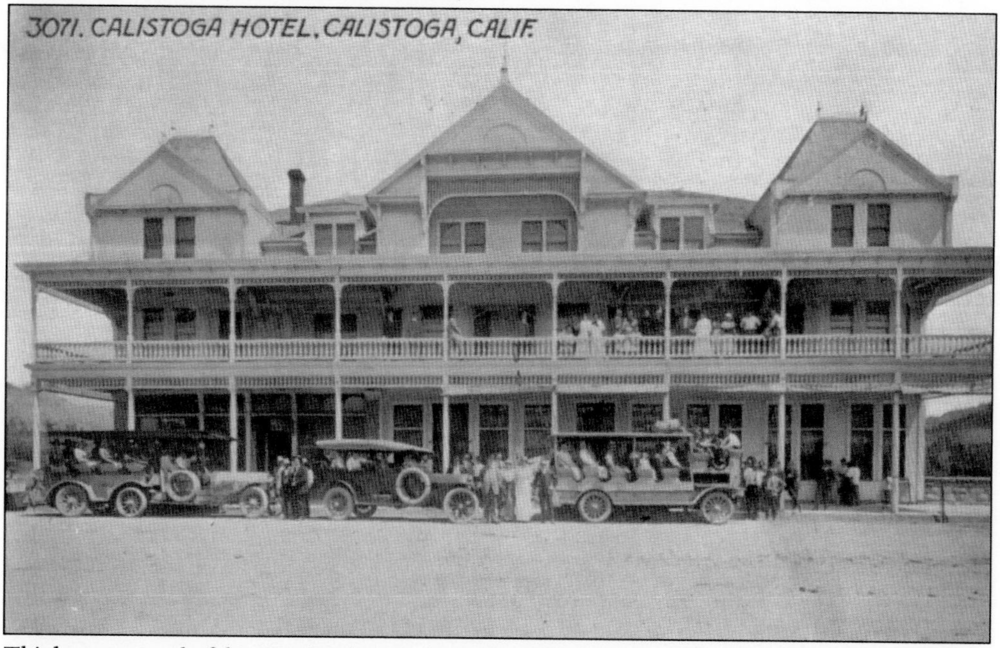

This later postcard of the Hotel Calistoga shows the full conversion from horse-drawn stagecoaches to horsepower under a hood. The hotel at this time was advertising its own hot sulphur baths, a 50-by-80-foot swimming pool that was naturally heated at 112 degrees, and room rates starting at $2.50 a night. (Courtesy of the Sharpsteen Museum of Calistoga History.)

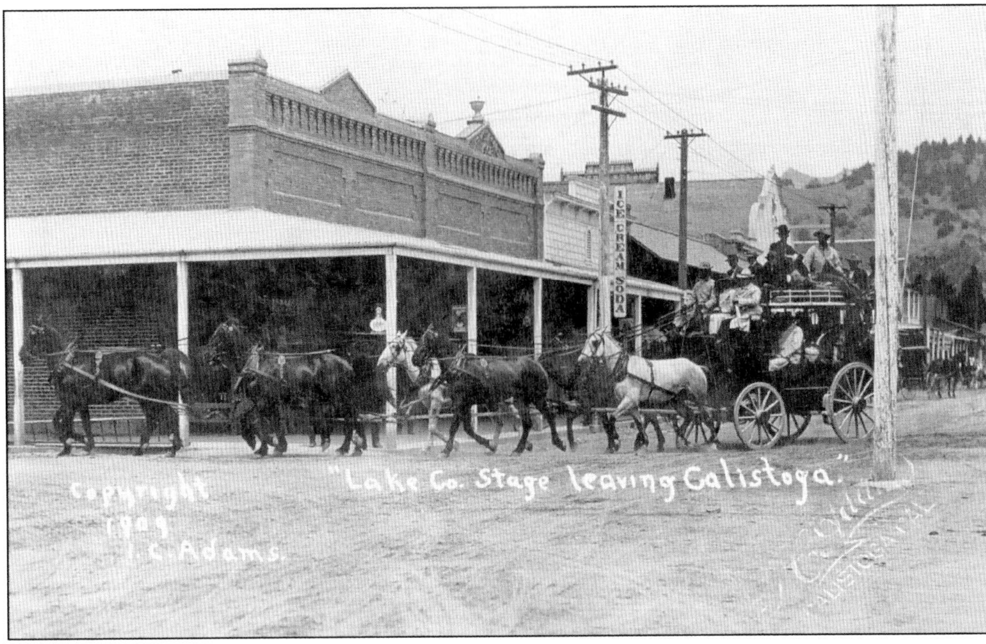

A stagecoach is pictured here at full gallop on its way out of Calistoga. William Spiers operated the Calistoga and Clear Lake Stage Line for many years, starting in 1888. A true transportation entrepreneur, Spiers converted his operation to automobile buses in the 1910s. (Courtesy of the Sharpsteen Museum of Calistoga History.)

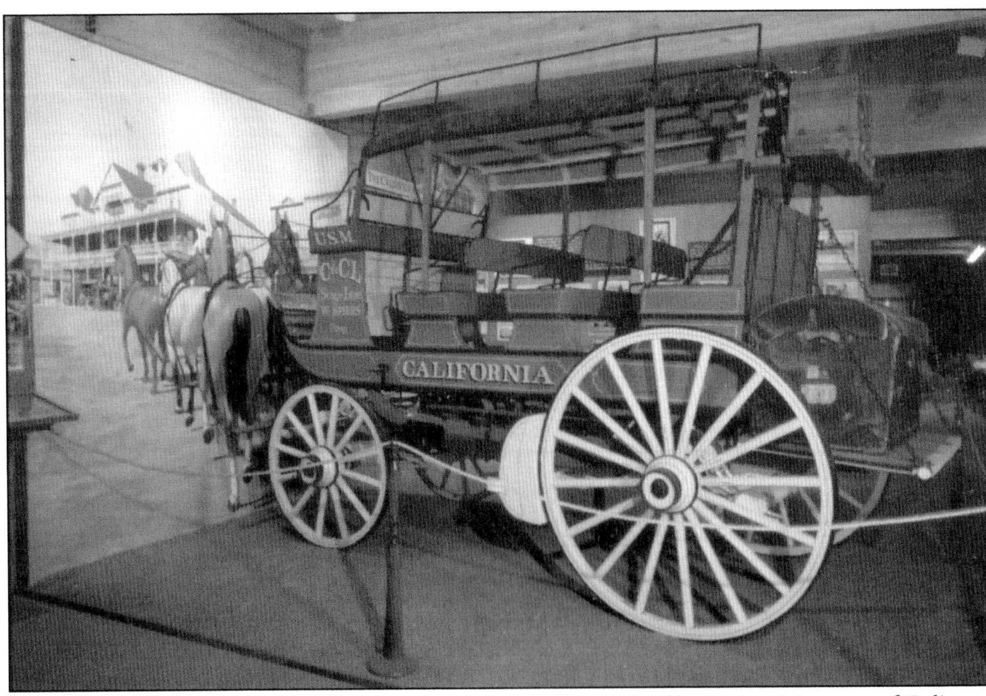

One of the Bill Spiers's original stagecoaches is on display at the Sharpsteen Museum of Calistoga History. The display includes a painted mural, which depicts the four-horse team pulling it towards the Hotel Calistoga. (Courtesy of the Sharpsteen Museum of Calistoga History.)

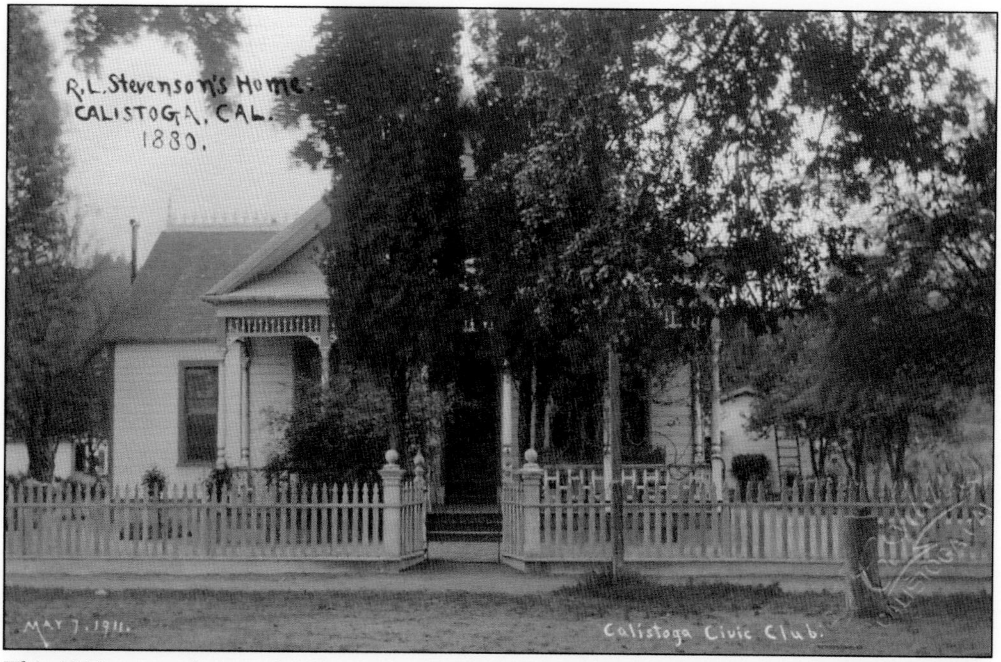

This 1911 postcard notes that this house, located at 913 Washington Street, was one of the places where author Robert Louis Stevenson stayed while visiting the Napa Valley in 1880. In actuality, the home was an 1885 expansion of a much smaller cabin that stood on Lincoln Avenue at the time Stevenson stayed there. It later became the residence of G. Iaacheri, a spa owner. (Courtesy of the Sharpsteen Museum of Calistoga History.)

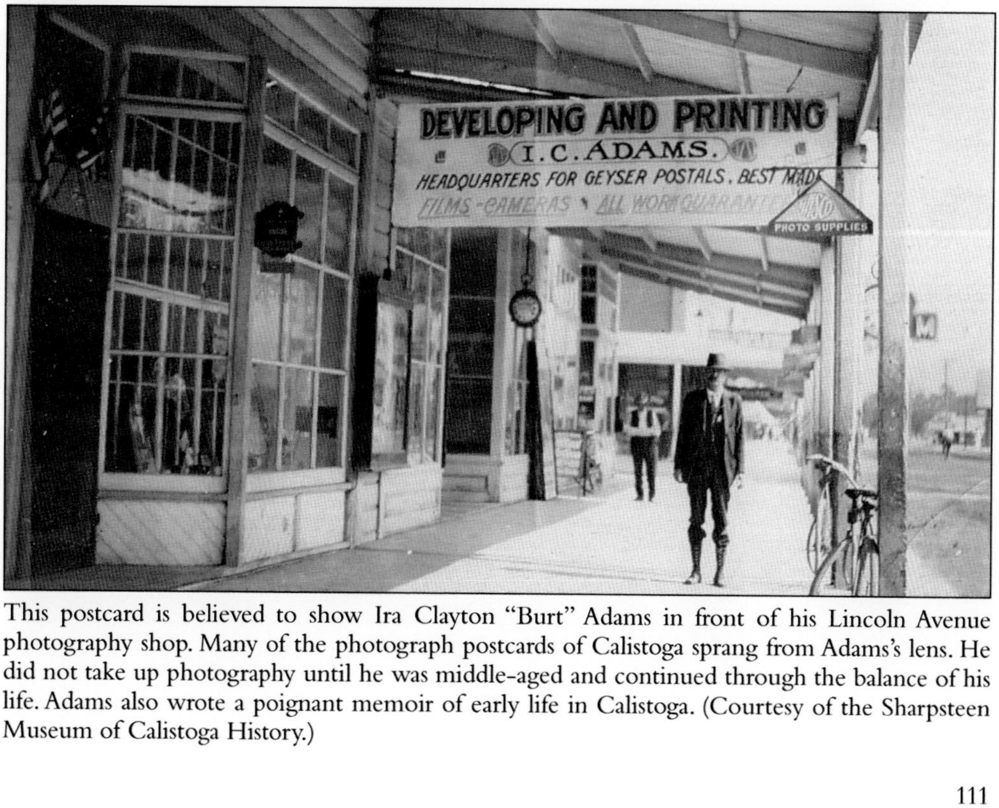

This postcard is believed to show Ira Clayton "Burt" Adams in front of his Lincoln Avenue photography shop. Many of the photograph postcards of Calistoga sprang from Adams's lens. He did not take up photography until he was middle-aged and continued through the balance of his life. Adams also wrote a poignant memoir of early life in Calistoga. (Courtesy of the Sharpsteen Museum of Calistoga History.)

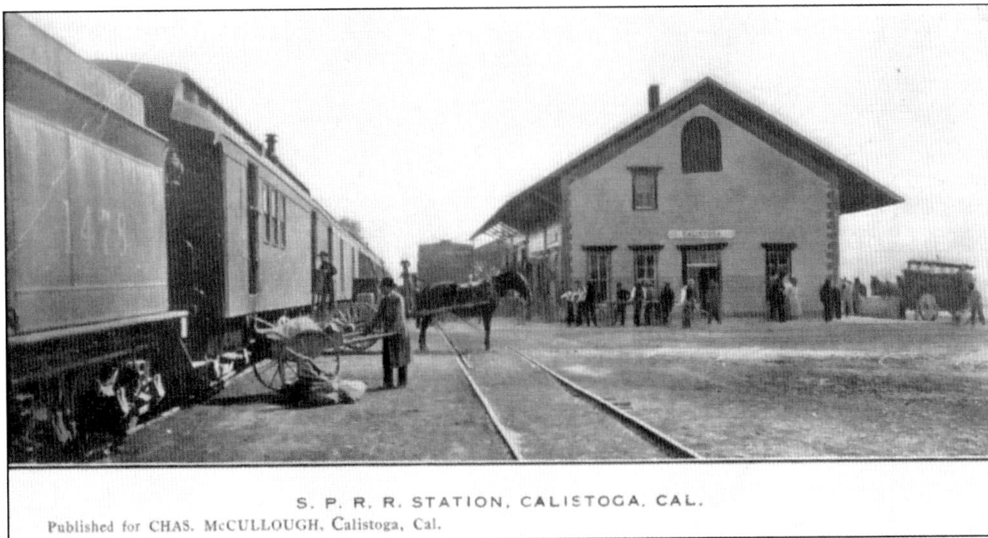

The Calistoga Train Depot appeared to be a busy place in this postcard. It was built in 1868 by Sam Brannan as a way to bring guests to his hot springs resort. It is the second oldest surviving train depot in California. It was restored in 1978 and currently houses several shops. (Courtesy of the Sharpsteen Museum of Calistoga History.)

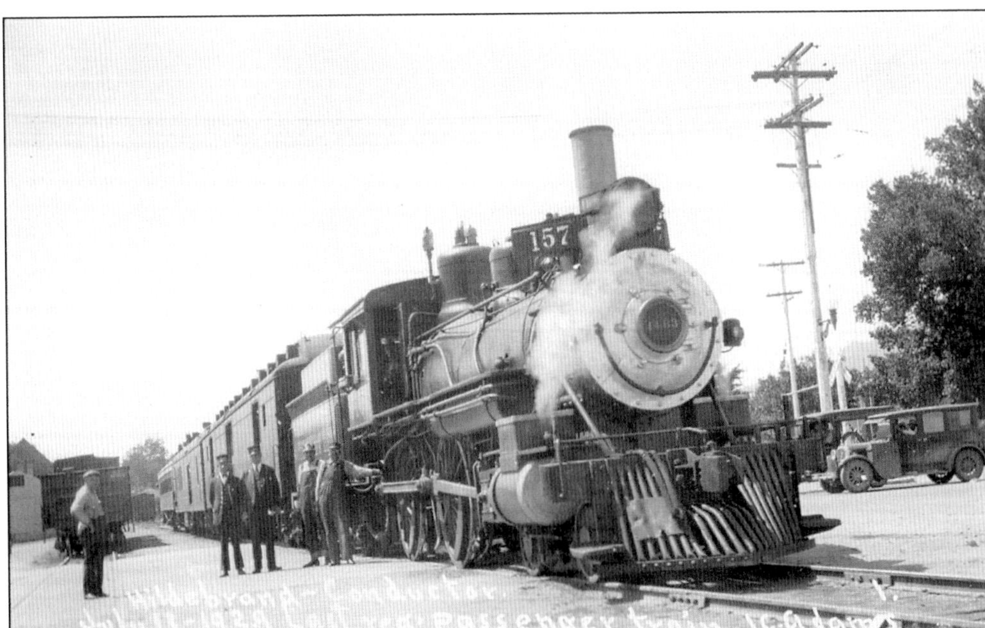

Calistoga photographer I. C. Adams snapped the photograph postcard to honor the last passenger train service to Calistoga, on July 13, 1929. The railroad, in the end run by the Southern Pacific Railroad, finally succumbed to the mounting competition from automobiles and bus transportation. (Courtesy of the Sharpsteen Museum of Calistoga History.)

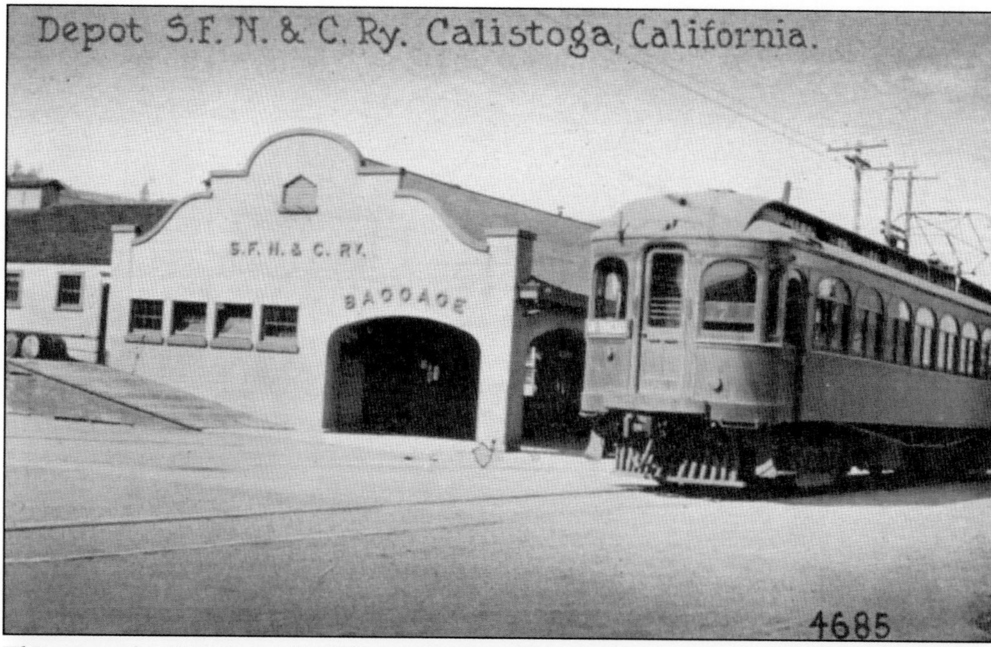

This postcard *c.* 1915 shows the Calistoga Depot of the San Francisco, Napa, and Calistoga Railway. Calistoga was the northerly terminus of the railway, 41 miles from its start in Vallejo; the depot was located at the southwest corner of Washington and Gerald Streets. After the demise of the electric railway, the station saw use as a terminal for the buses that replaced it. (Author's collection.)

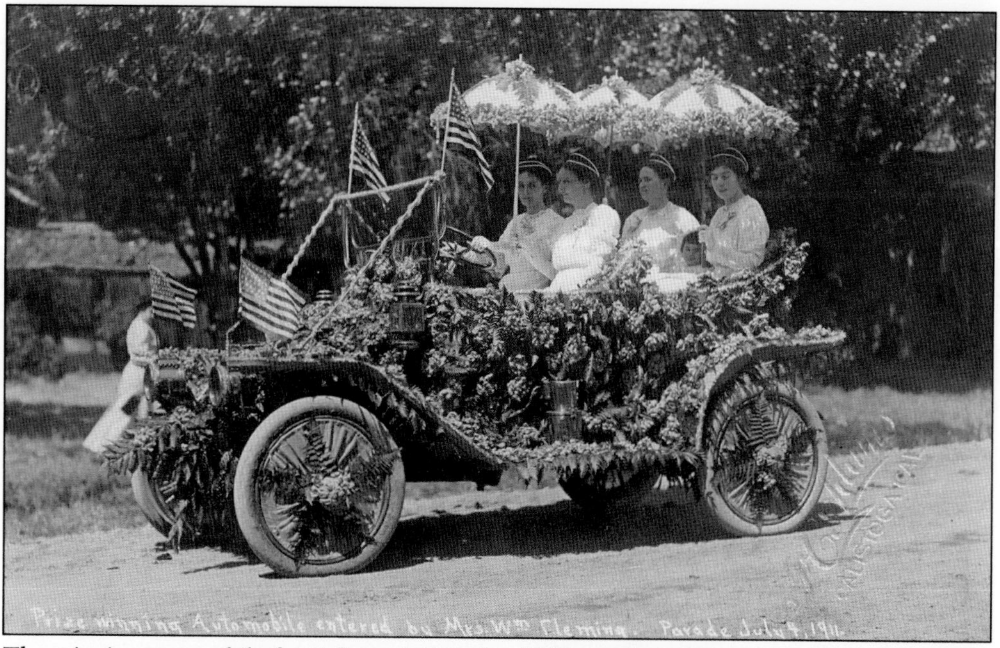

The winning automobile for Calistoga's Fourth of July parade is pictured in this 1912 postcard. The parade has been an important celebration in Calistoga since the start of the 20th century. The parade is now part of the larger Napa County Fair held in Calistoga. (Courtesy of the Sharpsteen Museum of Calistoga History.)

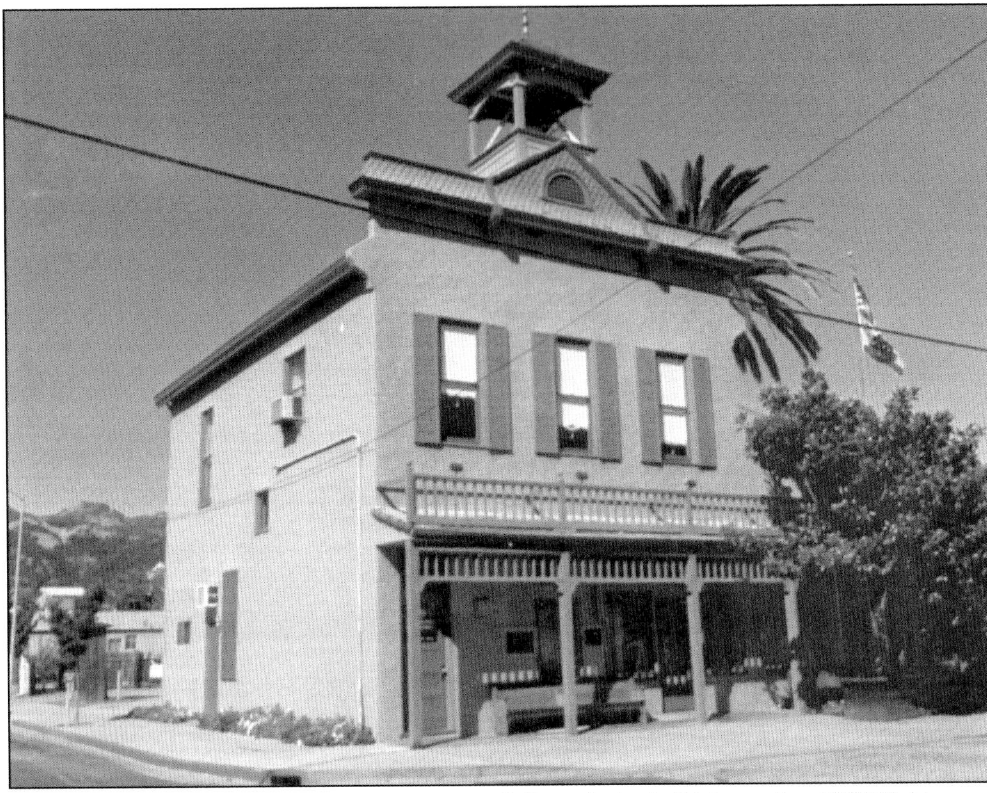

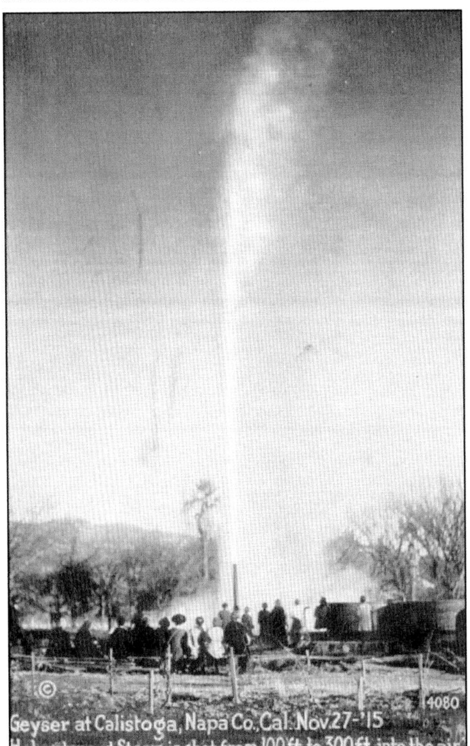

Calistoga's city hall is located at 1232 Washington Street. The structure was built in 1901 on the site of Badlams Opera House. The opera house burned to the ground during the conflagration that destroyed much of the town. The city hall building served many purposes over the years, including as a police station, jail, and the tax collectors office. (Author's collection.)

The Light Geyser was actually a man-made well dug by farmer Ephraim Light, who hoped to obtain a source of water to wash barrels and tanks at his farm off Tubbs Lane just north of Calistoga. When the well reached 150 feet, it struck a natural hot spring, which began erupting at regular intervals. The geyser is now known as the Old Faithful Geyser of California. (Author's collection.)

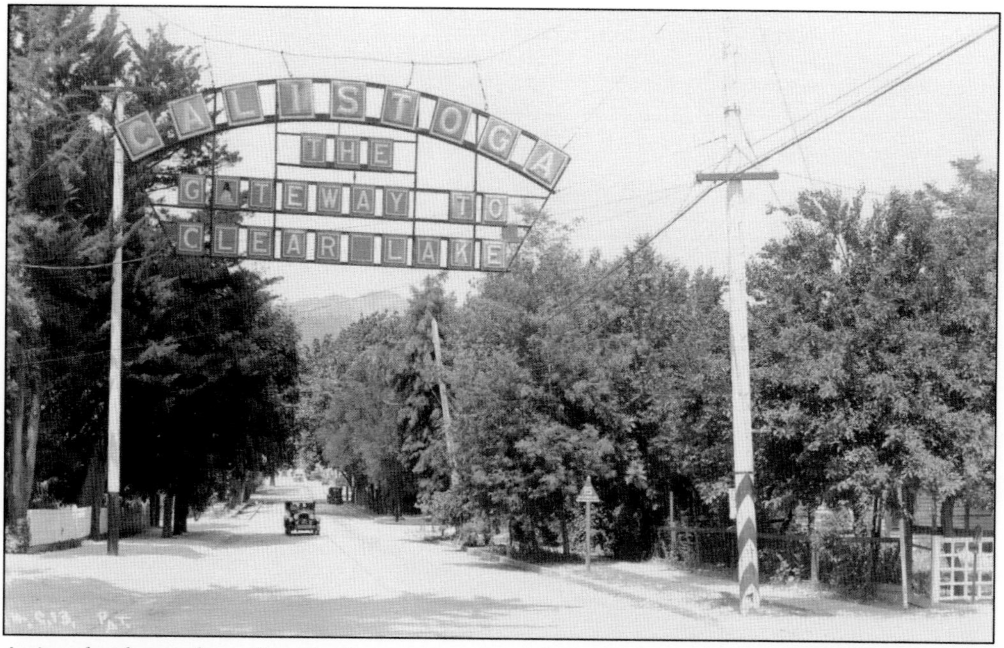

A sign that hung above Lincoln Avenue, just west of Myrtle Street, heralded Calistoga's location as a jumping-off point for the resorts of Lake County. By this time, the hot springs resorts in and around Calistoga were coming into their own as destinations for weary travelers and health seekers alike. (Courtesy of the Napa County Historical Society.)

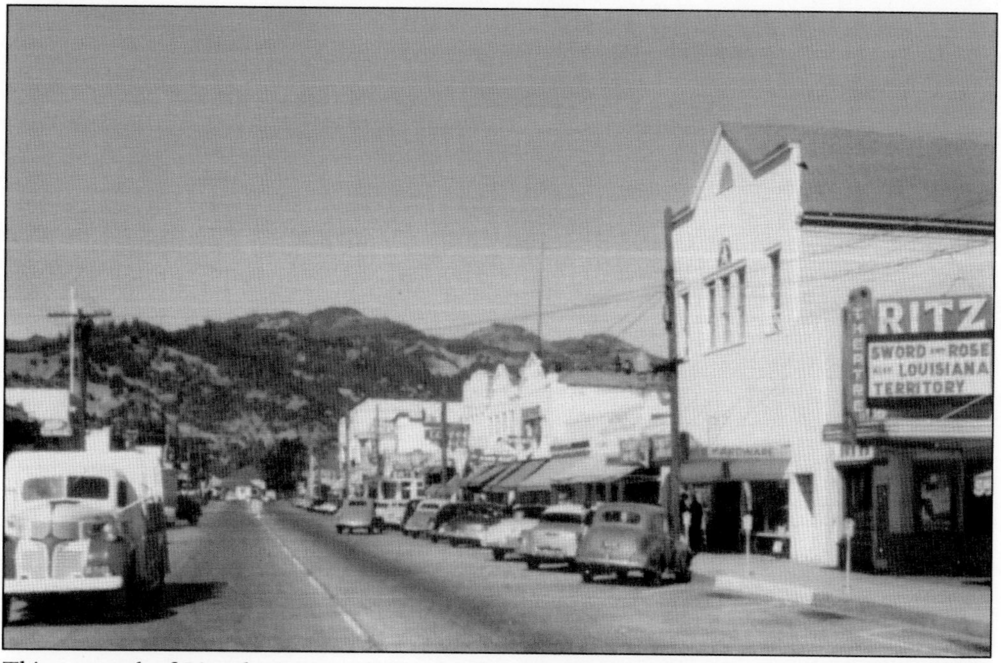

This postcard of Lincoln Avenue shows the Ritz Theater marquee; it was 1953, based on the movies playing at the time. The Ritz was located at 1348 Lincoln Avenue. The building began its life as an automobile repair shop. The theater has since been subdivided into several businesses. (Author's collection.)

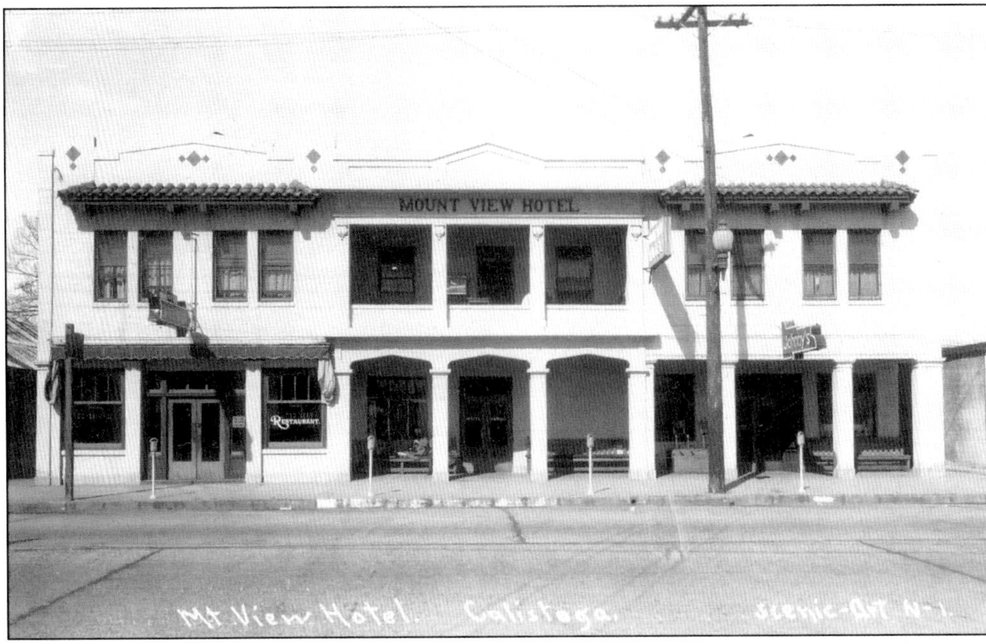

The Mount View Hotel is shown here as it appeared in the 1930s. The hotel, located at 1457 Lincoln Avenue, was built in 1917 in a Spanish colonial motif. It featured an ice cream shop and billiard hall on its first floor storefronts. It was also known for the Mount View Bar, which attracted Hollywood divas and political powers throughout its history. The hotel was most recently renovated in 2008. (Courtesy of Mike Vanwormer.)

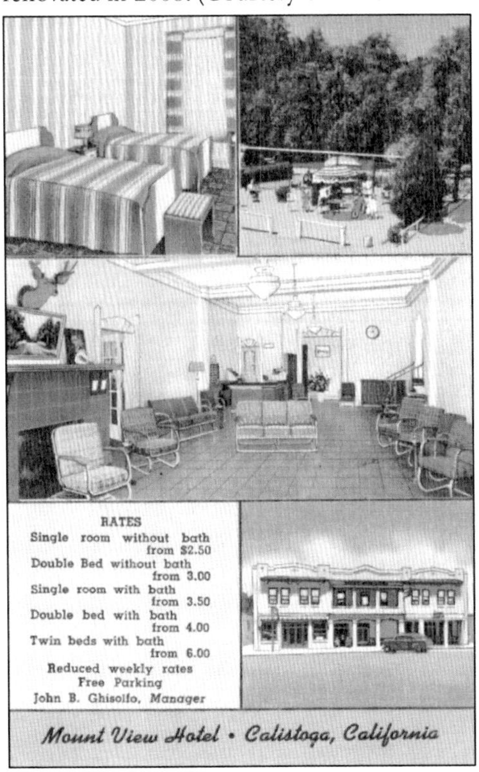

This 1950s postcard shows the comforts at the Mount View Hotel. Listed on this card as manager is Johnny Ghisolfo. He was a partner in the European Hotel, located at the site of the Mount View. In 1917, he tore the European down and built the Mount View. Ghisolfo was known around town as "Mr. Calistoga," and he served 32 years in civic service, including a term as mayor. In 1961, Calistoga's reservoir was named Lake Ghisolfo in his honor. (Author's collection.)

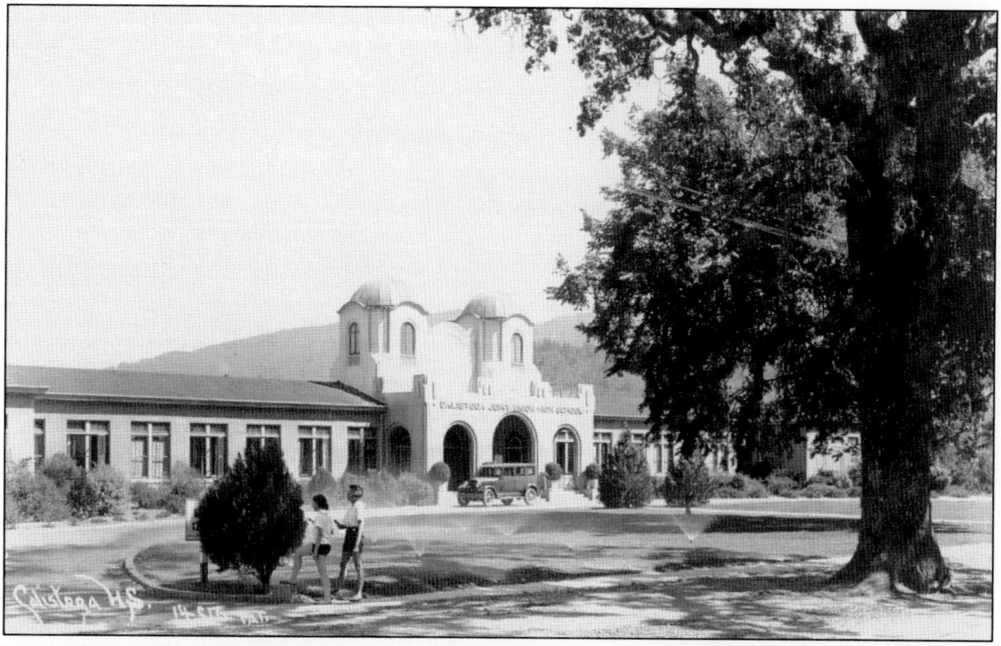

Shown here is the Calistoga Joint Union High School, located at 1608 Lake Street, as it appeared shortly after its opening in the 1920s. The building's distinctive towers and arched entryway were removed in the 1970s. It would go on to serve students through 1988, when it was demolished, and the current high school was built. (Courtesy of the Napa County Historical Society.)

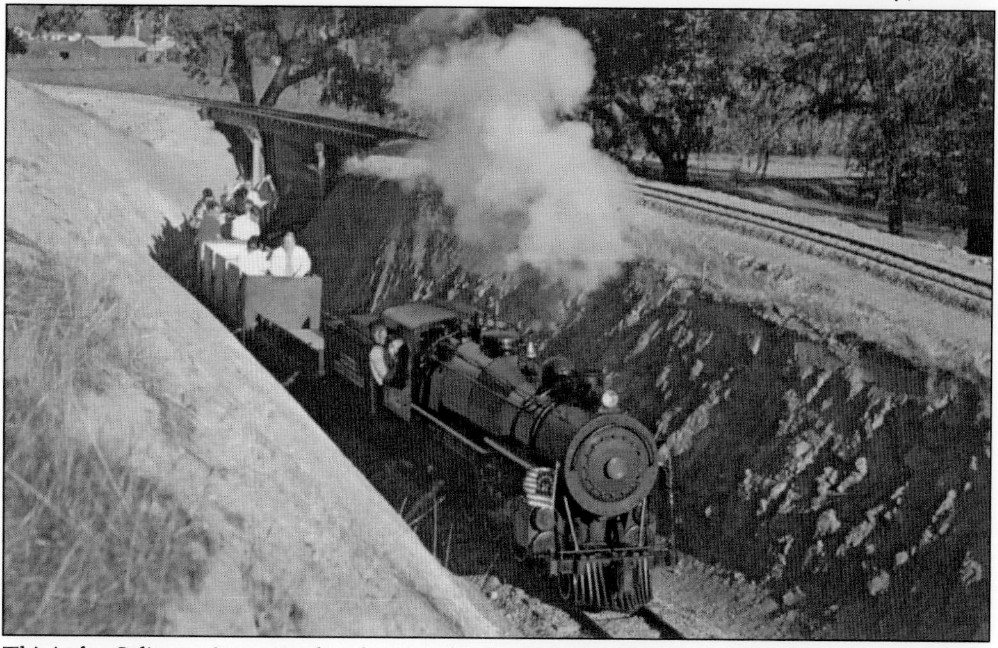
This is the Calistoga Steam Railroad, a one-third-scale railroad that was originally used in the 1915 Panama Pacific Exposition in San Francisco. The railroad featured a scaled-down depot, platform, and 2 miles of track. It operated just south of Calistoga from 1972 to 1975 and then was sold and relocated to San Luis Obispo County. A sister of this train is currently on display at the California State Railroad Museum in Sacramento. (Author's collection.)

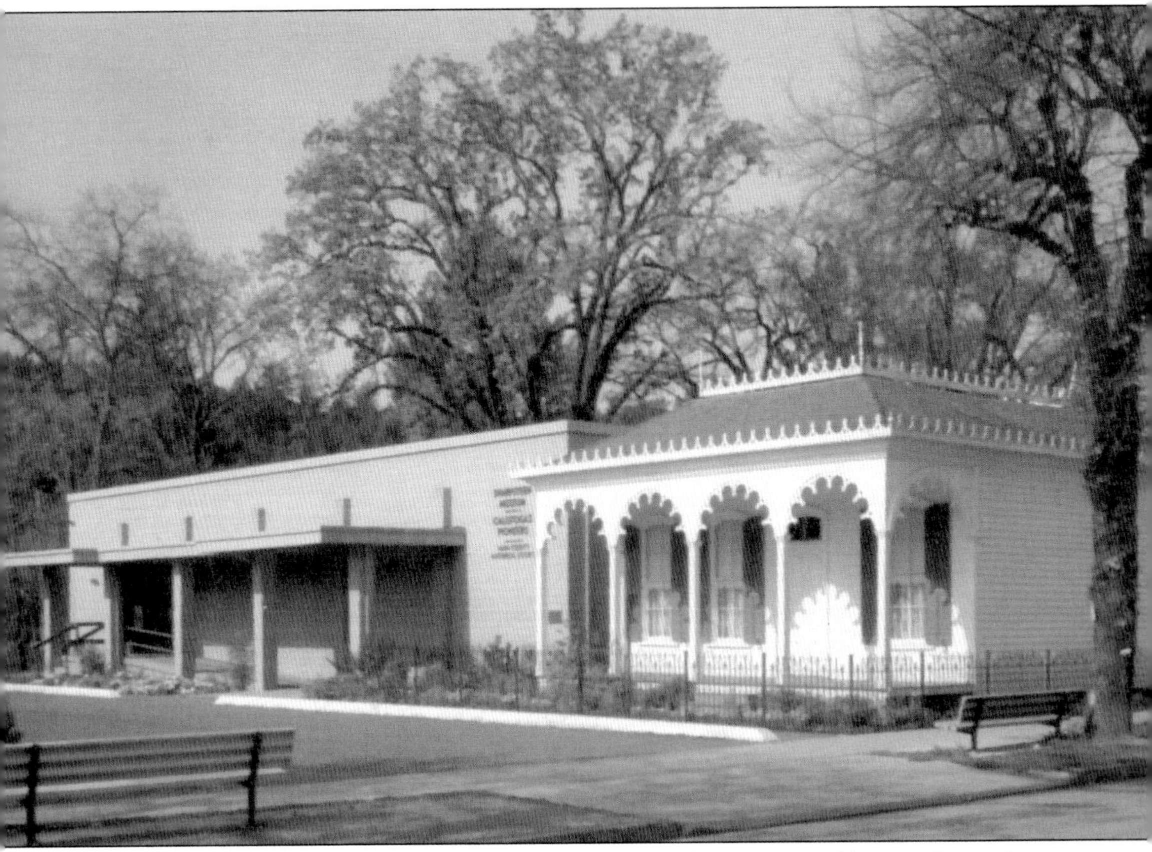

The Sharpsteen Museum of Calistoga History is located at 1311 Washington Street. It was a project of Ben and Bernice Sharpsteen. Ben was an Academy Award–winning animator, producer, and director for Walt Disney Studios. In 1978, the Sharpsteens completed construction of the museum building and dioramas that they donated to the City of Calistoga. The museum building adjoins a restored cottage from Sam Brannan's resort, which was moved to the site of the museum. (Courtesy of the Sharpsteen Museum of Calistoga History.)

Eight

A Thousand Words

The postcards in this book provide a snapshot of Napa County that can never be re-created. Perhaps as important as these visual windows into history are the handwritten messages scrawled on their backs or around the margins of the images themselves.

The senders of these postcards were trying to distill the sights and sounds they were experiencing into a few lines of text. Unknowingly their endeavors were part of the concerted tourism effort being mounted by the private resorts and chambers of commerce within the Napa Valley. Before the advent of Condé Nast, Frommers, or the Travel Channel, these postcards were advertisements to friends and relatives, touting the beauty and serenity that was and is the Napa Valley.

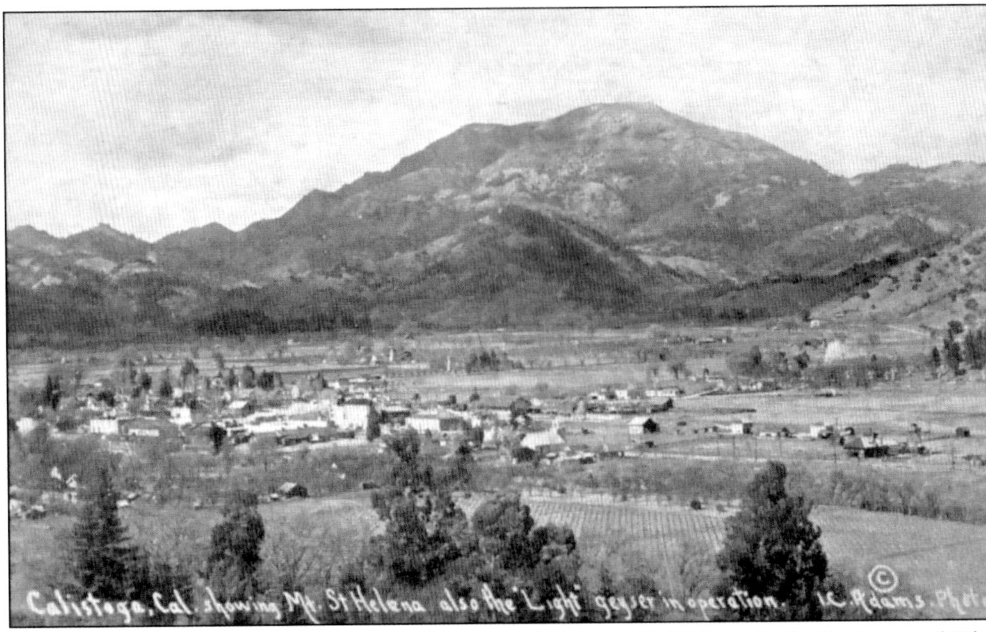

This postcard shows an early view of Calistoga, with Mount St. Helena in the background. The Light Geyser is visible at the right of the card. The sender of this card highlights the many attractions available to an early tourist: "Took a drive to St. Helena by way of a ranch, here to Calistoga where we saw the geysers and hot springs, home via petrified forest." (Author's collection.)

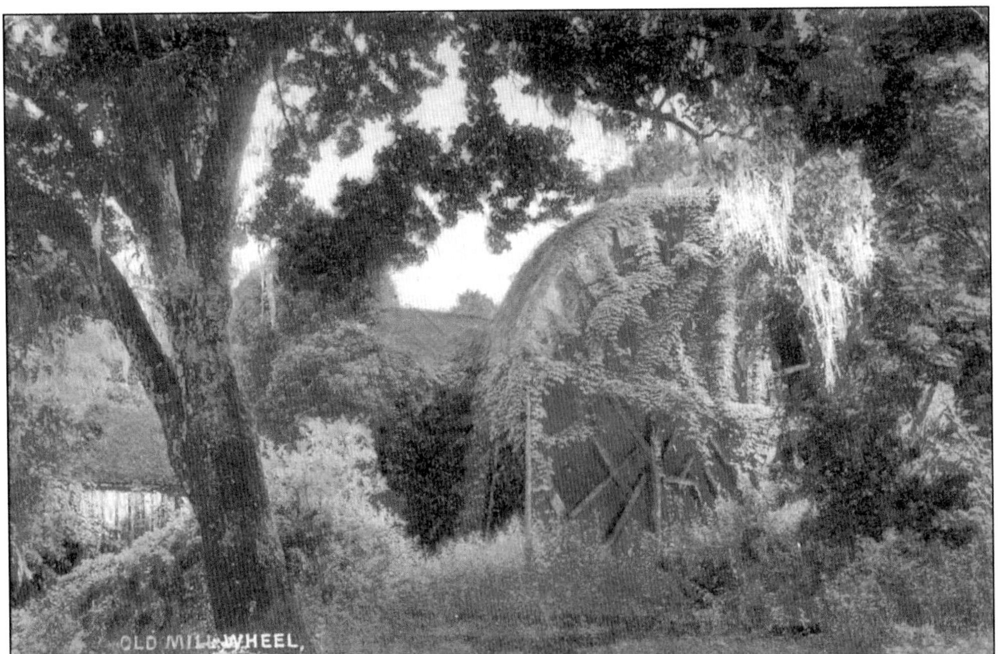

Although this 1914 postcard shows the ivy-covered Old Bale Mill, the sender was prouder of his hiking accomplishments and highlights the abundant outdoor activities available in the valley. He writes, "We went up Mt. George [east of Napa] and then around to Mardrone Falls, a walk of about 14 miles. I still feel the affects." (Author's collection.)

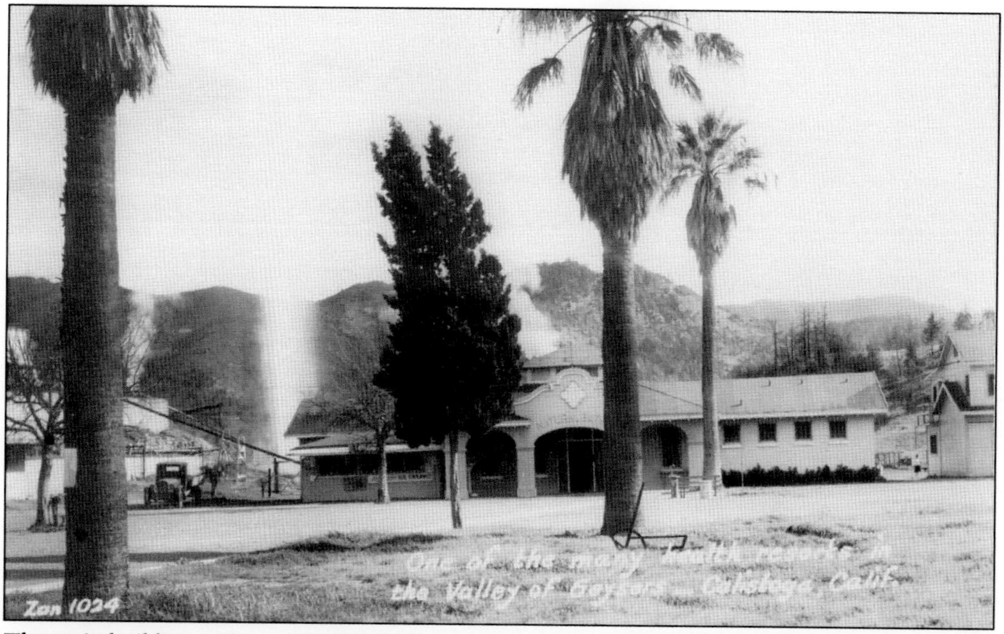

The main building and geyser at the Pacheteau Resort are visible in this 1945 postcard. The sender wrote, "We can see this picture from our cottage. The white foam in the back of the house is steam coming from the ground. Weather just right. Cold mornings and nites [*sic*]. We have a nice cottage." (Author's collection.)

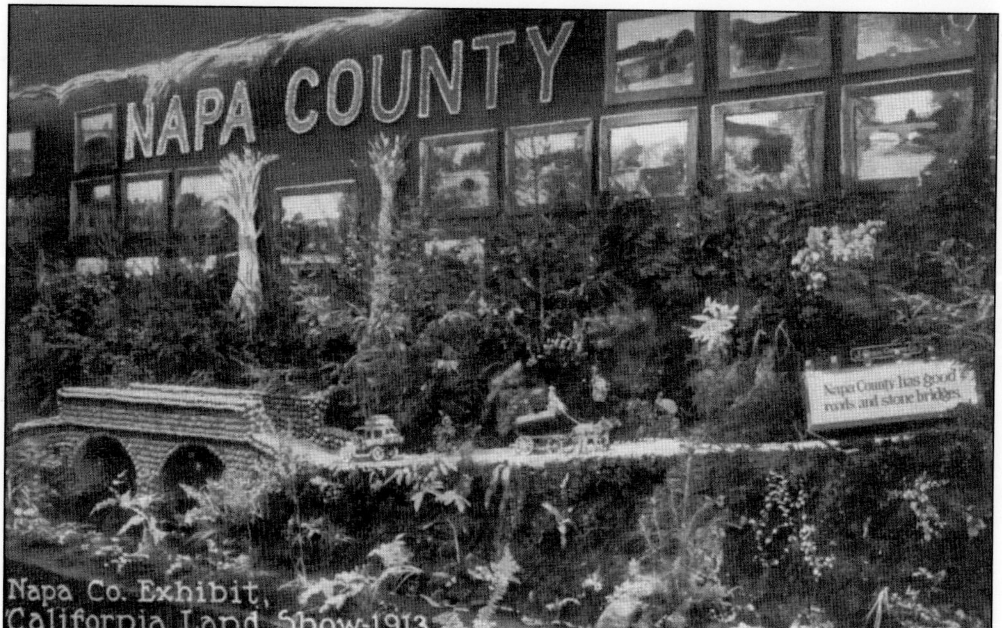

This 1913 postcard shows a rather elaborate display from Napa County at the California Land Show. The display highlights Napa's many stone bridges and includes a miniature diorama of one. This card was intended to be mailed as part of a PR campaign. Printed on the back are the following proclamations: "Crops grow without irrigation in Napa County" and "the residents of Napa County dwell in the valley of content." (Author's collection.)

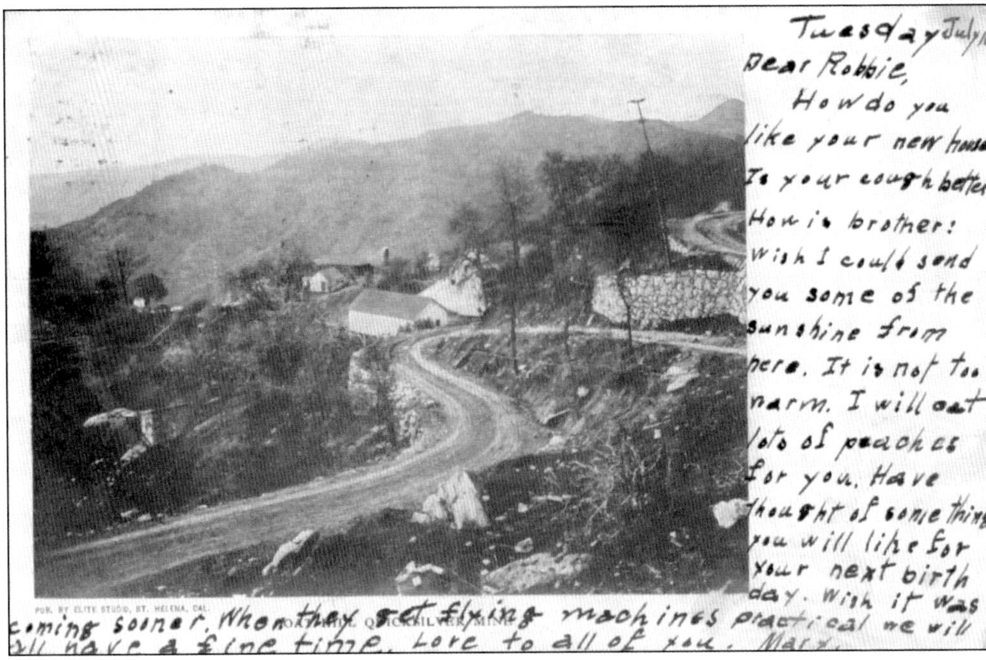

This postcard, mailed in 1907, features a picture of one of the quicksilver mines that dotted Mount St. Helena. The writer reflected on the new technology of flight by saying, "When they get flying machines practical we will all have a fine time." (Author's collection.)

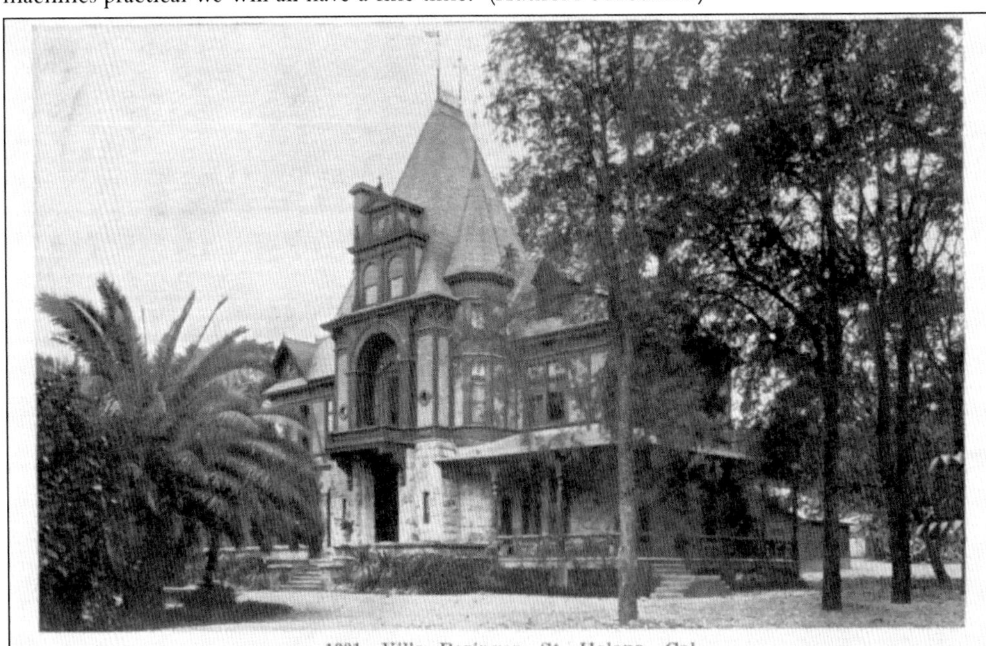

The Rhine House, the Beringer residence, was built in 1884. A St. Helena resident described the Beringer Winery as follows: "There is a large wine cellar dug into a hill near it, and they told me, come call, they had 400,000 gallons of wine in there. Four or five acres of grounds around that house with walks, flowers, shrubbery, palms, oranges, lemons, and roses. It is a fine place over there." (Author's collection.)

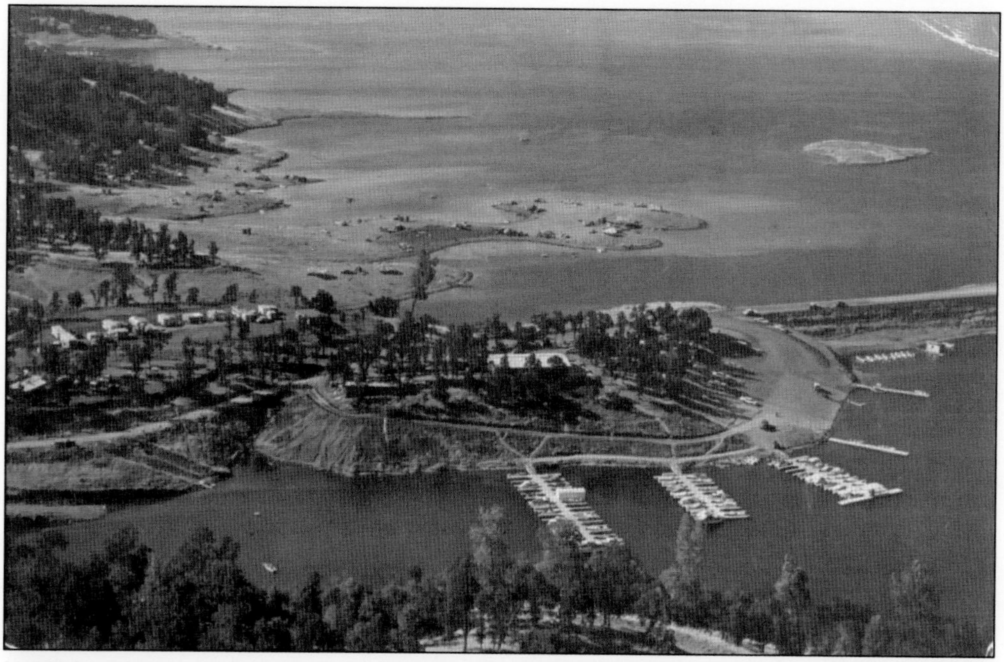

In 1961, a visitor to Lake Berryessa encapsulated a trip there as follows: "So beautiful here. The lake is about 22 miles long (enormous!) and this spot is just 'as shown' here. No bugs! Weather perfect! Fish, so far, too small to brag about—but tomorrow for sure!" (Author's collection.)

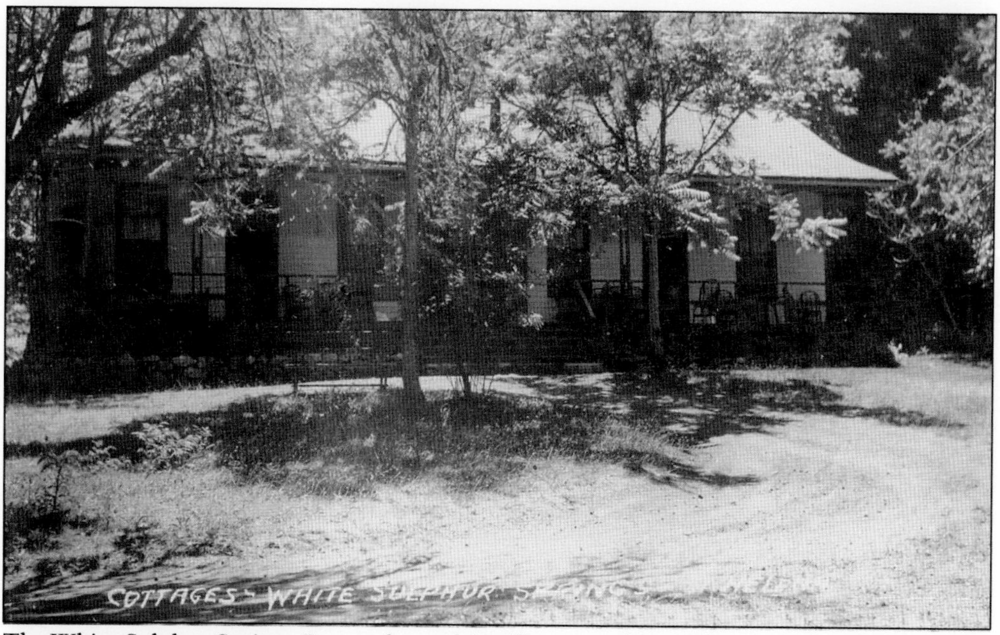

The White Sulphur Springs Resort, located 2 miles west of St. Helena, was first discovered by John York and David Hudson in 1848. A 1943 guest summed up her visit by writing, "I have enjoyed the sulphur baths each day, weather has been ideal and surroundings are lovely. Hate to leave for home." The resort was sold to the Methodist Church in 1957 and converted into a church retreat. (Author's collection.)

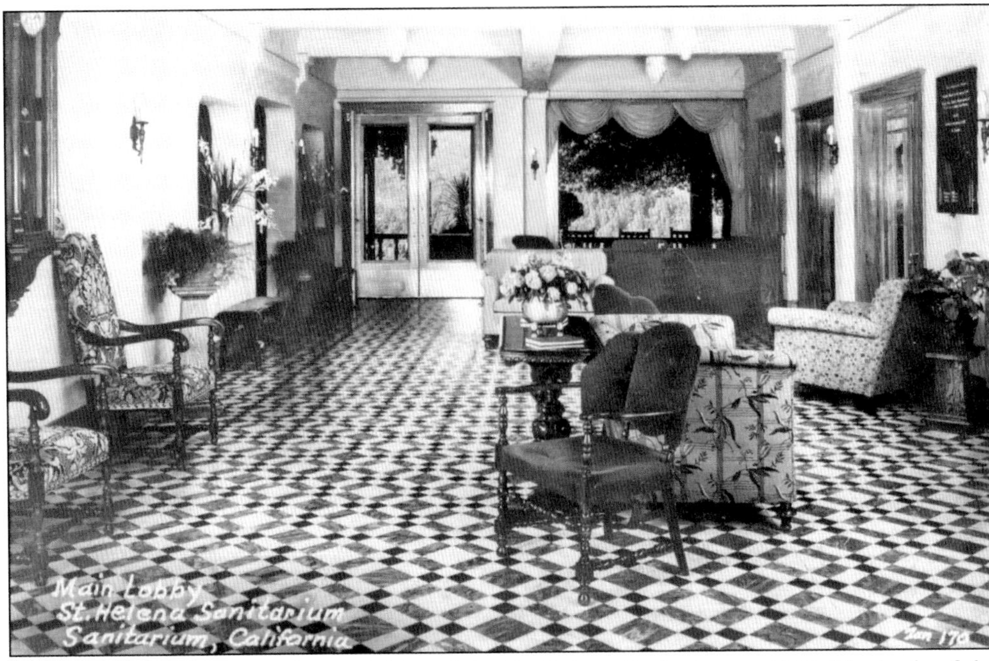

This postcard shows the elaborate lobby of the St. Helena Sanitarium *c.* 1911. The back of the card notes an alternate name for the sanitarium as Angwin's Health and Summer Resort. The sender noted, "Am taking a good rest this week, Next week we go gadding [a term for wandering without purpose]. The weather is about right. Was to the nickelodeon last night. We are going to have doves for dinner tonight." (Author's collection.)

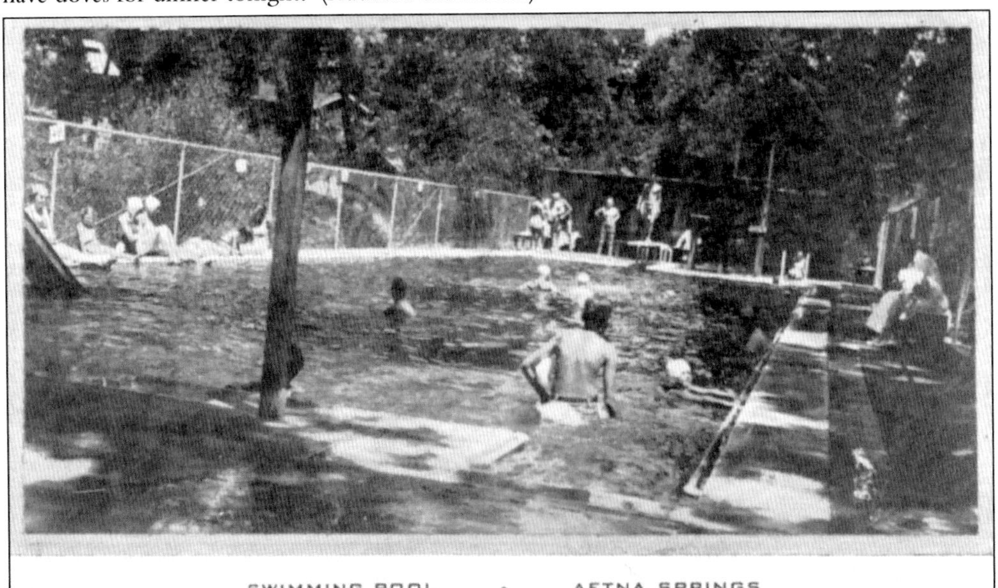

This 1945 postcard shows that Aetna Springs was a popular destination, even during World War II. The resort mailed this card to a guest instructing, "The O.P.A. regulations require us to collect ration points from all guests remaining a week or longer. Therefore, we ask your cooperation in bringing as many blue points as you can." The OPA was the wartime Office of Price Administration; they issued ration cards to the public, rationing many everyday staples. (Author's collection.)

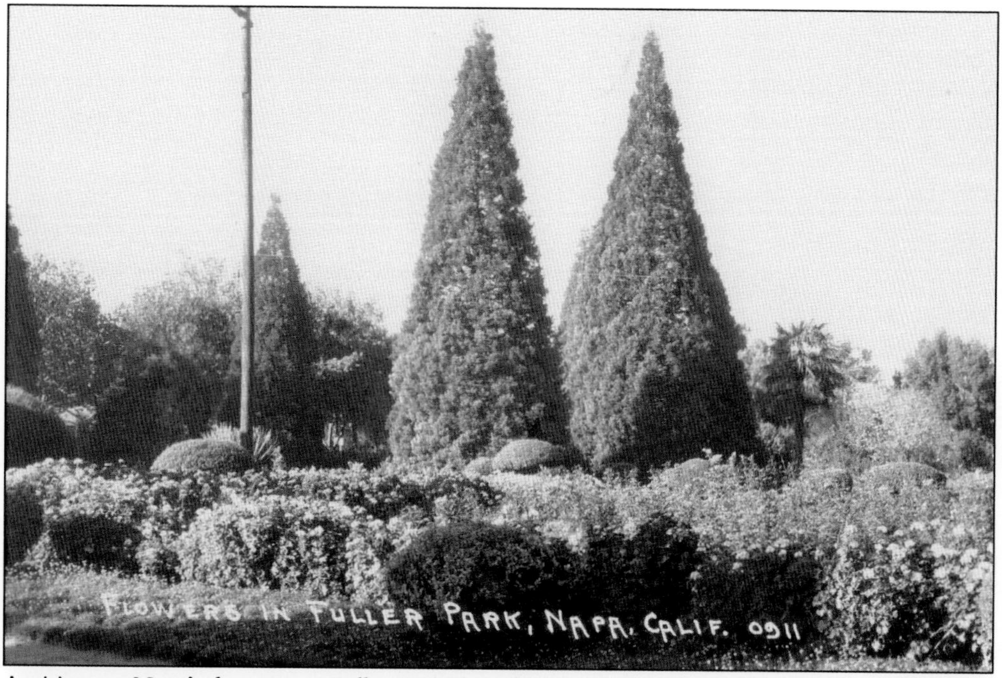

A visitor to Napa's downtown Fuller Park described it on this postcard as follows: "This is the nicest park I was ever in. Often wished I had a camera to take a snap shot of it. It's a block wide and two blocks long, with a playground in the center. All large trees and always full of people on Sunday, having picnic dinners." (Author's collection.)

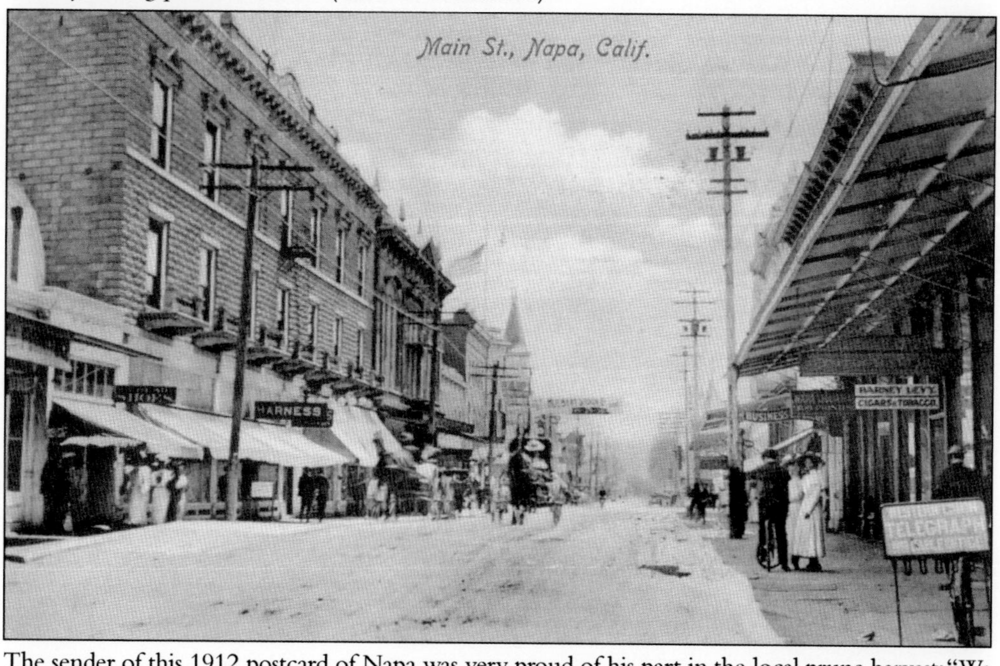

The sender of this 1912 postcard of Napa was very proud of his part in the local prune harvest: "We are pretty busy with the prunes. The first day I picked 600 pounds, ten boxes." Nut and fruit trees, such as prunes, were planted extensively in the Napa Valley at the start of the 20th century. They were an alternative to the grape crop, which had been decimated by phylloxera. (Author's collection.)

Bibliography

Adams, I. C. *Memoirs and Anecdotes of Early Days in Calistoga.* Calistoga, CA: 1946.

Coodley, Lauren and Paula Amen Schmitt. *Napa: The Transformation of an American Town.* Charleston, SC: Arcadia Publishing, 2007.

Darms, Herman A. *Napa City and County Portfolio and Directory.* Napa, CA: H. A. Darms, 1906.

Dillon, Richard H. *Napa Valley Heyday.* San Francisco, CA: The Book Club of California, 2004.

Domogalia, Kent V. *Looking for the Past in Calistoga.* Calistoga, CA: Sharpsteen Museum Association, 1998.

Eby, Gordon. *Napa Valley.* Napa, CA: Eby Press, 1972.

Grossinger, Robins and Erin Beller. *Landscape History of the Trancas: Historical Ecology Research Summary for the Trancas Crossing Park and Napa River Trail, City of Napa.* San Francisco, CA: San Francisco Estuary Institute, 2007.

Hanrahan, Virginia. *Napa County History: 1823–1948.* Napa, CA: Napa Chamber of Commerce, 1948.

History of Napa and Lake Counties. San Francisco, CA: Slocum, Bowen, and Company, 1881.

Kanaga, Tillie and W. F. Wallace. *History of Napa County.* Oakland, CA: Enquirer Print, 1901.

Kernberger, David and Kathy Kernberger. *Mark Strong's Napa Valley 1886–1924.* St. Helena, CA: Historic Photos, 1978.

Kernberger, Kathy. "History of a Small-town Newspaper: The St. Helena Star." *The Electrolier* (Summer 2003): 1.

Kilgallin, Anthony Raymond. *Napa: An Architectural Walking Tour.* Charleston, SC: Arcadia Publishing, 2001.

King, Norton L. *Napa County: A Historical Overview.* Napa, CA: Napa County Office of Education, 1973.

Loeber, Ivy. *Calistoga Centennial.* Napa, CA: Don Crawford Associates, 1959.

———. *History of St. Helena: A Century of Progress.* Napa, CA: Napa County Historical Association, 1955.

Maxwell-Long, Thomas. *Napa County Wineries.* Charleston, SC: Arcadia Publishing, 2002.

Pond, Fred. "Carneros Road Names." *Gleanings* (April 1972): 1–3.

Prchal, Dolly. "Mr. Calistoga: The Life and Accomplishments of John B. Ghisolfo." *Gleanings* (December 1985): 1–3.

Seeley, C. B., F. B. Mackinder, and I. C. Adams. *History of Solano and Napa Counties.* Los Angeles, CA: Historical Record Company, 1912.

Sheffer, Geneviere. *A History of White Sulphur Springs.* Napa, CA: Napa County Historical Society, 1970.

Smith, Clarence L. and Wallace W. Elliot. *Illustrations of Napa County California with Historical*

Sketches. Oakland, CA: Smith and Wallace, 1878.
Stanton, Ken. *Mount St. Helena and R. L. Stevenson State Park: A History and Guide*. Calistoga, CA: Illuminations Press, 1993.
Swett, Ira L. and Harry C. Aitken Jr., *Napa Valley Route*. Glendale, CA: Interurban Press, 1975.
Tortorolo, Mario. "History of the City of Napa Water Supply." *Gleanings* (May 1978): 1–2.
Verardo, Denzil and Jennie Verardo. *Napa Valley: From Golden Fields to Purple Harvest*. Northridge, CA: Windsor Publications, 1986.
Waters, John Jr. *Calistoga*. Charleston, SC: Arcadia Publishing, 2008.
Weber, Lin and the Napa Valley Museum. *Napa*. Charleston, SC: Arcadia Publishing, 2004
Weber, Lin. *Old Napa Valley: The History to 1900*. St. Helena, CA: Wine Ventures Publishing, 1998.
———. *Roots of the Present: Napa Valley 1900 to 1950*. St. Helena, CA: Wine Ventures Publishing, 2001.
Wichels, John. "Yountville in the Past." *Gleanings* (November 1973): 1–3.